DIVERSE
LEARNERS
in the Mainstream Classroom

DIVERSE LEARNERS

in the Mainstream Classroom

Strategies for Supporting **ALL** Students Across Content Areas

- English Language Learners
- Students with Disabilities
- Gifted/Talented Students

Edited by

YVONNE S. FREEMAN

DAVID E. FREEMAN

REYNALDO RAMÍREZ

Heinemann
Portsmouth, NH

Heinemann
361 Hanover Street
Portsmouth, NH 03801–3912
www.heinemann.com

Offices and agents throughout the world

The editors and publisher wish to thank those who have generously given permission to reprint borrowed material:

"Copla #1" by Gina Valdés from *Puentes y fronteras/Bridges and Borders* by Gina Valdés. Copyright © 1996 by Gina Valdés. Reprinted with permission of Bilingual Press/Editorial Bilingüe, Arizona State University, Tempe, Arizona.

Excerpt from "La Conciencia de la Mestiza" by Gloria Anzaldúa. In *Borderlands/La Frontera: The New Mestiza*. Copyright © 1987, 1999 by Gloria Anzaldúa. Reprinted by permission of Aunt Lute Books.

Library of Congress Cataloging-in-Publication Data
Diverse learners in the mainstream : strategies for supporting all students across content areas, English language learners, students with disabilities, gifted/talented students / edited by Yvonne S. Freeman, David E. Freeman, Reynaldo Ramírez

    p. cm.
  Includes bibliographical references
  ISBN-13: 978-0-325-01313-8
  ISBN-10: 0-325-01313-6
  1. Mainstreaming in education—United States. 2. Children with social disabilities—Education—United States. 3. Minorities—Education—United States. I. Freeman, Yvonne S. II. Freeman, David E. III. Ramírez, Raynaldo.

LC1201.D58 2008
371.9'046—dc22   2008004607

Editor: Lisa Luedeke
Production: Vicki Kasabian
Cover design: Catherine Hawkes | Cat and Mouse
Authors' photo on back cover: Christopher Trejo
Interior photographs: Julie Farias
Typesetter: House of Equations, Inc.
Manufacturing: Louise Richardson

Printed in the United States of America on acid-free paper
12 11 10 09 08 RRD 2 3 4 5

We dedicate this book to Dr. Juliet V. García, president of the University of Texas at Brownsville and Texas Southmost College. Dr. García's dynamic leadership and passion for making education accessible for all students in this border region have inspired faculty, community members, and the students themselves to achieve the highest possible levels of success. Dr. García's dreams for this rapidly changing region of the country have become reality, as is evidenced by the physical beauty and caring atmosphere of this growing campus and the accomplishments of all who are part of the university community. The faculty of the Department of Curriculum and Instruction in the School of Education view this book as a reflection of the positive atmosphere that has resulted from Dr. García's inspirational leadership.

In addition, we dedicate this book to future teachers who read this book and are influenced by its ideas, especially to future teachers of the Rio Grande Valley, who have shown the great promise Dr. García has always believed possible. They will need to meet the challenges confronting them, and it is on their shoulders that the future of this region rests.

Contents

PART 2: Meeting the Needs of Diverse Learners

Acknowledgments

We first would like to acknowledge the consistent support given us by the publishers of this book at Heinemann. Maura Sullivan, the managing editor, and Leigh Peake, the vice president and editorial director, supported this project from the beginning, as they have with the other Freeman books, trusting that the project could be completed and would fulfill a need. Our Heinemann editor for the book, Lisa Luedeke, read the manuscript over with care and gave us very useful suggestions. Vicki Kasabian, the production editor for many of the Freemans' books, has shown again how her professional expertise consistently produces the highest-quality books in the education market.

We would also like to acknowledge the authors of the chapters in this volume. They all wrote and edited their chapters with care and professionalism. Each chapter reflects the expertise of the authors, which they are now sharing with an audience beyond their own university classrooms. Information about these authors, including their research interests, is listed at the end of the book.

Finally, we, the editors, acknowledge the readers of this book as advocates for diverse students in schools everywhere. Our hope is that this book will challenge readers and enrich their teaching.

Introduction

Our teacher education program prepares students very well. They know a lot about the subject or grade they will teach, they know about classroom management, they know how to write objectives and connect them to standards, and they know how to assess student progress. When they go out to do their student teaching, they are well prepared, and they are confident. Most have successful student teaching experiences. But after they are hired for their first teaching job and have their own classrooms, things change. After a few weeks, many are often somewhat discouraged. They were well prepared to teach their subjects; however, they weren't ready to meet the needs of the students in their classrooms. They didn't realize that some were just learning to speak English, some were students with disabilities who had been mainstreamed, and some were gifted and talented students who already knew much of what they planned to teach. "How," they ask, "can I reach the diverse students in my classroom? There are so many different challenges that I am not sure where to begin."

This was the reflection from our department chair, Reynaldo Ramírez. It was these comments that planted the seed for the writing of this book. Faculty in the curriculum and instruction department at our university realized that although we were doing a good job of preparing teachers, one key element was missing. We thought that the students we were sending out were well prepared in every way, but listening to these new teachers' comments, we realized that there was an important gap in their preparation: they were not ready for the reality of today's classrooms, even though they themselves had graduated from high school only a few short years ago. Why was this?

For one thing, our nation is increasingly diverse, and this diversity is reflected in our schools. We often think of diversity as cultural or linguistic difference, and it is true that in almost every part of the country, new immigrants from around the globe are entering our schools. The number of students with limited English proficiency has increased dramatically. Nearly one in every ten students nationwide is an English language learner (ELL). While some ELLs are taught by English as a second language (ESL) or bilingual teachers, most are mainstreamed very soon after arrival.

But classroom diversity encompasses more than language or ethnic backgrounds. Because of new laws, more students with disabilities are now mainstreamed. Students who formerly studied in a resource room with a special education teacher now spend part or all of the day in a mainstream classroom. At the same time, there is a greater recognition that many students are gifted in some way. These students also deserve instruction that meets their varied needs.

Even among students who are native English speakers and who have not been identified as special education or gifted and talented students, there is considerable diversity. School districts often encompass different socioeconomic sections of a town or city, and the student population reflects these differences as well. Further, while some students come from a family with two parents, many have a single parent or live with other relatives.

Some of our teacher education students graduated from high school only three or four years ago. Diversity in the schools has increased during this time, but another factor also comes into play. Most students who go into teaching were not English language learners, at least not beyond their elementary years. They were not special education students either, for the most part, although with improved education for students with disabilities, that fact is changing. Some students in teacher education had been in programs for the gifted and talented, but not the majority. Since most teacher education students were not part of one of these diverse groups, they tended to associate with other students more like themselves. Even though their schools were diverse, many of our teacher education majors were not aware of the diversity when they were in elementary or high school. They were focused on their circle of friends.

However, when our students go back to school and become teachers, their perspective changes. Now they are responsible for differentiating instruction to meet the needs of all the students in their classes. For many new teachers, this challenge seems overwhelming.

Early in their teacher preparation, our students take a course designed to make them aware of different special populations in school. The course focuses on English language learners, students with disabilities, and gifted and talented students. Future teacher educators learn about these different groups and the laws relating to their education. However, the textbook that was being used did not make students fully aware of current classroom realities. Students in this class on special populations could answer questions about these different groups, but the course is offered early in their program, and most of the teacher education students approached the course as they would any other. They wanted to know what they needed to be successful academically, how they could pass the quizzes and tests rather than how they could use this information to prepare themselves to teach the students they would encounter in their classrooms.

The professors who taught this course did their best to supplement the textbook and bring issues of diversity to life, but they realized that one way to improve the course would be to find a better text. However, their search was not successful. They were unable to discover a textbook that contained essential information about each of the special populations and also provided concrete examples of how teachers in different subject areas could meet the needs of all their students. The more department members talked, the more we realized that if we could not find the kind of book we wanted, we would need to write it ourselves. The current book represents our efforts to provide the information and examples that we want our students to have.

Although this project started as a book for students in teacher education classes, as we have talked to administrators and veteran teachers, we have become aware that in many schools there are teachers who have struggled to cope with a rapidly changing student population. Approaches they used in the past don't seem to work too well with their current students. At the same time, teachers are under increased pressure to prepare all their students to meet high standards and pass high-stakes tests. As we talked with educators in the field, we realized that this book could also serve the needs of many practicing teachers by giving them background information and strategies they could use to more effectively teach all their students. Keeping in mind these two groups—new teachers and veteran teachers who find themselves in classrooms with a rapidly changing student population—we undertook the writing of this book.

Overview of the Book

This book is divided into two main sections. The first part describes each of the special populations. Luz Murillo and Patrick Smith open the book with a chapter that explores generally what cultural diversity is and then examines what diversity means for society and for schools. The authors end their chapter with a series of challenges that cultural diversity poses for teachers followed by suggestions for how to meet these challenges.

The following chapters each deal with one of the special populations. Chapters 2 and 3 discuss English language learners. In Chapter 2 Yvonne and David Freeman begin by showing the rapid increase in the number of students with limited English proficiency. The authors then discuss differences among ELLs and how schools identify and classify second language learners. The chapter also reviews the different kinds of programs available for ELLs. Following this discussion, the authors review best practices for teaching ELLs based on current research and theory. They close with an extended scenario that shows how a mainstream teacher works effectively with her limited English proficient students. In Chapter 3 Alma Rodríguez and Richard Gómez Jr. continue the discussion of ELLs, but with a focus on students in bilingual education settings. They explain what bilingual education is and the different kinds of bilingual programs. The chapter includes a discussion of the research and theory that supports bilingual education and concludes with a scenario showing how a teacher works effectively with second language students in a bilingual classroom.

Chapter 4 turns to a second group of students, those with disabilities. Steve Chamberlain begins with a review of the legal mandates for serving students with disabilities in a mainstream setting. He explains how a general education teacher can work with a special education teacher to identify and plan effective instruction for students with disabilities. This chapter concludes with scenarios showing how general education teachers can provide accommodations that students with disabilities need to reach their potential and prepare for a productive life.

In Chapter 5 Darwin Nelson discusses the different types of gifted and talented students and offers suggestions for working effectively with gifted students in a mainstream class, giving special attention to an often neglected intelligence: emotional intelligence. Kathy Bussert-Webb then expands on these ideas in her chapter (6, in Part 2) by discussing multiple intelligences in detail. She explains how teachers can assess and draw on eight different intelligences to provide the best possible education for diverse learners. Both Chapters 5 and 6 include scenarios showing how mainstream teachers can work with students who are gifted and talented in different ways.

Part 2 also contains a series of chapters that demonstrate how teachers can meet the needs of their diverse learners as they use technology, work with young children, and teach different content area classes. Each of these chapters follows a similar structure: theoretical foundations, characteristics of good programs and practices, an explanation of how to differentiate instruction for special populations, and a scenario showing how a teacher puts the theory into practice with his or her diverse learners.

Chapter 7 focuses on technology. Janice Wilson Butler describes a variety of technology tools and techniques available for teachers. This chapter includes an extended scenario showing how one teacher helps her students use a variety of technological tools to complete their class projects. In Chapter 8 Georgianna Duarte presents the theory and research related to early childhood education. This chapter focuses on students in preschool through third grade, a time when young children develop rapidly. The author discusses who these young learners are and what theories guide appropriate instruction for them. She elaborates on the importance of play, an appropriate physical environment for learning, and developmentally appropriate practices for young learners. In this chapter, teachers can see how to meet the needs of very young students who are ELLs or come to school with disabilities as well as those who, even at an early age, demonstrate that they are gifted and talented in various ways.

The final three chapters each deal with one of the major subject areas taught in school. In Chapter 9 James Telese explores math, in Chapter 10 Paula Parson and Renee Rubin review language arts, and in Chapter 11 Julio Noboa and Elsa Duarte-Noboa examine social studies. Like the earlier chapters, each of these chapters explains the theoretical foundations of the discipline, describes the characteristics of best practices, discusses how teachers can differentiate instruction for students from special populations, and then concludes with a scenario that shows how teachers can put theory into practice to meet the needs of all their students.

Each chapter in the book also contains a list of key terms and acronyms. When a term first appears in a chapter, it is italicized. Its definition can be found in the glossary at the end of that chapter. The authors of each chapter also list several applications. These are suggestions for ways readers can extend their understanding of key ideas from the chapter by engaging in an activity, such as observing in a school, interviewing a teacher, or summarizing main ideas. Many chapters also include a list of additional resources, such as websites, for students who wish to explore the ideas in more depth.

New teachers leave teacher education classes prepared to teach their subjects. They know how to plan lessons, use materials, and assess their students' progress. Veteran teachers bring years of experience and skills to their classroom each day. It is our hope that educators who read this book will come away better prepared to meet the challenges posed by the increasing diversity they encounter in their classes. It is only by educating all their students and ensuring that students from special populations are not left behind that teachers can truly succeed.

DIVERSE
LEARNERS
in the Mainstream Classroom

1

Understanding Special Populations

1

Cultural Diversity

Why It Matters in School and What Teachers Need to Know

Luz A. Murillo and Patrick H. Smith

Hay tantísimas fronteras
que dividen a la gente,
pero por cada frontera
existe también un puente.

There are so many borders
that divide people from one another,
but for each border
there is also a bridge.
Gina Valdés, *Puentes y fronteras: Coplas chicanas*

Introduction

Cultural diversity is an exciting and important issue facing educators in the United States and around the world. The ways that people are raised, socialized, and educated at home and at school are fundamental components of who we are. In our families and other social groups, these ways feel so familiar, so taken for granted, that often we become aware of them only through contact with people who have been raised and educated elsewhere. This is true for all members of society, but because teachers work closely with children, families, and colleagues whose backgrounds are different from ours, learning to understand and work successfully with cultural diversity is especially important for our profession. To borrow the metaphor in Gina Valdés' lovely poem, schools

3

have often acted as *fronteras*, borders between students from different cultural groups. This chapter is written for future teachers who would like to become cultural bridges for their students and communities.

To illustrate this idea, we begin with a brief discussion of how cultural diversity has motivated and shaped our own lives as educators. We then consider the question "What is cultural diversity?" before explaining why it matters for society and for schools. We look at some of the ways the topic of cultural diversity has been addressed in U.S. schools, including pedagogical efforts aimed at working with diverse learners. The chapter concludes with a description of six key challenges facing educators today and some suggestions for how to meet them.

Where We Are Coming From

Paulo Freire, a Brazilian educator whose work we admire, wrote that teaching people to read implies much more than teaching them to decode or sound out words and sentences. In the fullest sense, according to Freire, teaching people to read means helping them to "read the world," to interpret and connect the texts that they read to the everyday world around them. For educators, this approach offers exciting possibilities because the relationship between teachers and students is transformed from one of dispensers and receivers of knowledge. Instead, teachers guide students, who are interested and actively involved in their own education. This approach also holds the potential to keep teachers and teaching better connected to the world beyond the classroom. As with any theory of education, putting a Freirian approach into practice also poses challenges. For teachers, it means realizing and admitting when we don't know the answer, as well as having both the curiosity and the discipline to continue learning. For learners, it means accepting the challenge and hard work of questioning what we are learning, rather than simply accepting and rephrasing what we are taught.

We believe that these ideas are as true for authors and professors as they are for students and their families. With this in mind, we'd like to briefly describe our backgrounds and where we are coming from in terms of the fundamental matter of cultural diversity and what it means for education in the twenty-first century.

Luz was born and raised in the coffee-growing region of Caldas, Colombia, and Patrick grew up on farms in Michigan and Maine in the United States. Despite these different geographies, we are both children of career teachers and grew up in rural areas and small towns before moving to cities to study.

Although neither of us grew up planning to be a teacher (indeed, our parents recommended that we go into other fields!), our experiences and interests led each of us to become public school teachers working with linguistically and ethnically diverse students. Living and teaching outside our first communities and in new countries (Mexico, the United States, and Kenya) led us to learn new languages and to pursue graduate studies in order to better understand how to work with such learners. The topic of cultural diversity has come to matter to us personally as well as professionally; as parents of bilingual, multicultural children, we have seen firsthand the benefits of teachers who are well prepared to work with students who are different from their mainstream classmates, as well as the problems that can arise when teachers are not prepared.

How Our Approach Differs from Other Approaches to Cultural Diversity

The view of cultural diversity described in this chapter may be a bit different from those found in other works you will read as a student of education. For example, unlike approaches equating cultural diversity exclusively with membership in ethnic and linguistic groups (e.g., Hadaway 1995/2000), we make a connection between culture and ecological diversity. Our approach also incorporates issues of gender, sexuality, and ableism, including the identities formed around deafness and blindness. For this reason, we consider aspects of biology that are usually absent in discussions of cultural diversity.

We also believe strongly that teachers must understand the cultural and family backgrounds of the students from many different countries now studying in U.S. schools. For this reason, we illustrate our ideas about culture with examples from the contexts we know best, including the Rio Grande Valley, Mexico, and Colombia. Although some of these examples may seem unfamiliar to you at first, we encourage you to compare them with your own experiences as a student and future teacher. Finally, we are convinced that the best educators are intellectual actors and that learning to see ourselves as thinkers is fundamental for beginning teachers. Only in this way can we prepare our students to handle the many different situations they will face in and outside our classrooms.

No Single Best Way

One objective of this chapter is to introduce the basic theories that inform studies of cultural diversity. Because there are multiple theories, there is no single correct way of thinking about cultural diversity, just as there is no best way of teaching diverse students. Indeed, as your studies progress, you will find yourself questioning and perhaps challenging what you hear and read about cultural diversity. Our overall goal is not for you to learn the right approach to working with culturally diverse populations, but rather for you to understand the key issues that will allow you to become a successful teacher and lifelong learner about this exciting and important topic. If you wish to continue learning about this topic, consult the resource list at the end of the chapter.

What Is Cultural Diversity?

To begin to answer the question "What is cultural diversity?" let's first consider the related questions "What is culture?" and "What is diversity?"

What Is Culture?

> Anthropologists and many others have always wanted to celebrate culture as that which constitutes the humanity of human beings and allows them to build worlds that were not given by their biological endowments. Neither the pyramids, nor the Bill of Rights, nor the Chicago blues sprang forth fully formed from human muscles, neural networks, or hearts. (Varenne and McDermott 1999, 143)

We start with the observation that culture is not biology. More precisely, we can say that although human culture (like everything that humans do) has its roots in human biology, they are not the same thing. In talking about culture, we are referring to the ways in which human communities organize themselves to do certain things like form partnerships, raise children (including teaching them in formal institutions such as schools), work (including teaching), love, and play. In talking about biology, we are talking about brains and bodies and their capacity to perform activities that are culturally meaningful. We want to emphasize that apparent biological differences such as skin and eye color, hair texture, and facial features are actually quite superficial across human populations. Although fascinating to hairstylists, geneticists, and others interested in how humans came to look the way we do, they are not very useful in understanding how people learn. In fact, in contrast to nineteenth-century theories about racial differences and intelligence, contemporary research on human biology shows that humans around the world are remarkably similar when it comes to our brains and the mental processes by which we learn new things like language, how to read and write, and how to do arithmetic (Hall 2005; Diamond 1999/2003).

What does this mean for our understanding of culture? To begin with, it means that the values we assign to the skin-deep physical differences we observe are imbued primarily with social rather than biological meaning. Although humans are genetically programmed to take quick visual notice of characteristics such as size, age, and gender (indeed, it seems that we cannot help ourselves from performing rapid assessments of this sort, which explains why heads turn when a person enters a room), what we make of these apparent differences (like crossing the street to catch a closer glimpse of a person we find interesting or attractive or moving away from a person we consider threatening or scary) depends on interpretations that have their basis more in culture than in biology.

But just how much do people differ culturally, and in what ways? Recently, anthropologists influenced by descriptions of linguistic universals have examined different cultural groups to ask whether *cultural universals* might also exist. Here are a few of the items anthropologist Donald E. Brown (cited in Pinker 2002) believes are shared across contemporary societies:

- Men are, on average, older than the women they marry. They also engage in acts of collective violence (warfare) more than do female members of the same groups.
- Women are responsible for the bulk of child care.
- All societies have shared routines for how to talk to children and to adults of different social status.
- Homosexuality is present in all groups (although not all groups are equally open about or tolerant of gay people).
- All societies have developed shared means of marking group membership (including styles of dress, ways of speaking, and body piercing and other forms of adornment); conversely, all groups have developed criteria for establishing who is not a member.
- All societies have structures for raising children and passing on cultural knowledge that is regarded as essential for life.
- All groups appear to recognize transgressions of shared cultural values and have developed rules for dealing with people who are judged to have transgressed them.

Notice that none of the items from this list specifies exactly *how* groups go about enacting these shared understandings. What Brown's list demonstrates is not that all human populations are essentially the same or that people everywhere act the same, but that cultural variation across groups is limited in certain ways. In other words, rather than exhibiting random behavior, all cultures follow patterns that are fairly stable collective responses to situations and conditions confronting people in different contexts.

However, culture is far from fixed or monolithic. Juan Castañeda has observed that "culture is produced in the process of all social and community interactions, from art to television, to the ways we prepare food, dress ourselves, fall in love, face death, or dream of the future" (Castañeda 1999, 21). Thus, cultural understandings are reflected in all that we do, and culture is something that members of a group re-create and constantly modify as we live our lives. A scholar of Chicano origin, Renato Rosaldo adds that "culture is what gives meaning to human experience, selecting and organizing it. . . . Culture includes the commonplace and the esoteric, the mundane and the exalted, the ridiculous and the sublime. At all levels, culture penetrates everything. We learn from other cultures by living, reading, or by being there. Cultures are learned rather than inherited" (1993, 26). The notion of culture as constantly changing is nicely summarized by Spanish poet Antonio Machado, "Caminante, no hay camino, se hace el camino al andar," which, loosely translated into English, means "Traveler, there is no road. We make the road by walking" (Machado 1982, 142). In the end, we find it most useful to think of culture as a work in progress rather than a finished product.

What Is Diversity?

This brings us to our next question: "What is diversity?" Diversity means differences, of course, but differences from what? As noted in the previous section, humans are biologically programmed to recognize difference, and all cultural groups have developed ways to mark who is a member and who isn't. In this very basic sense, diversity simply means everyone who is different from me or us. In practice, however, this definition is too simple. Think, for example, of your (great) grandparents or your older aunts and uncles. Because of the circumstances in which they grew up—before email, chat, cell phones, and instant messaging existed—your older relatives are probably less adept than you at handling some of the communications technologies you may regard as basic for modern living. (You may want to test this out by handing your *abuelita* your cell phone and asking her to send a text message!) But don't start feeling too smug. If your elders grew up in times and regions with very different material resources and practices than those you grew up with, it is equally likely that they have certain forms of knowledge (for example, speaking a particular language, knowing how to work on a farm, preparing food in certain ways, observing certain religious practices) that you know less about. Although everyone can recognize these sorts of generational differences, would you say that your older relatives belong to a different culture? And, as we grow older and some of us have children and grandchildren with experiences that are very different from what we have known and done, would we claim that these newer generations belong to different cultures? Thus, thinking about culture means thinking about how people are different even within the same family.

A second problem with a simple definition of difference is that it is *essentialist*. By this we mean the kind of thinking that assumes (1) that all members of a particular group are fundamentally all the same and (2) that being a member of that group can somehow explain or even determine how an individual will act. According to essentialist thinking, all Vietnamese Americans, for example, are basically the same and therefore think and act in the same ways *because* they are Vietnamese Americans. This assumption, if true, would be a terrific tool for policy makers and educators. Imagine being able to predict how all Vietnamese American children and parents would react to a new math curriculum or a new form of bilingual education, or how all deaf parents would want their children to be taught to read.

In real life, of course, people are much more complex than essentialist thinking assumes. Think for a minute about all the different people you know of Mexican heritage. Do they all hold the same view about bilingual education? Does it matter that they were born and raised in different areas, such as Michoacán, Oaxaca, San Antonio, Chicago, or New York City? Does it make any difference that their parents, grandparents, or earlier generations were born and raised in different parts of Mexico (including those that became part of the United States!) or that they speak or spoke different *dialects* of Spanish or different indigenous languages? Does intermarriage with Anglo-, African, Asian, or other Americans, or with a person from another Spanish-speaking area like Puerto Rico, Cuba, or Colombia make someone less Mexican? Raising these sorts of real-life questions—which we can ask of any cultural group—demonstrates that an essentialist view of human nature fails to capture the ways people really are.

So far, we have been thinking about specific types of American status primarily as an example of an ethnic category. But people are far more than the sum of their ethnicities, and the picture gets even more interesting when we consider the other aspects of cultural diversity including language background, gender, age, sexual orientation, differing abilities, and so on. For example, do you act and talk the same way with your siblings as you do when you are with your grandparents? How about when you are with a group of all male or all female friends, or a group of straight friends or (openly) gay and lesbian friends?

What about with people who speak only English or Spanish and people who can speak both languages?

The kinds of slight adjustments we all make depending on the situations we encounter—yes, everybody does it!—mean that human individuals are shifters par excellence. Bilinguals and multilinguals are especially talented at this. Thus, in one context we can act more Mexican if we choose to, and we can act more gringo in another. Often we do these things, like *code-switching* with bilingual friends, without even thinking about them. At other times people are highly aware of what they are doing and choose very deliberately to adopt a particular way of speaking and acting. This is especially true when we sense that a certain aspect of our identity is viewed negatively. Sadly, this is often the case for Navajo children and other indigenous people, who attempt to hide their language and culture, and for some gay or lesbian teenagers, who hide their sexuality from their families and even from themselves because of *homophobia*. Sometimes, however, we celebrate our ability to shift between worlds, as in the poetry and prose writing of author and lesbian Chicana Gloria Anzaldúa (1987, 77):

> Because I, a mestiza,
> continually walk out of one culture
> and into another,
> because I am in all cultures at the same time,
> alma entre dos mundos, tres, cuatro,
> me zumba la cabeza con lo contradictorio.
>
> Estoy norteada por todas las voces que me hablan
> *simultáneamente.*

For these reasons, one of the myths that educators must avoid is interpreting cultural diversity as deviance from the norm. Culturally speaking, there really is no *normal* or standard group, just as there is no normal or right way to be a woman or a man, a Mexican American, an African American, a blind person, or a member of any other group. Instead, all people, including teachers, students, and parents, are diverse in multiple ways.

Anthropologists have described the ways that adult members of certain groups act in different contexts but have paid less attention to children and teenagers. Although teachers are taught that childhood and adolescence are times of development and change, the notion that identities are multiple is new in many schools. This means that teachers who give learners the freedom to express themselves, literally to try out different aspects of who they may choose to be as adults, are truly acting as leaders in a new era of education. For this reason, classrooms and all areas of schools need to be safe zones where cultural experimentation is respected and encouraged.

Defining Cultural Diversity Means Understanding Power Relations

Now that we have looked at the questions of what culture and diversity are, we are ready to tackle the larger question, "What is cultural diversity?" If you have read this far, you are probably not expecting a simple definition, and that is good because there really isn't one! There are, however, some excellent places to look for answers to this question. Rosaldo (1993) writes that cultural diversity is best understood by looking at historical change, socioeconomic inequities, and especially the differences salient to the members of specific groups themselves. He argues that contemporary ideas about cultural diversity have been shaped by social movements that have organized to protect the rights and interests of key groups including environmentalists, feminists, gays and lesbians, and Native Americans, African Americans, Chicanos, and Puerto Ricans. While this description refers specifically to the United States, these ideas have also been developed elsewhere around the world, especially in Latin America, Africa, and Asia (Canclini 1995; Martín-Barbero 2001). Rosaldo's nondefinition invites us to go beyond simply adding new groups to a list. Instead, by framing cultural diversity in terms of struggle and resistance, we can see that the power relations between different groups are critical for understanding cultural diversity.

This brings us to the confusing concepts of minority and majority groups. Federal and state departments of education use the term *minority* to refer mainly to nonwhites, as in this definition from a recent court decision in Texas: "A school district with a student population comprised of more than fifty percent minority students is commonly referred to as a 'majority-minority' district. For this purpose, the word 'minority' includes African American, Hispanic, and Asian" (U.S. Court of Appeals for the Fifth Circuit 2006). As you can see, this use of the term *minority* doesn't really make sense in schools in South Texas, where school populations are typically close to 95 percent Mexican origin, or in New York City, Detroit, Milwaukee, Philadelphia, Boston, and other communities, where some public schools are composed almost completely of African American and Latino students (Kozol 2005). Even in schools where the minorities are the numerical majority, they are still subject to the power differential that places one group (middle-class European Americans) as the standard by which all other groups are measured and evaluated. Thus, we cannot use these terms without carefully considering the specific local context and the power relations among the various groups involved.

Definitions of cultural diversity have expanded considerably in the past two or three decades. Whereas diversity training for teachers in the past focused mainly on issues of *ethnicity* and ethnic diversity, broader notions of diversity mean that twenty-first-century educators must also understand other forms of diversity including language background, migration and national origin, gender and sexual orientation, and diverse abilities such as deafness, blindness, and different learning styles (Banks et al. 2005). Although these issues were once viewed as completely separate, there is growing recognition that they actually combine to form individual and group identities.

Why Cultural Diversity Matters

At the most basic level, cultural diversity matters because it reflects the human condition. Human individuals, communities, and populations have always been diverse, although historically schools and other public institutions rarely have been organized to reflect and honor this fact. In the nineteenth century, for example, schools and universities across the United States were structured to exclude girls and women. And, as noted in the next section, up until the mid-twentieth century, education laws were enacted in many states to prohibit Native Americans and African Americans from attending white schools or from attending school at all.

Diversity also matters because unique and important forms of knowledge are embedded in specific cultures and their languages. Linguists Daniel Nettle and Suzanne Romaine (2000) describe the specialized knowledge that traditional fishermen in Polynesia have developed about fish species that formally trained ichthyologists are only beginning to understand. They argue that those of us schooled to accept the scientific method as the only way of discovering new knowledge are actually missing the boat in this case. As competition from large-scale, industrial fisheries pushes Polynesian fishermen to adopt nontraditional methods or to drop out of fishing altogether, these important forms of knowledge are lost to future generations. Murillo (2004) makes a similar case for land management practices developed over centuries by Arhuaco Indians in the Sierra de Santa Marta mountains in northern Colombia. The Arhuacos regard themselves as the keepers of this fragile ecosystem. Pointing to the devastation of the lands held by *bunachi* (non-Indians, literally "foolish little brothers"), they resist attempts to show them better ways of protecting the environment in the name of modernity and progress. Although we find it easy to dismiss local forms of knowledge, as these examples show, we do so at our own risk. As Maffi (2001) points out, many terms for describing plants, animals, and the practices that indigenous peoples have developed are simply untranslatable into English, Spanish, and other dominant languages. If the endangered languages spoken by these people are allowed to die out, a great deal of knowledge will be lost, with consequences for people everywhere.

You may be asking yourself at this point, as many students have asked us, what consequences follow when local forms of knowledge are lost? A famous example comes from the Navajo code talkers, Navajo speakers in the U.S. military during World War II who used their first language as an uncrackable and extremely valuable code for the Allies' communications. Banned in Arizona and federal Indian schools for many years, Navajo remains the Native American language with the greatest number of native speakers in the United States (Gordon 2005). Unfortunately, many Navajo children growing up today are rejecting Navajo in favor of English in order to appear less Indian and more white (McCarty, Romero-Little, and Zepeda 2006). Linguists predict that if this trend continues there will be very few native speakers of Navajo by the year 2050. Examples like this one show that diversity matters because human innovation and creativity—something that governments and businesses spend billions of dollars on each year—are fostered by access to multiple sources of new ideas and ways of thinking. By rejecting the ideas of individuals or groups because of who they are (or who we think they are), we risk homogenizing the sources of ideas and limiting our potential to find solutions to new problems that arise. Thus, protecting cultural diversity isn't just about respecting the past; it is also about keeping our options open for the future.

Why Diversity Matters for Schools and Education

In the most immediate sense, diversity matters for schools because international, federal, and state laws say that it does. At the international level, most nations have signed *UNESCO*'s declarations of human rights and cultural diversity, which means that they promise to protect the diversity of their populations, including the right to be educated in a language they understand. At the national level, various parts of the U.S. Constitution protect the rights of all citizens. And in Texas, competency standards for beginning teachers include knowing how to "use diversity in the classroom and the community to enrich all students' learning experiences" (Texas Education Agency 2006, 7). So in a very basic way, protecting and fostering the rights of culturally diverse learners matter because it is the law, and this powerful fact can be useful when students, parents, politicians, and other members of the public ask teachers if culturally responsible programs are really necessary in schools.

Legal protection is not absolute or permanent, however, as we can see in the case of women's right to vote in the United States. Although some western states permitted women's suffrage earlier, this right was not guaranteed nationally until the Nineteenth Amendment to the Constitution was ratified in 1920. And, despite the constitutional amendments adopted after the Civil War "guaranteeing" the rights of African Americans to vote (Fifteenth Amendment), hold office, and own property (Fourteenth Amendment), many states and cities found (illegal) ways to disenfranchise and oppress African Americans and other people of color for more than a century (Delpit and Dowdy 2002). In fact, most of the laws protecting culturally diverse populations now in place in the United States were developed only in the last forty years or so. For example, the Bilingual Education Act, first passed in 1968, must be periodically renewed by Congress, and this is also true for the Voting Rights Act, originally passed in 1964, and Public Law 94-142 (now the Individuals with Disabilities Education Act), first passed in 1977.

Protection of the rights of gays and lesbians is one of the most recent examples. For instance, the state of Texas outlawed homosexuality until 2002, when the U.S. Supreme Court upheld those rights and struck down the Texas law as discriminatory. Currently, only a handful of states permit civil unions between same-sex couples, and only Massachusetts permits marriage between people of the same sex. Like the rights of immigrants, rights for gay, lesbian, and transgender students are far from guaranteed in the United States today. Thus, while these examples illustrate the importance of establishing laws that protect culturally diverse populations, they also teach us how fragile and impermanent legal protections can be.

A more lasting rationale for cultural diversity in education is that educators can use this idea to promote equity and social justice. As teachers, it is our job to teach the students we have rather than to teach all students as if they were all the same. Teaching from an awareness of and a deep respect for cultural diversity is a step that teachers can take toward building "democracy in education, a tradition that insists . . . that all human beings have similar opportunities to develop themselves" (Varenne and McDermott 1999, 131). As we stated earlier, it is also true that different cultural groups hold knowledge that is potentially useful to anyone, including members of other groups. It follows, then, that all learners can benefit from learning new ways to approach problems.

Pedagogical Responses to Cultural Diversity

Following is a brief look at some of the ways that cultural diversity has (and hasn't) been addressed in U.S. schools. There is not space here for thorough treatment of this issue, but we mention a few early approaches, beginning with official policies aimed at exterminating Native American groups. Fortunately, most culturally different groups were not targeted for genocide, but many have experienced policies of exclusion and neglect. In some cases, they were simply not allowed to attend public schools at all. In others, schools were provided for nonwhite children, but these were typically greatly inferior to the schools attended by whites. A Mexican father in Nueces County, Texas, recognized the harmful effects of segregated schools, saying, "Having all children together is better. Then the teachers who teach the white boys have to do the same for the Mexicans" (Taylor 1971, as cited in San Miguel 1997, 144). This has also been the case for African Americans throughout the history of the United States. A half century after the 1954 Supreme Court ruling *Brown v. Board of Education*, which outlawed the concept of "separate but equal" schooling for blacks and whites, African American, Latino, and immigrant children in many cities now attend segregated schools characterized by *dumbed-down curricula*, inferior material resources, and inexperienced and poorly paid teachers (Kozol 2005).

Another common approach to addressing cultural diversity in schools was the policy of forced *assimilation*, typified by the *Americanization policies* common in southwestern states from the early 1900s and extending into the 1970s in some cases. Under such programs, Mexican-origin children, including many born in the United States, were educated in schools organized for white, English-speaking students and were taught by Anglo teachers with books and curricula designed to whitewash them, or transform them into monolingual speakers of English. A report on Hispanics in the United States recalls the period this way: "Until the Civil Rights era, these Mexican Americans, especially those in Texas, endured pervasive social and economic discrimination, reflected in segregated schools, churches, and residential neighborhoods" (National Research Council 2006, 21).

Because anti-Spanish and anti-immigrant practices continue covertly in many places, many Mexican-origin students today grow up feeling that they are inferior to mainstream or so-called majority culture, even though they now make up the majority population in many U.S. schools. An education student told us,

> Going to school in my town was very tough since my first language was Spanish. At the time I entered the first grade, teachers would still

slap your hands if you spoke Spanish at school. That meant I had to learn the English language no matter what. I went through first, second, and third grade having a very quiet, low self-confident attitude since I spoke English "funny."

Another reason that culturally diverse learners may feel "funny" in school is that they seldom see people who look or sound like them in instructional materials. For example, textbook publishers continue to leave Latinos, African Americans, and other minority groups out of social studies textbooks (Noboa 2006). And, despite research showing that American Indian societies were as complex and technologically advanced as the European societies that invaded them, U.S. history books continue to describe indigenous cultures as primitive and technologically inferior (Mann 2006).

Although individual teachers and advocacy groups like the *LULAC* and the *NAACP* were early champions of educational rights for students of color, it wasn't until the civil rights and brown power/*la raza* movements in the 1960s and '70s that equal educational opportunities for culturally diverse students started to become part of the national discourse through legislation. Some of these efforts did become law (such as the Bilingual Education Act and the Americans with Disabilities Act) and some did not (such as the Equal Rights Amendment, which sought to guarantee equal rights for women). One consequence of better access to higher education for members of groups historically denied an opportunity to attend college was the growth of academic departments and degree programs focusing on minority groups, including women's studies, African American studies, Chicano studies, Latin American studies, gay and lesbian studies, deaf studies, and special education. Although such programs have sometimes been criticized as too narrow in focus, they have given us valuable information about the social and economic history of the United States, information that was previously practically invisible in most schools and universities.

Multicultural education is another approach to culturally responsible teaching. Broadly, multicultural programs try to include the histories and literatures of various groups in the design of curriculum and instruction for all students. In their heyday in the late 1970s and early '80s, there were many different variations of multicultural programs, ranging from those that dealt with diversity in mostly superficial fashion (limited to celebrations of ethnic holidays, for example) to programs that aimed to use schools to resist and reverse inequities and injustice (Sleeter 1996). Although multicultural education programs were also criticized by progressive educators as not challenging the exclusionary biases of public education, the strongest criticism, beginning in the 1980s, came from conservative educators concerned that studying different cultural groups would water down the curriculum and divide the country by removing the core or basics that all Americans need to know (Hirsch, Kett, and Trefil 2002). This critique of multicultural education raises two fundamental questions all teachers should ask: "Who defines the content of our curriculum?" and "Which actors have the authority to make curriculum decisions that affect students and the teachers who teach them?"

The current economic and political dominance of the United States has led many people in this country and around the world to believe that U.S. ways of educating children are the best. However, important criticism of multicultural education has come from educators and researchers in Latin America and elsewhere outside the United States. Although supportive of the goals of inclusive education, international educators have pointed out that programs and materials developed in the United States convey dominant and colonizing ideologies that are harmful to societies in development. Because power relations are quite different in nations with a greater presence of Afro-Caribbean populations (Colombia, Venezuela, Cuba, and Brazil), indigenous groups (Bolivia, Guatemala, Mexico, Paraguay, and Peru), and *mestizos* (Mexico), scholars from such places have proposed *intercultural education*, a form of schooling that attempts to decolonize society (Walsh 2003). These programs are based on the idea that teaching about cultural diversity must include questioning why some groups have been excluded and others are more economically privileged and powerful (Muñoz Cruz 2002), as well as thinking about how schools and society can be reconceptualized and restructured to address these power imbalances. As U.S. schools receive more immigrant students and families from other countries, forms of education developed outside the United States are attracting attention and teachers are beginning to realize that there is much to be learned from schools in other places (Smith and Jiménez 2006).

A key lesson learned by educators working in and out of the United States is that students learn best when materials and teaching methods are familiar, an idea that can be termed *culturally relevant pedagogy*. The best-known example is an approach called *Funds of Knowledge* for Teaching, first developed in the U.S.-Mexico *borderlands* in the 1990s. Anthropologists doing ethnographic research with families in Sonora, Mexico, and Arizona were impressed by the many skills of Mexican children in these families, especially their ability to contribute to family businesses using math and literacy skills. However, when the researchers began to study the children's school performance, they were surprised to learn that the children had been judged as poor learners with few skills in math and reading. The researchers discovered that teachers knew very little about their students' home lives. When children did not do well on school tests, the teachers mistakenly assumed that the children had little knowledge of basic concepts of math, science, and reading.

The Funds of Knowledge Project (see González, Moll, and Amanti 2005) grew from the researchers' desire to work with border teachers to show them how smart and capable Mexican American children really are, and how the knowledge and skills they have developed at home can be built on in school. To gain this understanding, Funds of Knowledge teachers visit children's homes on a regular basis. Besides receiving special training in interviewing and interpreting life history, they also participate in teacher study groups where they read and discuss articles and books about teaching and compare these ideas with what they have observed and learned during the household visits and interviews. Although making the necessary release time to conduct home visits and study groups is often an issue, this approach to developing culturally relevant pedagogy has expanded from the Southwest to schools across the United States (McIntyre, Rosebery, and González 2001).

The final approach we discuss here is the current federal education policy, known by the name *No Child Left Behind* (*NCLB*). Aspects of the program such as rigid teacher certification programs, heavy reliance on standardized testing, and new accountability measures for schools that don't reach goals set by national and state departments of education were first tried out in Texas in the 1990s and then instituted at the national level by the Bush administration in 2001. Because of the emphasis on achieving high test scores in math and reading, and accountability in the form of penalties for not reaching them, many school districts have reduced the amount of time students spend learning about other subjects, including social studies and history (Meier and Wood 2004). This seems to be especially true for children in poor districts and for minority students (Goodman et al. 2005). In addition, increased reliance on mandated textbooks and scripted programs has taken away much of teachers' autonomy to select materials and pace lessons to fit the needs of their students.

Thus, although the primary argument behind the NCLB Act is that schools best serve children by holding all students to the same national standards, it appears that this goal cannot be reached without teachers who have developed a deep understanding of cultural diversity and have learned how to teach diverse learners. Unfortunately, despite teaching certification standards promoting cultural diversity and racial tolerance, many teachers probably find it more difficult to practice culturally responsible teaching in the era of NCLB than before the act was passed.

Challenges for Culturally Responsible Teachers in the Twenty-first Century

Six key challenges face teachers in the new century. Whether you teach in the community where you grew up or move to teach in a different state or even a new country, the increasing diversity of U.S. schools means that these are issues that all teachers will face sometime in their careers. In the "Applications" section at the end of the chapter, we provide some specific ideas you can try out with the diverse learners you will meet wherever you teach.

Challenge 1: Finding Out Who Your Students Are

The first challenge for *culturally responsible educators* is to learn who our students are. It is important but not enough to know something about the learners' ethnic backgrounds, the languages they speak, and what their parents do for work. *Amistad*, a Steven Spielberg film about an armed revolt aboard a slave ship in 1839, provides a powerful example of the importance of listening to stories. In this real-life case, decided by the U.S. Supreme Court during the international movement against the slave trade and the long buildup to the U.S. Civil War, the central question that developed was who the rebellious Africans really were. According to international law at the time, if born in West Africa, the *Amistad* Africans had been illegally enslaved and should therefore be awarded their freedom. On the other hand, if born into slavery in the Americas, they could be legally sold and held as slaves. This seemingly simple question proved very difficult to answer, in part because the Africans' lawyers did not speak any of the West African languages spoken by their clients and the Africans did not speak English, the language of the courts. With the help of a Mende-speaking interpreter, the Africans were eventually able to communicate with their lawyers, but it took a sort of superlawyer (former U.S. president John Quincy Adams, played by Anthony Hopkins in the movie) to convince the court to set them free. He did this by arguing that it isn't enough to know where people are from. Rather, you have to know their story. Here is an excerpt, in which Adams tells an abolitionist, a former slave named Joadson (played by Morgan Freeman), how to win the case:

> In a courtroom, whoever tells the best story wins. . . . What is their story, by the way? Mr. Joadson, you're from where, originally? Georgia. Does that pretty much sum up who you are, a Georgian? Is that *your* story? No! You're an ex-slave who has devoted his life to the abolition

of slavery, overcoming great hardships and obstacles along the way, I should imagine. That's your story, isn't it? You and this young so-called lawyer have proven you know *what* they are. They're Africans! Congratulations. What you don't know and, as far as I can tell, haven't bothered in the least to discover, is *who* they are.

Few cases facing teachers today are as dramatic or difficult as the case of the *Amistad* prisoners. However, over the course of a career in education you will surely participate in decisions about the best ways to teach students who are culturally different from students whose backgrounds are most familiar to you. To meet this challenge, you will need to listen carefully to your students in order to understand the many stories present in your classroom.

Challenge 2: Recognizing That All Students Are Diverse in Multiple Ways

Part of understanding who students really are lies in recognizing that all learners are diverse in multiple ways. Ironically, increased recognition of cultural diversity has led to the creation of new categories and terminology for describing students (limited English proficient, English language learners, bilingual, Hispanic/Latino, white, poverty, middle-class, single-parent family, gifted and talented, special needs, etc.). These labels, while required for recordkeeping purposes, can never capture the diversity of human beings. Teachers who wish to work with cultural diversity as a resource and tool for excellent instruction need to keep this in mind rather than accept essentialist labels that imply that children can be only one kind of person. The best tool that we have found to avoid pigeonholing our students is to spend time with them to find out who they are. In David and Yvonne Freeman's book *Between Worlds*, teachers talk about discovering the instructional value of getting to know their students better. One teacher reflected,

> I was amazed at Mony's proficiency in English and shocked at what I'd wrongly perceived it to be when she was in my class. It sounds so simple, but if we as teachers put more effort into *who* we're teaching, more of the *what* would take care of itself. When we concentrate on programs, or strict timelines, we lose sight of the important human element. (2001, 5)

Although discovering the diversities embodied by your students makes for richer teaching and increased opportunities for learning, it doesn't necessarily make teaching any easier. Another teacher commented on her experiences following a Hmong student in seventh and eighth grade: "This experience made me sadly aware that my students are all individuals with diverse and complicated needs and that I can never hope to solve them all. Just my one-on-one interviews with Tou and my special efforts to talk at least briefly with him every day pointed up that all my students need special attention. I feel stretched to the limit" (2001, 11).

Challenge 3: Understanding That Difference Is Not the Same as Deficit

As schools become more diverse in the ways that we have outlined in this chapter (and perhaps in ways we have not foreseen here), teachers must learn to see the cultural groups from which students come as representing resources rather than problems. Schools need "teachers who regard color, ethnicity, and language variations among children as strengths to be drawn upon instead of deficits to be overcome" (Berliner 2005, 182). At the level of individual learners, you will need to see abilities rather than only what children are (currently) unable to do. Ultimately, this requires you to be able to see your students and their families as actors, not victims. It means understanding that people are capable of making choices in social circumstances that, while difficult at times, do not reduce them to the role of passive bystanders in their own lives.

Challenge 4: Teaching in and Outside the Classroom

As teachers, our first responsibility is the intellectual growth and well-being of our students. For new teachers, juggling the myriad tasks involved in curriculum planning, materials development and selection, lesson planning, teaching, and assessment of your own students will probably seem like more than enough work! And yet, as any middle school teacher will tell you, articulation with the abilities developed at earlier levels is also of great importance. The same is true for the transition between middle school and high school and between high school and college. Therefore, no matter what grade level or content area we teach, our jobs are inevitably linked with the teaching done by colleagues working in earlier and later grades.

But teaching does not stop at the classroom door or even at the door of the school. Culturally responsible educators also need to consider how our teaching connects to the outside world. As the principal of a successful dual language school once told us, her greatest challenge is not in educating students bilingually, but rather in keeping parents and community members informed about how bilingual education works. The same is true for all forms of culturally responsible teaching. We cannot assume that everyone will automatically understand the thinking underlying culturally responsible programs. Because these efforts are probably very different from the ways parents were educated, you need to be able to clearly explain to parents and community members what you are doing and why you are doing it.

Challenge 5: Keeping Up with Change and New Ways of Thinking About It

At the beginning of this chapter we described our own growth as multicultural educators, noting that learning about cultural diversity never stops. While not all teachers end up specializing in diversity issues, none of us can afford to stop paying attention to them. The children we teach certainly cannot afford it! Keeping up with change means keeping up with new ways of thinking about how the world and the worlds of our students are ever changing.

Technological developments are one example of rapid change, as well as the educational consequences of not keeping up. For example, many learners today have access to new forms of information technology, including the Internet, email, cellular phones, and text messaging, that parents and teachers are less familiar with. These technologies are changing the ways children learn and process information outside school, but what does this mean for teaching? Some scholars believe that teachers who don't become familiar with these new ways of learning, those who stick to "the subject-based curriculum based on texts and academic teachers as authority[, are] in trouble" and at risk of being outdated (Lankshear and Knobel 2003, 176). Similarly, even in the most culturally homogenous communities, digital technologies make a wide variety of new cultural influences available to learners. Thus, teachers who want to be able to teach effectively in a variety of contexts (with students of different ages, in different schools, and in different regions) need to be lifelong learners about the population movements and globalization that characterize life in the twenty-first century.

Challenge 6: Understanding the Limits of Culturally Responsible Education

Given our focus on the importance of cultural diversity for education, it may seem strange that we conclude by cautioning teachers to recognize the limits of culturally responsible teaching. There are two parts to this challenge. First, teachers need to recognize that culturally responsible teaching is not a panacea for the many real-life issues facing schools and their culturally diverse students. For example, as you will read in the subsequent chapters of this book, culturally responsible teaching is certainly not a substitute for content area preparation. Although current policies embodied in No Child Left Behind have motivated schools to emphasize reading and math, teachers of science, social studies, art, and physical education still need to be well prepared to teach their respective subjects *in addition to* keeping in mind the issues we have outlined in this chapter.

Finally, policy makers and the public tend to be overly optimistic about the power of schools to redress the historic and current inequities between white, middle-class students whose first language is English and the growing number of students with less privileged but equally legitimate backgrounds. As scholars and many veteran teachers have observed, schools are not wholly responsible for the wide disparities in income and access to quality health care and housing that characterize many U.S. communities. It is illogical to expect that schools can make the whole difference without support from other parts of society. But we do what we can. For those of us who dare to teach (Freire 1998), accepting the challenge of learning to be culturally responsible educators can be an important *first step* in doing a better job of serving all learners.

Conclusion

Clearly, cultural diversity matters for schools and for learning, and educators who base their teaching practices on this understanding will be better prepared to teach the students of today and tomorrow. Schools can be very conservative institutions, but they are also places in which new members are always arriving and others leaving. Thus, schools are continuously changing, whether we like it or not. Understanding how to work with these changes presents a significant challenge to beginning and experienced teachers alike, and we invite you to continue this important journey with classmates and colleagues. We close with a quote about the power of teacher collaboration from a participant in a bilingual teachers study group:

> Learning how to learn together and to work together was a major transformation. It did not happen quickly, smoothly, or easily. We experienced dissonance and frustration as we struggled to understand what we were learning and sharing with each other. We tended to want to find ideal solutions, to try to resolve hard issues and lay them to rest once and for all. It took considerable work before we were able to welcome ambiguities. But as we persisted in the inquiry process to

which we had committed ourselves, we began to experience some profound and exhilarating changes. (Saavedra 1999, 308)

Like these collaborating teachers, we find that working with culturally diverse learners requires us to look at people and issues in new ways, ways that are not always comfortable or easy. In the process of becoming a successful teacher for all students, especially learners whose language and cultural backgrounds, identities, and abilities are unlike your own, you will continue to grow too.

Applications

Because teaching is a complex activity that changes with each new group of learners, we offer the following strategies not as recipes to be followed but as possibilities to be modified to fit the needs of your students as well as your own interests and developing strengths. With experience and reflection, you will be able to find what works best for you and your students.

Applications for Challenge 1

1. In *Teacher Man*, Frank McCourt recalls how he relied on the power of story-telling as a first-year teacher in New York City: "I'm twenty-seven years old, a new teacher, dipping into my past to satisfy these American teenagers, to keep them quiet and in their seats. I never thought my past would be so useful. Why would anyone want to know about my miserable life?" (2005, 26). McCourt's more experienced colleagues warn him against this tactic ("You can never get back the bits and pieces of your life that stick in their little heads. Your life, man. It's all you have. Tell 'em nothing"), and it backfires initially when students begin to ask about his love life, and he isn't sure how to respond. As a new teacher, you will want to think carefully about which life experiences are appropriate to discuss with your students and then plan how you will incorporate them into a lesson. With these words of caution in mind, consider sharing parts of your life story. Like McCourt, you might be surprised by how interested the students are and by the assumptions they make about teachers. For younger learners and less proficient readers, you can tell your story in oral form; older students and more advanced readers can read an autobiography you prepare ahead of time, and English language learners can write sentences or a short biography based

Applications for Challenge 5

1. James Gee (2004) believes that video games require students to use more higher-order thinking skills than typically called for in school. Test Gee's claim by observing a child or young adult complete an in-school or school-based activity. Then observe the same learner using digital technology for school or play (outside school). What are the differences in the number and complexity of tasks the learner is called on to perform? Based on your observations of what a child is able to do outside school, would you say that the school curriculum is actually holding back this student's learning?

2. Is there a special topic you've been meaning to learn more about? Teach yourself more about it via the Internet or another type of information technology. Keep a journal of how your learning is different using this new kind of tool. What aspects are easier or more difficult than with the ways you are used to learning?

Applications for Challenge 6

1. Talk to veteran teachers to find out what their aspirations for social change were when they first began teaching. How have those aspirations changed? Are they as optimistic about the role of teachers and schools to change society for the better? What barriers do they see hindering the power of schools to promote social change? One interesting project is to interview teachers at the beginning and others nearing the end of their teaching careers and compare their ideas about how teaching and schools have changed.

2. Look in the library or online for articles and websites that claim a positive relationship between education and equity in schools. Identify the claims in the articles you find. What evidence do they give in support of this assumption? Do you agree with the authors' claims? Why or why not? Some places to look include websites for FairTest, Rethinking Schools, and the Center for Research on Education, Diversity and Excellence, listed in the "Online Resources" section at the end of the chapter.

3. Think across disciplines. One fascinating way to keep up with change and new knowledge is to discuss issues with students majoring in other disciplines. Just as this chapter draws on ideas from anthropology and biology, you can invite students and professors from those disciplines to read the "What Is Diversity?" section with you and to discuss the points raised there.

How does your thinking about culture and human diversity change as a result of your discussion?

Key Terms and Acronyms

Americanization policies. A series of laws passed in the early and mid-twentieth century in southwestern states such as Texas, Arizona, and New Mexico aimed at turning Mexican-origin and other migrant students into monolingual speakers of English and thus (so the thinking went) into better Americans.

assimilation. A process in which migrants lose their distinct cultural traits and develop new customs and practices consistent with mainstream culture.

borderlands. Term describing the geographical area on both sides of the physical border between the United States and Mexico, but also the cultural spaces occupied by people who share characteristics of Mexican and U.S. cultures.

code-switching. The use of two or more languages in a single sentence or conversation. Rapid code-switching is a marker of highly fluent bilinguals.

cultural universals. The idea that some aspects of human behavior and social organization are shared by all cultural groups.

culturally relevant pedagogy. Instruction that is designed to fit the cultural needs of the learners.

culturally responsible educators. Teachers who shape their teaching to meet the cultural needs of their students.

dialect. A way of speaking, writing, or signing a language that is noticeably different from other ways, including differences in pronunciation, accent, and vocabulary. World languages such as Arabic, English, Mandarin, and Spanish are composed of many different dialects, often associated with a particular region.

dumbed-down curriculum. A plan of study that is beneath the learners' intelligence. Whether the curriculum is well intentioned or cynical, the long-term effect is that students leave school poorly prepared for advanced study or well-paying jobs.

essentialist. The idea that a group of people share all the same characteristics and, therefore, their actions are determined by membership in that group.

ethnicity. A group identity based on shared characteristics such as race, language, and culture.

funds of knowledge. Knowledge that children acquire in their homes and communities.

homophobia. Fear of and discrimination against gays, lesbians, and transgender individuals and groups.

intercultural education. A form of schooling based on the idea that teaching about cultural diversity must include questioning why some groups have been excluded and other are more economically privileged and powerful. Compare with *multicultural education*.

LULAC. League of United Latin American Citizens.

mestizo. A Spanish word describing a person of mixed indigenous and European heritage.

multicultural education. A form of education that attempts to incorporate important elements of different cultures. Compare with *intercultural education*, which explores why some groups have greater prestige and power than others.

NAACP. National Association for the Advancement of Colored People.

No Child Left Behind Act (NCLB). A federal policy requiring schools to meet standards as measured by testing all students.

normal. The popular idea that there is a single value-neutral or natural way to be human. A persistent fiction that is used to present others as abnormal and deviant.

UNESCO. United Nations Educational, Scientific and Cultural Organization.

Resources for Further Study

Online Resources

Center for Research on Education, Diversity and Excellence: http://crede.berkeley.edu/index.html

The Deaf Resource Library: http://deaflibrary.org/

Ethnologue: Languages of the World, fifteenth edition: www.ethnologue.com/

Houston Teachers Institute: http://teachers.yale.edu/league/hti/index.php

The National Center for Fair and Open Testing (FairTest): www.fairtest.org/

Rethinking Schools: www.rethinkingschools.org/

Teaching Tolerance: www.splcenter.org/center/tt/teach.jsp

U.S. Census Bureau: www.census.gov/

Audiovisual Resources

Esparza, Moctesuma, and Robert Katz, producers. 2006. *Walkout*. HBO Films. www.hbo.com/films/walkout/.

Nava, Gregory. 1983/2000. *El norte*. Island Alive/Artisan Films.

———. 1995. *Mi familia/My Family*. New York: New Line Cinema.

Public Broadcasting Service. 1994. *For a Deaf Son*. Arlington, VA.

Public Broadcasting Service. 2001. *Sound and Fury*. Arlington, VA. www.pbs.org/wnet/soundandfury/lesson.html.

Spielberg, Steven, dir. 1997. *Amistad*. Universal City, CA: DreamWorks Entertainment.

2

English Language Learners

Who Are They? How Can Teachers Support Them?

Yvonne S. Freeman and David E. Freeman

Introduction

In 2004 one in every ten students in U.S. schools was an *English language learner* (ELL). The U.S. Census Bureau predicts that by 2030, nearly 40 percent of the school-age population will speak a language other than English at home (Ramírez 2004). Some states, such as California, Texas, New York, Florida, and Illinois, have had large numbers of ELLs in the public school system for many years. Other states have had only small and scattered pockets of second language students, often concentrated in one or two schools.

Despite these differences among and within states, one fact stands out: the number of ELLs has increased dramatically in the last decade. According to statistics compiled by the National Clearinghouse for English Language Acquisition (2006), in the 1994–95 school year, the total K–12 enrollment in U.S. schools was 47.75 million students. Of these, a little over 3 million, or about 6 percent, were ELLs. By the 2004–5 school year, ten years later, the total number of K–12 students in U.S. schools had risen by only 1.23 million, a 2.59 percent growth. During that same period, the ELL population had soared by almost 2 million to over 5 million, a 60 percent gain. During this ten-year period, nearly every state recorded gains in its ELL population, and eleven states reported a greater than 200 percent increase. The graph in Figure 2.1 compares the K–12 growth with the ELL growth.

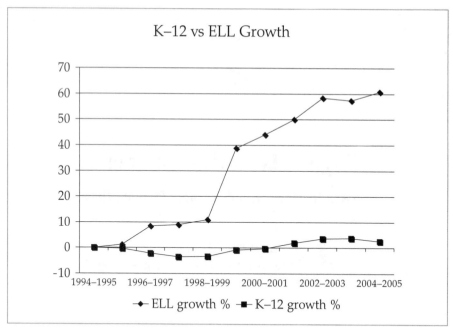

figure 2.1 K–12 and ELL Population Growth

National statistics show that ELLs are three times as likely as native English speakers to be low academic achievers. They are also twice as likely to be retained to repeat a grade. These statistics point to the challenges schools face in meeting their goal of enabling every student to succeed academically. This rapid growth in the ELL population has left many districts searching for teachers with the experience and training necessary to work effectively with second language students.

This chapter addresses how to meet the needs of ELL students in schools. It is first important to understand the learners themselves. There are different types of English learners and each has different characteristics. We describe these types of students and provide examples of each. In addition, teachers need to understand how schools identify and classify ELLs for instruction. Once students are classified, they are provided with different kinds of support programs. Some of these programs are more appropriate than others, so it is important for educators to understand the programs and their effectiveness.

After reviewing learners and programs, we turn to effective practices for English learners based on second language acquisition theory. *Krashen's theory of second language acquisition* provides a framework for best practices for second language learners. Based on this theory, we suggest three keys for working with ELLs. We bring these keys to life through an extended classroom scenario.

Types of Learners

"José and Felipe arrived here from Mexico at the same time last year, but Felipe is doing quite well while José seems completely lost. I think José isn't trying to learn English." This comment is typical of those we hear from teachers across the country. *Limited English proficient* (LEP) students enter classes at different ages and with different academic backgrounds. Some do very well while many struggle. Teaching these diverse students is complex. García, in a review of the research on concerns about English learners, points out that "there is no typical LEP child" (2000, 3). When teachers ask us what is most important for working with ELLs, we always tell them, "Know your students." English language learners vary a great deal, and in order to teach them well, it is critically important to know who they are, where they have come from, and what strengths they bring to the classroom. Teachers should consider some basic differences among English learners as they plan instruction, including differences in their academic backgrounds and their academic language proficiency. Let's take a look at three types of learners.

Students with Adequate Formal Schooling—Guillermo

Sixteen-year-old Guillermo arrived in Tucson, Arizona, in 1984 a week after he had watched as his father, an important military official, was assassinated in front of his home in San Salvador. Guillermo narrowly escaped being arrested and probably murdered himself. In fact, Guillermo had two bullet wounds in his leg when he arrived in this country. Guillermo sought asylum in the United States with his aunt, a doctoral student and teaching assistant at the University of Arizona in Tucson, because his stepmother in El Salvador distanced herself from him for her own safety and that of a two-year-old daughter, Guillermo's stepsister.

Although Guillermo had studied English at private bilingual schools in San Salvador, his comprehension of English was extremely limited when he first arrived. His aunt enrolled him in a local high school almost immediately and put him on a strict study schedule. She warned him that education was his only road to success, that there was no time to be wasted, and that she would not tolerate irresponsibility.

The aunt supported her nephew financially the best she could. He also received some sporadic financial help from aging grandparents in El Salvador. Guillermo was very social. He worked hard to make friends and joined high school clubs almost immediately. He talked to anyone who would try to understand him.

After only one semester, his grades were good for a new arrival. He took regular college preparatory academic course work, he earned Bs and an occasional A in his classes, and his average qualified him to attend the local university.

Guillermo studied engineering and international economics at the university. He served on the university's student government team several times and spent one summer as an aide to a senator in Washington, DC. After completing his bachelor of science degree, he went on to the University of Southern California and completed a master of arts in architecture. Presently, he is considering setting up his own architectural firm in Los Angeles.

Guillermo represents the first of the three types of English learners, *students with adequate formal schooling*. These students are recent arrivals who are at grade level in their native language studies. Though they may still struggle with standardized tests, they catch up with course work quickly. Guillermo attended private schools while living in El Salvador. He was at grade level in his content studies and had even studied some English there, though he certainly was far from a fluent English speaker, reader, or writer when he arrived. In addition, Guillermo's family had traveled to Europe and the United States. He had background knowledge of school subjects in Spanish that often exceeded that of his native English-speaking classmates in the United States. ELLs like Guillermo who arrive with adequate formal schooling generally succeed in school. However, this group of newcomers is usually the smallest group of English learners found in schools. The other two groups are more numerous and struggle more to achieve school success.

Students with Limited and Interrupted Schooling—Laura

Laura represents a second group of English learners, *students with limited formal schooling*. She spent the first nine years of her life in a rural farming village located at the base of the Popocatepetl volcano in the state of Puebla, Mexico. Her elementary schooling experience before coming to the United States was sporadic. During these years, Laura lived with her grandparents because her parents had moved to Texas to find work. Her elderly grandparents found it very difficult to transport her to school from their rural ranch. At the end of third grade, her parents came and took her to Houston, Texas. Her mother had a job cleaning office buildings at night, and her father did construction work for a home builder. In Houston, Laura and her parents lived in an apartment shared by an aunt, an uncle, and two cousins.

Laura's mother enrolled her in the bilingual program of a school that served mainly middle- to upper-middle-class families. Based on her age, Laura was placed in fourth grade. She and her cousins lived in the only zone of the school district that had low-income housing. Philip, her teacher, soon realized that Laura spoke no English. His evaluations of her academic Spanish showed that she was at about a first-grade level in reading and writing, and her math skills did not go beyond some very basic computation.

When Philip talked to Laura about how she felt about school in the United States, she told him that everyone else seemed to understand what was being taught and could speak at least a little English. She explained that she couldn't understand her homework, even in Spanish, and her mother was the only person who could read or write in their family, but she worked at night when Laura was at home. Because of this, she often did not turn in her homework. Laura was frightened because she had no friends and felt different from everyone else. At this point of the interview, she started to cry and told Philip that she wanted to go back to Mexico, where she didn't even have to go to school and her grandparents would be at home to be with her.

Philip realized that Laura was so far behind the other students that it was highly unlikely she would be able to pass fourth grade. The school identified her as an at-risk student within the first three weeks and placed her in the intervention program. Laura represents a child who has gone from her familiar rural environment in a country where she understood everyone to one of the largest cities in the United States where many other languages besides Spanish are spoken. Besides the culture shock, her lack of schooling made her educational experience in Texas all the more difficult.

Laura fit all the characteristics of a limited formal schooling student. She was a newcomer who was confused and frightened by school in this country. She spoke almost no English. Although she was in a bilingual classroom where the teacher provided some instruction in Spanish, she was far behind her peers in reading and writing as well as math as evidenced by her limited math computational skills. The extra tutoring provided would probably also overwhelm Laura as she desperately tried to learn in a language she didn't understand.

Long-Term English Learners—Andrew and Teresa

Some ELLs are *long-term English learners*. An example is Andrew, a middle school native Chinese-speaking student who has attended schools in the San Francisco area since kindergarten, struggles in classes, and is reading four grade levels below his peers. His parents work in a restaurant in the Chinese section of the city, and he attends the large, multiethnic high school nearby. Andrew doesn't seem to be trying very hard to do well in school, and because he speaks

English well but struggles with reading and writing English, his teachers have recently referred him to be tested for special education. In fact, school officials are baffled by the growing number of Asian students like Andrew who struggle academically (Chang 2001).

Andrew is a challenge for both his parents and school officials. His general attitude toward school is quite negative. Andrew's parents are confused by his rebellion and lack of respect for their traditional Chinese values. School officials suspect that Andrew has joined a neighborhood gang. Andrew can speak and understand English, but he can't read or write English at grade level. In addition, he has not developed knowledge and skills of the different academic subject areas and struggles on standardized tests. Despite his academic deficiencies, Andrew thinks he is doing well in school because he gets mainly Bs and Cs on his report cards.

Teresa's story is somewhat different from Andrew's. Teresa's parents are farmworkers who do not speak English. She is an only child but has a great deal of responsibility at home for cooking and cleaning because her parents work long hours in the fields. She has an extended family with whom she spends time, and she often serves as a caretaker for her younger cousins.

Like Andrew, Teresa has attended schools in the United States since kindergarten and speaks English well; yet, according to her seventh-grade language arts teacher, she arrived in junior high school without being able to write complete sentences in English. Far from being a troublemaker, Teresa has gone through school as an extremely quiet and shy student. She has learned how to remain unnoticed. Because she was quiet and turned in assignments, she was promoted each year. She received some *English as a second language* (ESL) support in early grades, but she arrived at junior high without grade-level literacy in either Spanish or English.

Andrew and Teresa are typical long-term English learners. They do not read or write in their primary language. In fact, all their schooling has been in English. They have attended schools in this country since kindergarten and appear to have mastered English. Andrew understands how schools work and interacts socially with native English speakers easily. Teresa also understands the system. She knows how to remain unnoticed. Both struggle academically. They are below grade level in reading and writing. They get average grades but probably will not pass the secondary exit exam.

Teachers and other school officials often label long-term English learners like Andrew as lazy because they speak and understand English well but perform so poorly on standardized tests. Teresa's teachers have trouble remem-

Newly Arrived with Adequate Schooling (Guillermo)	• recent arrivals (less than five years in United States) • adequate schooling in native country • soon catch up academically • may still score low on standardized tests given in English
Newly Arrived with Limited Formal Schooling (Laura)	• recent arrivals (less than five years in United States) • interrupted or limited schooling in native country • limited native language literac • below grade level in math • poor academic achievement
Long-Term English Learner (Andrew, Teresa)	• seven or more years in the United States • have had ESL or bilingual instruction, but no consistent • program • below grade level in reading and writing • mismatch between student perception of achievement • and actual grades • may get adequate grades but score low on tests

figure 2.2 Types of Older English Learners (adapted from Olsen and Jaramillo 1999)

bering who she is, and when asked, they say she is a nice girl but not very motivated. What is most disturbing about long-term English learners is that there are so many of them. The dropout rates among these students has begun to alarm educators (Bridgeland, Dilulio, et al. 2006).

Figure 2.2 summarizes the characteristics of the three types of English language learners.

Identifying English Language Learners

To determine which category an ELL fits into, a teacher needs detailed information. In most cases, teachers are not given this information about their ELLs. In fact, different states use a variety of ways to identify students as ELLs. The U.S. Department of Education uses the term *limited English proficient* (LEP) to refer to students in elementary or secondary schools who were born outside the United States or students who speak a language other than English at home and who do not have sufficient mastery of English to meet state standards or excel in an English language classroom. States use different measures to determine whether a student meets these requirements. For example, in Texas an LEP student is defined as a student whose primary language is other than

English and whose English language skills are such that the student has difficulty performing ordinary class work in English.

According to Wiley (1994), the most common ways to identify LEP students are to use information from the U.S. Census, to use information that parents put on a *home language survey*, or to use a test of language proficiency. Each of these methods has problems. Both the census and the home language survey are reports by people of how well they or their children speak English and of what language is usually spoken at home. Parents who want to have their children placed in an English language classroom rather than a bilingual classroom may say that English is the language spoken at home even if the family uses some other language. Language proficiency tests are also problematic. Different states use different tests. They are a single measure of a student's proficiency in English. The student may be suffering from culture shock or simply be very nervous about taking a test in a new language. As a result, the score on the single test may not reflect the student's actual knowledge of English.

Even if methods for identifying English language learners were consistent across states and based on better information about students' actual level of English proficiency, simply classifying the student as LEP or as an ELL would still not provide important information that a teacher needs. For example, the teacher would not know how well the student reads and writes in his primary language even though primary language literacy is an important indicator of academic success in English.

Much more information is needed. Various experts in the field (Crawford 2004; Gottleib 2006; Short and Fitzsimmons 2007) suggest using many sources of information to assess students. Students' native language content knowledge and literacy skills should be assessed. This information should be combined with results of an appropriate assessment of ELLs' vocabulary and content knowledge in English, an assessment that should be made using rubrics specifically designed for ELLs. Classroom portfolios, including student work samples, provide teachers with much more useful information about students than a single language proficiency test score. Parents and school records can provide additional information. It is important to know about students' schooling outside the United States and to know if students have moved often or if their previous schooling has been interrupted. Students' socioeconomic status often helps explain how much access students have to resources, and past and present participation in special services helps teachers understand ELLs. Clearly, the assessment of ELLs is a schoolwide or districtwide task. In order to plan appropriate instruction, teachers need this kind of information about each of their students.

Instructional Support Programs for ELLs

It is important for schools to gather accurate information about ELLs in order to provide the kinds of instructional support these students need. Districts with large numbers of new arrivals often establish a *newcomer center*. This is a place where students can be assessed and given some initial instruction. For students who speak very little English, a newcomer center can offer intensive ESL classes. These classes help new arrivals develop the basic English they need to understand classroom directions. In addition, newcomer centers teach students about how school works in the United States. For example, older students need to understand such things as changing classes for different subjects, keeping their books in a locker, and eating in a cafeteria. For students who have had very limited experience with schools or whose schools are very different from those in the U.S., this induction period is extremely important. Newcomer centers also work with parents to help them adjust to life in a new community. Many families suffering from culture shock struggle to adjust to life in a new country, and they need this kind of support. Newcomer centers play an important role in assessing students and preparing them to enter the U.S. school system. However, in many districts there are no newcomer centers to provide these kinds of support, and ELLs are placed directly into their neighborhood schools.

In school, ELLs may receive different kinds of support. The best programs are those that use both the students' primary language and English. These bilingual classes draw on the language strengths students bring and have been shown to be the most effective programs for ELLs. The following chapter discusses bilingual education in more detail. Although bilingual programs have been shown to be the most effective option for ELLs, schools may not be able to offer them. There may not be enough students at the same grade level who speak the same first language to justify a program, or there may not be enough qualified bilingual teachers in the school. In some states, laws prohibit the establishment of bilingual programs under most circumstances. In these cases, ESL support is the best instructional model for ELLs.

Schools provide various types of ESL support. At the secondary level, students may receive one or two periods of ESL instruction each day. During the other periods, the ELLs attend regular classes. ESL classes provide additional support for ELLs, and, in the best of circumstances, the ESL teacher and the regular content teachers work together to plan instruction for the ELLs in their classes. However, this coordination seldom takes place. ESL teachers with recent preparation in second language teaching methods use current methods and teach their students language through content, but, unfortunately, there are still many ESL teachers who use very traditional techniques, and this approach does not prepare students to perform well in mainstream classes.

A common practice at the lower grades is to have an ESL teacher who works with the ELLs part of the day. The ESL students may be pulled out of their regular class to work with the ESL teacher. This approach poses two problems. First, when they are pulled out, the ELLs miss out on the regular instruction the mainstream teacher provides. Second, the ESL teacher often works with students from several different classes, so it is hard for the ESL teacher to coordinate instruction with the mainstream teachers. In addition, the students lose time during the transition to and from the mainstream class.

In some schools, the ESL teacher comes into the class and works with the ELLs. This push-in approach can work well because it is easier for the mainstream teacher to coordinate with the ESL teacher. Although ELLs may need the extra help the ESL specialist can provide, many ELLs want to work with the mainstream teacher, not an ESL specialist, because they want to fit in with their native English-speaking classmates. The social stigma of being pulled out for extra help or of having a teacher come in to work with them often outweighs the benefits students can receive from the ESL teacher.

At both the elementary and secondary levels, many ELLs receive extra help from a paraprofessional who spends at least part of the day in the class. Often, paraprofessionals speak the first language of the ELLs. In some cases, the regular teacher may delegate almost all the instruction of the ELLs in the class to the paraprofessional. Some paraprofessionals do an excellent job, but they have not been trained as teachers, so they are not well qualified to work with a group of students on a regular basis. The best approach is for ELLs to be placed with a mainstream teacher who has received training on ways to meet the needs of second language students and can modify instruction to teach them effectively. Figure 2.3 lists the different options schools may adopt for working with ELLs and the advantages and disadvantages of each.

Effective Instruction for ELLs

Schools offer different kinds of support for ELLs. Each approach has advantages and disadvantages. ELLs in any program benefit when teachers use effective methods based on current theory and research on second language acquisition and second language teaching. There are three keys to effective teaching for ELLs. When teachers apply these keys, all their students, including their ELLs, benefit.

Type of Support	Advantages	Disadvantages
One or two periods of ESL (middle and secondary schools)	• provides ELLs with special attention • may provide extra help with difficult subjects	• seldom coordinated with regular classes • ESL teacher may use traditional methods
ESL pullout (most common in elementary schools)	• provides small-group support • tailors instruction to the needs of ELLs	• difficult for ESL teacher to coordinate with mainstream teacher • ELLs miss out on the instruction in the regular class • ELLs may feel stigmatized for being pulled out
ESL push-in	• ESL teacher works in the regular classroom • easier to coordinate with regular teacher • provides extra help tailored to needs of ELLs	• ESL and regular teacher may not have time to coordinate instruction • ELLs still miss out on some regular class activities • ELLs may feel stigmatized
paraprofessional	• paraprofessional may speak ELLs' language • paraprofessional offers extra support for ELLs	• paraprofessional is not qualified as a teacher • paraprofessional may not use current methods
mainstream teacher with special training	• can include ELLs in all class activities • can use techniques to make the instruction understandable	• requires extra plan-ning to differentiate instruction

figure 2.3 Types of Support for ELLs

Key 1: Teach Language Through Content

The first key is to teach language through content. Traditional approaches to teaching language focused on the language itself. Students learned the grammar and vocabulary of the new language. The problem with the traditional approach was that students learned *about* the language, but they did not learn the language. Communicative approaches to language teaching replaced traditional approaches. Rather than studying grammar and vocabulary, students practiced dialogues and did role plays using the new language. They learned how to introduce someone, order food, or make an apology. Communicative approaches helped students to speak and understand the new language in daily settings.

Content-based language teaching builds on the communicative approach. However, instead of learning to communicate in everyday situations, students learn to communicate in the different academic subjects taught in school. They learn to speak, understand, read, and write like scientists, social scientists, mathematicians, and literary scholars. This is the language they need to succeed in schools. Krashen (1982) developed a theory of second language acquisition that forms the basis for content-based language teaching. In the following sections we describe his theory. Then, we explain how teachers can teach language through content and the reasons they should take this approach.

Krashen's Theory of Second Language Acquisition

Krashen's theory comprises five hypotheses: (1) the *learning/acquisition hypothesis*, (2) the *natural order hypothesis*, (3) the *monitor hypothesis*, (4) *the input hypothesis*, and (5) the *affective filter hypothesis*.

The learning/acquisition hypothesis • Krashen (2003) uses the term *learning* to refer to a conscious process of language development that occurs as a result of direct teaching. In contrast, *acquisition* is a subconscious process of language development that occurs as the result of exposure to meaningful messages in a language. Most researchers agree that many aspects of a child's first language are acquired. All normally functioning children acquire the phonology, syntax, and semantics of the language used by their caretakers. Within a fairly short time, they can understand and produce messages in the language those around them use. This knowledge is acquired, not learned, because no one teaches a child this information. Krashen argues that people acquire a second language in the same way that children acquire their first language, without explicit teaching. People can pick up a new language because humans have an innate capacity for acquiring languages.

The natural order hypothesis • Krashen reviews research that shows that language, both first language and second language, is acquired in a natural order. Simply put, some aspects of language appear in the speech of language learners before other features. For example, babies acquiring English first produce sounds with vowels (usually the low, back "ah" sound) and later add consonants beginning with those formed with the lips, like *p* and *m*. This helps explain why the first word of many infants is something like *mama* or *papa*, much to the delight of a parent. Sounds like *r* come later. That's why young children might say, like Elmer Fudd, *wabbit* instead of *rabbit*. Other parts of language also appear in a natural order. Statements come before questions. Positive statements come before negatives, and so on.

Researchers of second language found the same phenomenon. The natural order of second language acquisition differs slightly from that of first language, but there is a definite order. Dulay and Burt (1974) studied Spanish and Chinese speakers acquiring English. They looked at the order in which certain morphemes appeared. They noted that the plural *s* in a word like *toys* showed up in children's speech earlier than the third-person *s* of present tense verbs in sentences like "He plays." Whether researchers look at the acquisition of sounds, word parts, or sentence patterns, they find an order of acquisition that is the same, even for children whose first languages are different. The order seems to come from the language being acquired, not a transfer of features from the first language.

The monitor hypothesis • The monitor hypothesis helps explain the role of learning in the process of language acquisition. Acquired language forms the basis for the ability to understand and produce language. The phonology, morphology, syntax, and semantics are acquired. Acquisition is what enables native English speakers to tell what sounds right in their dialect. They may not be able to explain why "He is married to her" sounds better than "He is married with her," but because native speakers have acquired the language, they can make these kinds of judgments.

Learned knowledge also plays a role in language competence. The rules that people learn can be used to monitor spoken or written output. People can use these rules to check what they say or write. In order for monitor use to be effective, language users must have time, they must focus on language form, and they must know the rules. Even in the first language, most people monitor their speech in formal situations such as giving a lecture to a large group of people. To use the monitor effectively, one must have learned the rules. Is it *different from* or *different than*? Unless the speaker has learned the right answer, she can't monitor the output very well.

Spoken language is difficult to monitor using learned rules because if we start focusing on form, we cannot also focus on meaning. However, editing during the writing process represents an ideal situation to apply the monitor because there is time, and one can focus specifically on the correctness of the language—learned knowledge—to be sure that sentences are complete and words are spelled right.

The input hypothesis • How does acquisition take place? According to Krashen, the key is comprehensible input: messages, either oral or written, that students understand. Not all input leads to acquisition. Krashen says that students acquire language when they receive input that is slightly beyond their current level. He refers to this as i+1 (input plus one). If students receive input that is below or at their current level (i+0), there is nothing new to acquire. However, if the input is too much beyond their current level (i+10, for example), it no longer is comprehensible.

Providing comprehensible input is not an exact science. Teachers can't possibly ensure that everything they say or write will be exactly at the i+1 level for every student. The students in a class are all at different levels of proficiency. Nevertheless, as long as students understand most of what they hear or read in a new language, they will acquire the language. Different students will acquire different parts of the language depending on their current level. Krashen is an especially strong advocate of reading for language acquisition. He cites research showing that reading provides excellent comprehensible input and is the source of one's knowledge of vocabulary, grammar, and spelling.

The affective filter hypothesis • How do affective factors such as nervousness, boredom, and anxiety influence language acquisition? If language is acquired when a person receives comprehensible input, that input has to reach the part of the brain that processes language. Boredom and anxiety can serve as a kind of filter to block out incoming messages and prevent them from reaching the language acquisition device. As a result, even though a teacher may present a very comprehensible lesson, some students may not acquire the language of the presentation because their affective filters operate to block the input. Students cannot acquire language that never reaches the language acquisition device. On the other hand, when their filters are open, when students are relaxed and engaged in a lesson, even messages that are not easy to comprehend will trigger the acquisition process.

Krashen's theory of second language acquisition claims that second languages are acquired, not learned. The process is the same as for first language acquisition. Acquisition occurs in a natural order when people receive comprehensible input and their affective filter is low. Rules that people learn can be used to monitor the output, either oral or written. Although other theorists have pointed to the importance of output and interaction in the process of developing a second language, most researchers agree that languages are largely acquired rather than learned.

English language learners can acquire the language of social science or literature if their teachers make the academic content comprehensible and if the classroom is a place where students are engaged, not bored or nervous. There are several ways that a teacher can make academic input comprehensible (Freeman and Freeman 1998); see Figure 2.4 for a sampling.

All of the strategies listed in Figure 2.4 help make the input comprehensible because they supply extra support for the new language. Rather than simply lecturing, teachers scaffold instruction by using visuals and by having students work in groups. These techniques make lessons more understandable for all students, including ELLs.

There are four reasons that ELLs benefit when teachers teach language through content (Freeman and Freeman 2002; Freeman and Freeman 2006b). First, ELLs get both language and content. They acquire English as they learn the different school subjects. They don't need to learn English first and math or science later. They can do both at the same time. Second, language is kept in its natural context. Students in a math class acquire words like *triangle* and *rectangle* as they study different shapes. This approach is much more effective

---

1. Draw on students' first languages to preview and review the lesson.
2. Use visuals and realia (real things). Try always to move from the concrete to the abstract.
3. Scaffold content learning through the use of graphic organizers including Venn diagrams, webs, and charts.
4. Use gestures and body language.
5. Speak clearly and pause often, but don't slow speech down unnaturally.
6. Say the same thing in different ways (paraphrase).
7. Write key words and ideas down. (This slows down the language.)
8. Use media, slideshow presentations, overheads, and charts whenever appropriate.
9. Make frequent comprehension checks.
10. Above all, keep oral presentations and reading assignments short. Collaborative activities are more effective than lectures or assigned readings.

figure 2.4 Strategies to Make the Input Comprehensible

than having students try to memorize vocabulary first and later try to use it to do math.

A third reason for teaching language through content is that students have a purpose for learning the new language. They are not just studying some grammar rule to pass a test. Instead, they might be studying how democracies are different from monarchies. In the process, they pick up the language of social studies, almost without realizing it.

The final reason to use content-based language teaching is that students begin to acquire the vocabulary of the different content areas. It is estimated that adult English speakers know about sixty thousand words. Students can't possibly learn that many words by direct study. However, they can acquire a large vocabulary, including academic terms, as they discuss, read, and write about different content areas.

Key 2: Organize Curriculum Around Themes

A second key for working effectively with ELLs is *organizing curriculum around themes*. Thematic teaching works well at every level of schooling. At lower grades, in a self-contained classroom, the teacher can integrate the different subjects around a theme. At upper grades, teachers can team to provide thematic instruction, or a teacher may provide thematic instruction within one content area.

Themes should extend over several weeks and should be based on big questions such as "How does food get from the field to the table?" "How does where we live influence how we live?" and "What contributions do immigrants make to a country?" These big questions can be formulated by looking at grade-level standards. State and national standards list what students at each grade level should know and should be able to do. Teachers can use these standards to develop questions that students can answer as they carry out investigations in the different content areas. The scenario at the end of this chapter illustrates how one teacher effectively teaches language through content based on a big-question theme.

When teachers organize curriculum around themes, all their students, and especially their ELLs, benefit in several ways (Freeman and Freeman 2002; Freeman and Freeman 2006b, 2007). In the first place, the thematic focus provides a context within which students can better understand instruction in a second language. In the same way that it is easier to assemble a jigsaw puzzle if we can look at the picture on the cover of the box, it is easier to make sense of individual lessons when we know they all focus on the same big question. Kindergartners engaged in the study of a question such as "How do animals and people change as they grow?" know that each lesson will relate to this topic. Since the students have the big picture, they can make better sense of a math lesson in which they compare the growth rate of two animals or of a science lesson in which they study the stages of growth from a tadpole to a frog.

A second benefit of organizing around themes is that teachers can help students make connections across subject areas. Students investigating a big question like "How does where we live affect how we live?" might learn about the conditions that cause hurricanes during science, locate areas where hurricanes have struck during geography, and read a story about a family whose home was devastated by a hurricane in language arts. In math, students can study charts showing changes in wind velocity as hurricanes travel across water and then chart these changes themselves. They can study how meteorologists use data to predict the course of a hurricane. Knowledge gained in one subject area can be used in studying another area. Teachers can also remind students of what they learned during math or science as they read a story or write a report.

Third, when subject areas are interrelated through the focus on a central theme, students keep thinking and learning about the big question as they move from subject to subject or class to class. What they learn in math they may apply in social studies or science. They can't simply put math out of their minds once the math lesson is over. The more that subjects are interrelated, the greater the chance that an ELL will understand the instruction. What the students don't fully comprehend during science might become clear when the topic is revisited during social studies or language arts.

A fourth reason to organize around themes is that maintaining the same topic through the focus on a big question also ensures that key vocabulary will be repeated naturally in the different subject areas. In the past English as a second language teachers used repetition to help students learn vocabulary. A teacher might have the class or a student repeat a word or phrase as a way of improving pronunciation and memorizing the word. However, second language acquisition research has shown that we do not learn a new language through imitation and repetition. The problem with repetition is that it can become mindless, much like writing out each spelling word ten times. To acquire some aspect of language, like a word or phrase, students need to encounter it several times in meaningful contexts. By organizing around themes, teachers provide the repeated exposure to meaningful language that students need. Instead of hearing a word like *temperature* only in science class, an ELL might hear or see it again during language arts, social studies, and math. When some of the same vocabulary comes up in each subject area, it increases a student's chance of acquiring important academic vocabulary.

Fifth, listening to someone speak a language we do not understand well is mentally tiring. Our brains naturally attend to things that make sense, so if a reading passage or a lecture is hard to understand, our attention turns to something else, something we can understand. For this reason, it is critical that teachers do everything possible to make instruction comprehensible for ELLs. One way to do this is to organize around themes. Even when students don't fully understand the language of a new lesson, they know it is connected to the theme, and they stay engaged for a longer period of time. It is this engagement that leads to both language development and increased subject matter knowledge.

If ELLs can stay focused on the lesson being delivered in English, there is a greater chance that they will learn the concepts and acquire more of the new language. The result is more success in writing papers, presenting reports, and taking quizzes on the subject. And success increases motivation to make that mental effort needed to comprehend new subjects in a new language. Thematic organization makes curriculum more comprehensible, and this leads to more sustained engagement and greater success.

A sixth benefit of organizing around themes is that teachers can more easily differentiate instruction to meet the needs of ELLs at different levels of English proficiency. Even when teachers have only three or four ELLs in a class, these students may be at quite different proficiency levels. One might be a beginner while another is at the intermediate level and two more are advanced. As long as all the students are studying the same theme, teachers can adjust assignments to suit the varied proficiency levels of the students. For example, during the theme based on the question "How does food get from the field to the table?" the beginning student might read a picture book that shows how the fruit, juice, milk, cereal, and toast some Americans eat for breakfast get from the farm to the store. This student could represent his understanding by drawing and labeling pictures of each step. Intermediate and advanced students could read more challenging books on the topic and demonstrate their understanding by making a complex chart or writing a list or a paragraph to explain how food gets from the field to the table.

The final reason to organize around themes is that themes based on big questions are universal. Animals and people everywhere change and grow. The weather affects our lives no matter where we live. Since the curriculum focuses on such big questions, teachers can connect subject area studies with students' lives. In fact, ELLs can often make important contributions to a class by giving examples from countries where they or their parents have lived. Some students who have grown up in the United States might eat cereal, toast, and juice for breakfast while a student from Vietnam might have rice and fish. Both students can draw on their own background experience as they learn how food gets from the field to the table. At the same time, the variety of examples coming from a class with students from different backgrounds expands the curriculum and enriches the learning experience for all the students in a class.

All students, and especially ELLs, benefit when teachers organize around themes based on big questions and taken from the standards. Students comprehend instruction more fully and retain the new knowledge longer.

Key 3: Draw on Students' Backgrounds—Their Experiences, Cultures, and Languages

Some English language learners come to schools in the United States with limited amounts of formal schooling, but all ELLs come with a variety of experiences. They also come from different cultural backgrounds and speak languages other than English. When teachers build on the backgrounds their ELLs bring, all students in a class, and especially the ELLs, benefit. Two ways that teachers can draw on the cultures and languages of their ELLs are by reading *culturally relevant books* and by using the *preview, view, review* technique.

Culturally relevant books • Books are easier to understand when readers have background knowledge about the setting, the characters, and the events. Teachers who provide culturally relevant books improve reading instruction for all their students (Freeman, Freeman, et al. 2003; Freeman and Freeman 2004). Figure 2.5 contains a rubric teachers and students can use to determine whether or not a book is culturally relevant. Teachers can use this *cultural relevance rubric* to evaluate books, they can ask individual students to rate books they read, or the whole class can judge a book.

A book that many Latino students find to be culturally relevant is *América Is Her Name* (Rodríguez 1997), the story of a girl from Oaxaca whose family moves to Chicago. América sees gang violence on the streets and struggles in her ESL class with a very traditional teacher. Her father doesn't believe education is important for girls, and América's home life is tense because her parents find adjusting to a new culture to be very difficult. However, a visiting poet asks students in América's class if they know a poem they can recite. The poet speaks Spanish, and América recites a poem she learned in Mexico. The poet encourages this shy girl to write poetry. When she wins a citywide poetry contest, even her father realizes that school can help his daughter succeed.

1. Are the characters in the story like you and your family?
   Just like us .... Not at all
       4   3   2   1

2. Have you ever had an experience like one described in this story?
   Yes .... No
       4   3   2   1

3. Have you lived in or visited places like those in the story?
   Yes .... No
       4   3   2   1

4. Could this story take place this year?
   Yes .... No
       4   3   2   1

5. How close do you think the main characters are to you in age?
   Very close .... Not close at all
       4   3   2   1

6. Are there main characters in the story who are boys [for boys] / girls [for girls]?
   Yes .... No
       4   3   2   1

7. Do the characters talk like you and your family do?
   Yes .... No
       4   3   2   1

8. How often do you read stories like these?
   Often .... Never
       4   3   2   1

figure 2.5 Cultural Relevance Rubric

Many ELLs find the characters in this book and the difficulties they encounter to be much like their own. América and her family look and talk like many ELLs. Upper-elementary school girls relate particularly well to this story. It is a good example of a book that would be rated high on the cultural relevance rubric by many students. Teachers can try to find books that connect with the students in their classes. Many culturally relevant books are now available for students from almost any cultural background. ELLs can understand these books because their own backgrounds are like those of the characters. They are also much more motivated to read culturally relevant books.

Preview, view, review • Another way teachers can draw on the strengths ELLs bring to a class is through strategic use of their first language. Preview, view, review is a strategy that can work in classes with English learners from one or several primary language backgrounds, and it can work whether or not the teacher speaks the students' languages (Freeman and Freeman 2000; Freeman and Freeman 2001). An example comes from a teacher who has organized around the theme "How does the weather affect our lives?" This lesson is designed to teach students about different kinds of clouds.

The teacher, a bilingual peer, a bilingual paraprofessional, or a parent briefly tells the ELLs in their native language that this will be a lesson about five kinds of clouds. This introduction provides the ELLs with a preview of the lesson. Other ways to provide a preview include having a bilingual student, paraprofessional, or parent read a book about clouds in the students' primary language. In addition, a teacher could show a video clip about clouds with narration in the students' first language. A teacher could also have students brainstorm in same-language groups what they already know about clouds. Students could use their first languages in their groups and then report back in English.

During the view, the teacher conducts the lesson using strategies to make the input comprehensible. The teacher shows pictures of different kinds of clouds and writes the names of the cloud formations and their characteristics under the pictures. With the help of the preview, the students can follow the English better and acquire both English and academic content.

Finally, it is good to have a short time of review during which students can use their native language. For example, students who speak the same first language could meet again in groups to review the main ideas of the lesson, ask questions, and clarify their understanding, and then report back in English.

The preview, view, review technique provides a structured way to alternate English and native language instruction. Students are given access to the academic concepts they need to know and, at the same time, acquire English. Simply translating everything into a student's first language is not productive because the student will tune out English, the language that is harder to understand. This concurrent translation method does not lead to either concept or language acquisition. Using preview, view, review can help teachers avoid concurrent translation while still drawing on students' first languages.

Nutrition Unit: Effective Teaching for ELLs

We conclude this chapter with a scenario that illustrates how one teacher works effectively with the ELLs in his class. This teacher knows his students well, and his teaching reflects the three keys we have described. As a result, all his students, including the ELLs, experience academic success.

David is a sixth-grade teacher at a school in a rural farming community in South Texas where his Mexican-origin students, many of whom began school speaking Spanish, now receive their daily content and literacy instruction in English. In addition, some of his students are native English speakers. David works hard at planning curriculum that will lead his students to academic success. He is aware that many of his ELLs never developed literacy at grade level in Spanish. The majority of his students are long-term English learners who speak English well but struggle with reading and writing in English. Some students are newer to this country and do read and write in Spanish although they have not fully developed conversational English. Others arrive in his classroom from Mexico with little English and limited formal schooling in Spanish. All these students need to be able to read, write, and learn academic content in English.

David teaches language through content and organizes his curriculum around themes that draw on the standards. His unit on nutrition is an example of how he carefully chooses culturally relevant materials and organizes his teaching around big questions to help his students develop academic English and subject matter knowledge.

Before beginning his unit, David reviewed the social studies, health, math, and language arts standards. He incorporated social studies standards in economics that require students to compare ways in which various societies organize the production and distribution of goods and also require them to identify and differentiate among traditional, market, and supply and demand economies in selected contemporary societies. In math he worked on estimation, and in health education he focused on standards that call for students to analyze healthful and unhealthful dietary practices. The language arts standards require students to compare and contrast texts from different genres, to paraphrase and summarize texts and organize ideas, to draw inferences using text evidence and experience, and to draw on background knowledge to interpret readings.

To meet these standards and to encourage his students to read extensively, David provided his students with books related to nutrition in both Spanish and English at differing levels of difficulty. Students who were stronger readers in Spanish could read the books in English but also refer to the versions in Spanish to help support their reading comprehension.

To begin the unit and to encourage students to begin talking about the topic of the food traditions of different cultures, David introduced the big questions "How do traditional foods from around the world compare with our foods?" and "Which of the traditional foods are nutritious?" He read *Everyone Cooks Rice* (Dooley 1991) to his class. In this book the main characters go from house to house, and in each home they are served rice prepared in the style unique to a particular culture. David divided his students into groups. Each group chose one section of the story and reported on the special rice preparation described in that section. This activity stimulated lively discussion and led students to talk about their own families' favorite rice dishes.

As the discussion progressed, students began to express their food preferences. This provided an excellent opportunity for David to take out *Judge for a Day* (González-Jensen 1997b). It is the story of an Anglo boy whose principal asks him to judge the Latino dishes in an international food festival. He is very nervous because he doesn't like spicy food. This story helps dispel the myths that all Hispanics are alike and that all Hispanic food is spicy. It encourages students to be adventurous eaters and to appreciate the variety of foods that different countries have to offer.

Since David had multiple copies of this book, he paired more proficient readers with struggling readers so they could help one another. David then asked his students to brainstorm questions they might use to interview one another about their food preferences. They asked each other about the foods they liked and didn't like. David listed the class preferences on the board. Then he showed the students how to make a bar graph to illustrate the results.

In addition to graphing, David also wanted students to work on estimating. He had multiple copies of the book *That's About Right: A Book About Estimating* (Burke 2004). He put his students into groups to read about estimating. Each group chose a favorite food and estimated how much of each ingredient they would need if they were going to cook the dish for the entire class. The next day, David brought in newspaper ads from local grocery stores, and his students first estimated and then calculated how much money they would need to buy the ingredients for their favorite dish. Students concluded that feeding the whole class would be very expensive. They compared and contrasted which groups had the most expensive dishes and decided which ingredients were the most expensive. They discovered, for example, that dishes without meat were not so expensive as dishes calling for meat.

David then read *Saturday Sancocho* (Torres 1995b), a book about a traditional Central and South American stew. He asked his students if they had ever eaten a dish like *sancocho*. Some students explained that their families prepared a similar dish, but it didn't have yucca or *plátano verde* (green plantains) in it. They enthusiastically described the ingredients and preparation of stews and soups their relatives served, including typical Mexican stews such as *posole* and *menudo*.

Saturday Sancocho brought up a social studies topic for David and his students to discuss. In the story, María Lili and her grandparents, who traditionally have *sancocho* on Saturdays, have a dozen eggs but no money. María Lili and her grandmother go to the market, and through some clever bargaining and trading, end the afternoon with all the ingredients they need for *sancocho*, including a chicken.

David asked his students if they could do what the characters in the story did here in the United States with no money, only something to trade. Some students brought up experiences they'd had with bartering in Mexico with relatives at the market or in small villages, but all agreed that in this country, this would not happen.

David asked the students to move into groups to read three different books related to this discussion: *Mexican Immigration* (Pile 2005), *To Trade or Not to Trade* (Hirsch 2004), and *Golden Opportunities* (Rigby 2004). He asked the students reading *Mexican Immigration* to find out why Mexican immigrants came to this country and what they found here. The students reading *To Trade or Not to Trade* were asked to trace the history of economics in this country from early bartering to the present trade industries. The group reading *Golden Opportunities* was asked to find specific examples of new immigrants who became entrepreneurs in this country by taking advantage of the free enterprise system.

After gathering the information, each group prepared a short electronic slideshow presentation to share with the whole class. As each group made their presentation, the class engaged in discussion of the topic. The presentation on *Golden Opportunities* led several students to tell how their families had started little businesses, including a restaurant, a shoe repair shop, and a bakery, in this country. Others told how their families had a business of their own in their dreams.

David continued this unit for several weeks using different texts, both fiction and nonfiction, to explore various aspects of nutrition and to help his students build academic content knowledge and academic English in different content areas. He chose a content theme of interest to his students and used books that drew on his students' cultural backgrounds. Throughout the unit students read books at different levels of difficulty. In this way, all the students were able to succeed with reading. Figure 2.6 lists the books David used in his unit, including Spanish versions that were available.

Burke, Melissa Blackwell. 2004. *That's About Right: A Book About Estimating.*
    Barrington, IL: Rigby.
Dooley, Norah. 1991. *Everyone Cooks Rice.* New York: Carolrhoda.
González-Jensen, Margarita. 1997a. *Juez por un día.* Crystal Lake, IL: Rigby.
———. 1997b. *Judge for a Day.* Crystal Lake, IL: Rigby.
Hirsch, Charles F. 2004. *To Trade or Not to Trade.* Barrington, IL: Rigby.
Pile, Murray. 2005. *Mexican Immigration.* Washington, DC: National Geographic.
Rigby. 2004. *On Our Way to English Fourth Grade Golden Opportunities.*
    Barrington, IL: Rigby.
Torres, Leyla. 1995a. *El sancocho del sábado.* New York: Farrar Straus Giroux.
———. 1995b. *Saturday Sancocho.* New York: Farrar Straus Giroux.

figure 2.6 Bibliography for Nutrition Unit

Applications

1. At the beginning of the chapter, we discuss the growing numbers of English language learners in U.S. schools. Find demographic information about ELL growth in your local school district and compare that growth with national figures.

2. Three types of ELLs are described in the chapter: students with adequate schooling, students with limited formal and/or interrupted schooling, and long-term English learners. Interview several older ELLs in a local school. Determine which type of ELL each student would be according to the examples and explanations given in the chapter. Be prepared to discuss these students and their characteristics in class.

3. ELLs are identified and assessed in different ways in different places. There are problems with many methods of identifying and assessing students. Find out how ELLs in your school district are identified and assessed. Do the methods used seem appropriate? Refer to concerns and suggestions discussed in the chapter.

4. The chapter lists several different types of ESL support found in schools and discusses advantages and disadvantages of each. Find out what kinds of ESL support ELLs at the elementary, middle, and secondary levels are given in your local district. Is the support organized on a districtwide basis, or do individual schools do different things? What did you learn from your investigation?

5. In discussing Krashen's theory of second language acquisition, we list five of his hypotheses: learning/acquisition, natural order, monitor, input, and affective filter. Think back over a language learning experience you have had. Which of the hypotheses apply to your own experience? How? Be specific.

6. We suggest that the best approach for teaching ELLs is to teach language through content themes organized around big questions. David's unit provides an example of this type of teaching. With a partner, choose a grade level and review standards in language arts, social studies, math, and science. Drawing on the standards, identify a big question and plan several activities for teaching the theme.

7. Using culturally relevant texts and preview, view, review are two strategies suggested in the text. With a partner, plan a lesson using the cultural relevance rubric or the preview, view, review strategy. If possible, implement the lesson and report back on the experience.

Key Terms and Acronyms

affective filter hypothesis. The hypothesis that affective factors such as nervousness and boredom can block input from reaching the part of the brain where acquisition occurs.

content-based language teaching. An approach to teaching ELLs using academic content as the vehicle for language learning rather than using traditional grammar and vocabulary instruction.

cultural relevance rubric. A rubric teachers or students can use to determine if books are culturally relevant.

culturally relevant books. Texts that connect to students' backgrounds, age, language, gender, or past experiences.

English as a second language (ESL). Instruction for English language learners.

English language learner (ELL). Student with limited English proficiency.

ESL pullout. One model of instructing ELLs in which the students are taken out of their regular classes to be given extra help in English by the ESL teacher.

ESL push-in. One model of instructing ELLs in which the ESL teacher goes into the regular classroom and provides support to ELLs as needed.

home language survey. A survey on which parents report their first language and the language spoken in the home.

input hypothesis. The hypothesis that second language learners acquire language when the input is comprehensible and slightly above their present level of understanding, referred to as i+1.

Krashen's theory of second language acquisition. Stephen Krashen's theory of how language is learned, including several hypotheses.

learning/acquisition hypothesis. The hypothesis that there is a distinction between formal learning in school and natural learning that takes place inside and outside of school.

limited English proficient (LEP). Designation for students who do not speak English well enough to benefit from instruction in English.

long-term English learners. ELLs who have had all or most of their schooling in this country, never developed their first language, and learned to speak English but lack competency in reading and writing English.

monitor hypothesis. The hypothesis that ELLs can monitor their output if there is time, a focus on correctness, and if they know the language rules to apply.

natural order hypothesis. The hypothesis that children acquire certain features of language in a certain order that resists direct teaching.

newcomer center. A location where students new to schooling in the United States are tested and usually given some basic instruction in English in order to prepare them for schooling here.

organizing curriculum around themes. An approach to teaching ELLs that helps them make sense of the curriculum because the content is connected through investigating questions of importance.

preview, view, review. A strategy for using students' first language to teach content. The preview is in the students' first language, the view is in the second language (English), and the review for clarification is in the first language.

strategies to make the input comprehensible. Activities that teachers use to help ELLs understand the content instruction.

students with adequate formal schooling. ELLs who arrive in schools at grade level in their native language because of schooling in their native country.

students with limited formal schooling. ELLs who arrive in schools with very little or no schooling in their native language.

Resources for Further Study

Center for Applied Linguistics (see "English Language Learners"): www.cal.org/

Interactive map of Hispanic population in United States: www.drtango.com/usmap.asp

Stephen Krashen's website: www.sdkrashen.com/

Website on language policy: http://ourworld.compuserve.com/homepages/jwcrawford

National Clearinghouse for English Language Acquisition and Language
Instruction Educational Programs: www.ncela.gwu.edu/

TESOL (Teachers of English to Speakers of Other Languages):
www.tesol.org/

3

Bilingual Education

Alma Dolores Rodríguez and Richard Gómez Jr.

Introduction

Chapter 2 discusses the growing population of English language learners (ELLs) in the United States, the types of ELLs, how they are identified, and best practices for teaching them English. Although ELL students come from many backgrounds and speak many languages, many areas of the United States have large numbers of ELLs who speak the same first language, often Spanish. This chapter addresses how the needs of ELLs who speak the same native language can effectively be met through bilingual education.

This chapter provides a general description of bilingual education programs. We explain what bilingual education is, how it came about, the basic requirements of bilingual education programs, and how students are identified. We also explain the theory and research that supports bilingual education. We give special attention to dual language programs, since research has shown that they are the most promising for closing the academic achievement gap between English language learners and their native English-speaking peers.

What Is Bilingual Education?

The term *bilingual education* is used to refer to instructional programs that provide students with an education in two languages, English and the student's own native language. However, bilingual education is more complex than one would think. Ovando, Combs, and Collier (2006) explain that bilingual education is not a single method to teach English language learners. Some bilingual programs instruct students in their native language only for a limited amount of time, until they can transition to all-English instruction. Other programs are designed to maintain and develop students' native languages and teach English simultaneously. Krashen (2000) states that bilingual education has two goals: English language development and native language development. A third type of bilingual program is designed to provide bilingual instruction not only to students whose native language is other than English but to English-dominant students as well. We discuss the different types of bilingual program models later in the chapter. At this moment, it is important to realize that the term *bilingual education* may be considered an umbrella that encompasses a wide variety of instructional models structured quite differently and with different purposes.

English Language Development: The First Goal of Bilingual Education

Krashen (2000) states that the first goal of bilingual education programs is to teach students English. As was explained in Chapter 2, Krashen believes that children acquire a language when they understand it, that is, when they receive comprehensible input. Therefore, English as a second language (ESL) instruction is an essential component of bilingual education programs.

Native Language Development: The Second Goal of Bilingual Education

Krashen (2000) further states that native language development is the second goal of bilingual programs. He explains that native language development has both cognitive and social advantages for individuals. That is, students who develop their native language do better in school and are more marketable in society. Krashen argues that all the instruction that students receive in their native language "help[s] English language development enormously" (21). Moreover, research has consistently shown that native language development has positive effects on the academic achievement of ELLs (Cummins 1981; Greene 1998; Ramírez 1991; Rolstad, Mahoney, and Glass 2005). Bilingual education programs usually provide initial literacy instruction and at least some content area instruction in the students' native language. The theory shows that the skills and knowledge that students develop in their native language transfer to English.

Theory Supporting Bilingual Education

Effective bilingual education programs incorporate Krashen's theory of second language acquisition, explained in detail in Chapter 2. Comprehensible input is a central component of Krashen's second language acquisition theory, and Krashen explains that first language instruction is the best kind of comprehensible input. Since English language learners cannot wait until they develop adequate English language proficiency to begin to learn academic content and must keep up with grade-level academic instruction, native language instruction is critical.

Students develop academic and literacy skills more easily in their native language. Cummins states that concept development in the students' native language provides a "foundation for long-term growth in English academic skills" (2000, 12). Cummins (1981) distinguishes between social and academic language proficiencies and argues that academic language proficiency transfers from one language to another. Several of Cummins' theories support bilingual education.

BICS: Basic Interpersonal Communicative Skills

Cummins describes *basic interpersonal communicative skills* as the "surface" manifestations of language, or perceptible features such as "pronunciation, grammar, and basic vocabulary" (1981, 22, 23). BICS, or conversational language, is the language that individuals use in everyday, face-to-face situations where there are clues to make language comprehensible (Cummins 1981). For example, ELLs who have developed BICS in English are able to talk to their English-speaking peers on the playground or understand and follow basic classroom directions. They are able to understand and participate in activities like games and hands-on activities when there are visuals and gestures that provide clues to meaning.

Collier (1989) and Ovando, Combs, and Collier (2006) state that conversational language is developed fairly quickly, in two to three years. In addition, they point out that conversational language does not just include the ability to understand and speak the language. It also includes the ability to read and write in informal, everyday situations. For example, ELLs who have developed BICS in English are able to read and comprehend a menu in English at a restaurant and help their Spanish monolingual parents order their food.

CALP: Cognitive Academic Language Proficiency

Cummins describes *cognitive academic language proficiency* as the "manipulation of language in decontextualized academic situations"(1981, 22). In other words, CALP is the language of school. CALP is the language proficiency that allows students to comprehend instruction and complete assignments such as reading textbooks, listening to a lecture without visuals, and writing a long composition. Students who have developed CALP can read a poem and interpret the author's purpose or write an essay explaining the process of photosynthesis. CALP constitutes deeper language skills than those which underlie BICS.

Freeman and Freeman explain that "students need to be able to think, act, comprehend, speak, read and write using language appropriate to the context" (2006b, 2). Therefore, academic language does not refer exclusively to literacy, reading, and writing. It also involves speaking and comprehending oral academic language. For example, ELLs need CALP to comprehend a lecture on the Civil War or to deliver a formal oral presentation on the water cycle. Because of the complex nature of academic language, it takes longer than conversational language to develop. The development of academic English takes ELLs anywhere from five to ten years to develop when they are instructed only in English. On the other hand, it takes them from four to seven years when they receive instruction in their native language as well as in English (Collier 1989; Ovando, Combs, and Collier 2006).

Linguistic Interdependence

Cummins (1981) explains that the knowledge that students acquire in their first language transfers to the second language. In other words, students develop concepts, knowledge, and skills, or CALP, and these concepts are the same in any language. That is, the concepts themselves do not change when students learn a second language, only the labels for those concepts are different. For example, the concept of a mammal being a warm-blooded vertebrate that gives birth to live young is exactly the same as the concept of the Spanish word *mamífero*. The deep structure of *mammal* and *mamífero* is the same. Therefore, if students receiving science instruction in their first language learn what a *mamífero* is, when presented with the concept in English, they need to acquire only the surface structure, the term *mammal*. Students need to learn only how to say in English what they already understand in Spanish. They do not have to learn what a mammal is again because academic concepts transfer from one language to another. This concept of transfer is the linguistic interdependence hypothesis.

Cummins (1981) argues against the idea of a *separate underlying proficiency* (SUP). Advocates of the SUP theory state that if we want students to acquire English, then we need to expose them only to English. There must be an underlying belief that what is learned in the native language is not useful in learning a second language. If individuals learned and stored academic concepts by language, a Spanish-English bilingual student who learned the multiplication tables in Spanish would not know the multiplication tables in English. This is not logical. Students need to acquire the vocabulary of multiplication in English, but they do not have to memorize the multiplication tables again.

Therefore, Cummins (1981) challenges the SUP theory and has replaced it with that of CUP, or *common underlying proficiency*. He explains that all the knowledge that we acquire is stored in our brain and can be retrieved in any language. Academic concepts constitute this underlying proficiency, which is accessible to bilingual students in their two languages. Literacy skills are also part of CUP. Literacy skills transfer from one language to another. Students who are literate in their first language do not have to learn to read again in the second language.

Students acquire academic language and literacy skills more easily in the language they understand best, their first language. In addition, students whose CALP is well developed in their first language acquire English faster than those students whose CALP is not developed (Cummins 1981). Therefore, it makes a lot of sense to provide ELLs with native language instruction. However, this has not been the norm in the United States. Bilingual education has gone through phases of acceptance and rejection throughout the history of our country.

History of Bilingual Education

People who speak languages other than English have been part of the population of the United States since its origins. Our country was colonized by English, Spanish, French, German, Dutch, Russian, and numerous other immigrant groups. In addition, there were hundreds of Native American languages spoken in this country when early colonists arrived (Wolfson 1989).

Early settlers established schools that provided education in their home languages (Crawford 1991). In the 1800s, states such as Ohio, Louisiana, and New

Mexico passed laws authorizing instruction in German, French, and Spanish, respectively (Crawford 1991). But in the early 1900s, a new stream of immigration from southern and eastern Europe threatened established settlers, and an increasingly negative attitude toward languages other than English began to grow (Wolfson 1989). With the breakout of World War I, anti-German sentiments, and *isolationism*, a government policy based on the belief that national interests were best served by avoiding economic and political alliances with other countries, came a movement to assimilate all groups into one language and one culture. American schools were seen as the best way to ensure that all citizens spoke the same language and assimilated. The results of this movement meant that bilingual education was almost nonexistent in the United States from 1917 to 1950 (Ambert and Melendez 1985).

After World War II, the launching of the satellite *Sputnik* in 1957 by the former Soviet Union brought about a change in the perspective toward other languages (Ambert and Melendez 1985). Americans realized they needed to speak languages other than English to keep up with the rest of the world. This, along with the Cuban revolution, caused changes in antibilingual views. Well-educated Cubans who arrived in Florida, escaping Castro's communist government, established the first Spanish-English dual language school in 1963, Coral Way School in Dade County. Cuban and American children received English and Spanish instruction side by side. The successful results initiated a rebirth of bilingual education (Crawford 1991).

These events as well as the civil rights period of the 1960s lead to legislation that supported *bilingualism*. The Civil Rights Act of 1964 guaranteed, for the first time, nondiscriminatory education for English language learners (Ambert and Melendez 1985) and gave way to the passing of the *Bilingual Education Act* of 1968, or Title VII of the federal *Elementary and Secondary Education Act*. Although it did not mandate bilingual education, it allowed bilingual programs to be established, provided funding, and promoted research on bilingual education (Malakoff and Hakuta 1990). However, not all English language learners were being adequately educated.

In 1974, 1,856 Chinese American students filed a class action suit, *Lau v. Nichols*, against the San Francisco Unified School District for failing to provide them with meaningful educational opportunities. The Supreme Court declared that providing students who do not speak English with the same materials, teachers, and facilities as English-dominant students does not constitute equal treatment since such instruction all in English is not comprehensible to them (Ambert and Melendez 1985). Although the Lau decision did not go so far as to mandate bilingual education, it opened the door for the use of native language instruction to give students access to the curriculum.

In the late 1970s bilingual education again lost popularity as immigration waves and the growth in the Hispanic population led to anti-immigrant sentiment. The Bilingual Education Act was amended in 1978. Bilingual programs became strictly transitional, that is programs that offered first language support for only a short time. *English-only* movements became popular during the 1980s (Crawford 1991). In 1998, Proposition 227, which dismantled bilingual education in California, was passed into law (Cummins 2000). With Proposition 203, the state of Arizona did away with bilingual education the following year (Steinberg 2000). In 2002, the Elementary and Secondary Education Act was reauthorized as the No Child Left Behind Act. Title VII, the Bilingual Education Act, was replaced by Title III, the English Language Acquisition, Language Enhancement and Academic Achievement Act. As its name implies, there was "shift in emphasis" from native language support and bilingualism to English language development and academic achievement in English (Lessow-Hurley 2005, 134).

Bilingual education programs are still being implemented in many states despite the recent setbacks from English-only legislation. The *Office of Civil Rights (OCR)* has specific guidelines for the establishment and operation of programs for ELLs as well as for the identification, treatment, and exit of participating students.

Establishment of Bilingual Programs

Title VI of the Civil Rights Act of 1964 prohibits discrimination of students on the basis of race, color, or national origin. However, because many school districts failed to provide appropriate instruction for students who did not understand English, the Office of Civil Rights issued a memorandum in 1970 clarifying that when students of different national origins do not speak English, they are not able to participate fully in and benefit from instruction (OCR 1970). The memorandum was updated in 1985 and 1991. OCR realizes that individual school districts have varied needs depending on the number of ELLs they serve and the languages that these students speak. Therefore, it does not require districts to establish bilingual programs. School districts are granted the authority to determine the type of instruction that will provide an equal educational opportunity for their ELLs. Nevertheless, there are a number of procedures that all school districts must follow: (1) proper identification of English language learners; (2) development of a sound alternative program; (3) appropriate implementation of the program; (4) monitoring of student progress and establishment of exit criteria; and (5) assessment of the effectiveness of the program (OCR 2000).

Identification of Students

Districts are given the flexibility of setting the criteria and measures they will use to identify English language learners. Most districts request information from parents to begin to assess students' proficiency in English (OCR 1985). The state of Texas, for example, administers a home language survey to every student who initially enrolls in a Texas public school. Parents are asked if a language other than English is spoken at home. An affirmative response to this query identifies the student as a potential ELL (TEC 2007). Many states make a final identification of ELL status through formal and/or informal language assessments. For example, students in Texas public schools whose home language survey reveals a potential need for an alternative instructional program are given a formal English language proficiency test along with a language proficiency test in their home language. Students entering kindergarten or first grade are assessed orally, while students entering second to twelfth grades are assessed both orally and in writing. The results are used to determine whether students meet the ELL criteria, as well as to place them in the most appropriate instructional program.

Development of a Sound Alternative Program

Although the OCR does not require school districts to implement bilingual education to instruct their ELLs, a school district must be in compliance with OCR requirements as outlined in the 1981 *Castañeda v. Pickard* Fifth Circuit Court of Appeals decision. *Castañeda* requires school districts to establish alternative instructional programs that are designed based on sound theory. That is, experts in the field should have recognized such instructional practices as being effective. Some of the most common alternative programs include transitional bilingual education, developmental bilingual education, and English as a second language (OCR 1991). Transitional programs provide some native language support while students are acquiring English. Developmental programs strive to support the development of students' first languages and English. ESL programs provide specialized instruction in English for nonnative speakers. Later in this chapter, these programs are explained in more detail. Because of the requirements of the *Castañeda* decision, it is important for educators to understand the theory covered in Chapter 2 and in previous sections of this chapter. In addition, school districts must make careful decisions as to which instructional program would benefit their student population the most. Examining existing research on the effectiveness of different alternative programs is one way of accomplishing this task. Therefore, a brief discussion of the most relevant research on the effectiveness of bilingual education follows.

Major research studies on bilingual education

In 1988 Krashen and Biber conducted a survey of bilingual programs in California and found that well-designed bilingual programs are effective (Krashen 1991). Other longitudinal studies, those that examined the effect of bilingual education over a long period of time, found that ELLs who receive long-term instruction in their native language perform better in all content areas than those ELLs who do not, and that ELLs who receive long-term instruction in their first language reach higher levels of English language proficiency (Collier 1992; Ramírez, Yuen, and Ramey 1991).

Thomas and Collier (2002) conducted a nationwide study examining eight different types of instructional programs and identified two-way bilingual or dual language as the only programs that close the academic achievement gap between ELL and English-dominant students. The researchers found that the more formal schooling students receive in their first language, the higher their achievement in English, and that ELLs who receive instruction in two languages for at least four years outperform those who receive instruction only in English. Rolstad, Mahoney, and Glass (2005) conducted a meta-analysis, or study of studies, to determine the effectiveness of different alternative programs for ELLs. Their findings showed that bilingual instruction is more effective than all-English instruction. They identified long-term bilingual programs as more effective than short-term programs. In short, when comparing bilingual and ESL programs on long-term academic achievement, researchers found that the more native language was utilized, the more English proficient a student became, and conversely, the more English instruction was utilized, the less English proficient a student became. In other words, more English instruction does not equal more English. This counterintuitive finding is key to the importance of long-term native language instruction for high academic English proficiency.

Program Implementation

Designing a program that is based on sound theory does not guarantee effective results unless it is properly implemented. Proper program implementation is also a standard set by *Castañeda v. Pickard*. In order to properly implement programs, school districts need to have adequately trained teachers and aides. Teachers must have the necessary training according to the instructional program. Teachers in bilingual programs must be proficient in both languages. They must be able not only to speak and understand but also to read and write in their students' native language. ESL teachers, on the other hand, are not necessarily required to be bilingual (OCR 1991). In addition, school districts must also have the necessary resources such as instructional materials and equipment to implement the program correctly (OCR 1985). For example, a bilingual program cannot be properly implemented without sufficient materials in the students' native language.

Student Progress and Exit Criteria

School districts must closely monitor the progress of ELLs in alternative programs to ensure continuous equal educational opportunity. ELLs should not exit the program until they are able to fully participate in and benefit from a regular educational program (OCR 1991). In the state of Texas, for example, students in a bilingual program must demonstrate oral and written English language proficiency before exiting the program. Students must perform satisfactorily on the reading and/or language arts state assessments in English, or score at or above the fortieth percentile in the reading and language arts sections of a standardized test in English (TEC 2007).

Program Effectiveness

Castañeda v. Pickard requires school districts to design programs based on sound theory and to implement such programs properly. *Castañeda* also requires districts to evaluate the effectiveness of such programs. If the selected program is not the most appropriate for the ELLs in that district, the district is required to make the necessary changes to the program to ensure students are receiving the best possible instruction (OCR 1991).

Bilingual Education Program Models

The most common bilingual and ESL programs utilized in the United States for purposes of providing ELLs with equitable education opportunities in order from least effective to most effective are

1. ESL pullout

2. content ESL

3. early exit

4. late exit

5. one-way dual language enrichment

6. two-way dual language enrichment

The first two models, ESL pullout and content ESL, by design provide ELLs with 100 percent English-only instruction. These programs are discussed in Chapter 2. These programs, which do not provide native language instruction, have been identified as the least effective in closing the achievement gap between ELL and native English-speaking students (Collier and Thomas 2004). Models that do provide native language instruction vary in their effectiveness.

Early-Exit Bilingual Education

Early-exit bilingual models are designed to move ELLs from their native language to English in the first years of their schooling. These programs, also known as transitional bilingual programs, provide students with native language instruction only from one to three years (Freeman, Freeman, and Mercuri 2005). Most of the instruction ELLs receive at the beginning of the program is in their native language. However, there is a gradual reduction in the amount of native language instruction and an increase in the amount of English language instruction as the school year progresses. Students exit the transitional program as soon as they are able to function in a mainstream or all-English class. The major goal of transitional programs is the acquisition of the English language and not the preservation of students' first languages. Therefore, these models are sometimes referred to as *subtractive bilingual programs* because students eventually lose their native language (Freeman, Freeman, and Mercuri 2005, 15). Early-exit bilingual programs were found by Collier and Thomas (2004) to be more effective than English-only programs, content ESL, and ESL pullout, but the least effective among all of the bilingual programs that utilize the native language of ELLs.

Late-Exit Bilingual Education

Late-exit bilingual models, just like early-exit models, are designed for English language learners exclusively. This model, also known as maintenance or developmental bilingual education, is designed to move ELLs from their native language to English over the five- or six-year period of their elementary grades. Although the main goal of this type of instruction is the acquisition of English, late-exit programs maintain and develop the students' first language (Freeman, Freeman, and Mercuri 2005, 11). In contrast with early-exit programs, maintenance bilingual education is an *additive bilingual program*, that is, students acquire English but also maintain their first language. In a late-exit program, students become "bilingual and biliterate" (Freeman, Freeman, and Mercuri 2005, 16). Late-exit programs were found to be more effective than early-exit models but less effective than either of the two dual language programs analyzed by Collier and Thomas (2004).

Dual Language Education

Two *dual language enrichment* (DLE) models, one-way dual language enrichment and two-way dual language enrichment, were included in the Collier and Thomas' 2004 study. Both of these enrichment models achieved their goal of completely closing the academic achievement gap between ELL students and native English-speaking students. A major goal of dual language programs is for all participating students, ELL and English-dominant students, to become bilingual and biliterate. This makes dual language education an additive program (Freeman, Freeman, and Mercuri 2005, 16). Rather than being considered a remedial program, like early-exit and late-exit models, dual language is an enrichment program because it promotes the development of high levels of proficiency in two languages (Freeman, Freeman, and Mercuri 2005, 11).

A number of features distinguish DLE from other bilingual models and facilitate its effectiveness. First, the language other than English is used for a considerable part of the instructional time. Second, languages are kept separate (Lindholm and Molina 2000). That is, instruction is delivered in only one language at a time. For example, in an English-Spanish DLE program, the content areas may be assigned to be taught in specific languages. Math may always be taught in English while science may always be taught in Spanish. This is only one possibility. Other options include separating languages by time of day, by day, or by week. Therefore, careful scheduling is an important aspect of DLE programs. A third feature that characterizes DLE programs is it gives both languages the same status. Students must value the language other than English and are encouraged to learn it (Lindholm and Molina 2000). Fourth, unlike previously explained models, DLE programs are open to all students, English-dominant children and ELLs. There are two DLE options available for different student groups.

Two-way dual language enrichment model • Two-way DLE is a bilingual program in which students come together in two different ways to learn:

1. Students learn from a school curriculum that is taught in two languages, for example, English and Spanish.

2. The students, in approximately equal numbers, come from two different language backgrounds. For example, eleven native English-dominant and eleven Spanish-dominant students might come together to form one DLE classroom.

To create two-way DLE programs, a school can serve only as many ELLs as there are English-dominant students choosing to participate in a DLE program.

One-way dual language enrichment model • One-way DLE bilingual programs are taught the same as two-way DLE programs, but the makeup of the participating students differs. Students in one-way DLE programs come together to learn a school curriculum in two different languages. However, in a one-way DLE program, students come together in only one way to learn. All or the greater majority (more than two-thirds) of the students are from the same language-dominant group. Therefore, it is possible to have a one-way DLE program where 100 percent of the students are Spanish dominant or, for that matter, where 100 percent of the students are English dominant. A school may serve virtually all of its ELLs in one-way DLE programs without the participation of even a single English-dominant student. Usually, however, there are at least a few English-dominant speakers. In fact, in these types of programs that serve native Spanish-speaking ELLs in the United States context, students may come to school as Spanish-dominant speakers, English-dominant speakers, or with some proficiency in both languages. A well-known one-way DLE model in Spanish and English that is being widely implemented in the states of Texas and Washington as well as in other states is the Gómez and Gómez model (Gómez, Freeman, and Freeman 2005; Gómez 2006). In this model, students begin literacy instruction in their first languages but always study math in English and science and social studies in Spanish. After second grade students study language arts in both languages. Other features of the program allow students to build vocabulary in both languages. Time is given for announcements, opening activities, physical education, computers, music, and art, which alternate languages each day. This is called language of the day, and it provides a variety of rich instruction in both languages throughout the day.

The similarities and differences between one-way and two-way DLE programs can be seen in Figure 3.1.

Two-Way Dual Language Enrichment	One-Way Dual Language Enrichment
50% English-dominant students 50% English language learners	66% to 100% English language learners
50% school curriculum taught in English 50% school curriculum taught in second language	50% school curriculum taught in English 50% school curriculum taught in second language
ELL students close academic achievement gap High academic success for all students	ELL students close academic achievement gap High academic success for all students
Bilingualism and *biliteracy* is a fifth-grade goal	Bilingualism and biliteracy is a fifth-grade goal

figure 3.1 Two-Way Versus One-Way DLE Programs

Enrichment Versus Remedial Bilingual Education: David and Timo's Story

Five-year-old David and Timo lived just two blocks from each other. Their mothers were sisters, which made David and Timo first cousins and, even better, the best of friends! Linda was troubled by a pamphlet that arrived from the new school located no more than four blocks away. The pamphlet, written in Spanish and English, described a program starting up at the new school. It was called a dual language program. The new program was described as being very successful where it had been implemented before. The program taught the curriculum in two languages. One-half of the curriculum would be taught in English and the other half in Spanish. It promised English proficiency for little David and academic success too. But Linda was still uneasy. How can you learn English by learning in Spanish? It just did not make sense. She had spoken with her husband, Franco, about this, and he was leery as well. They both knew how difficult a future could be for little David if he did not become English proficient. Linda's sister had also read the pamphlet and decided right away against enrolling Timo at the new school. She would enroll Timo in an all-English school.

Linda and her husband studied the pamphlet and the model described. The school would be using the Gómez and Gómez dual language enrichment model.

English-dominant students and English language learners would be receiving the same type of instruction side by side. The pamphlet explained that because children learn to read once, Spanish-dominant children in the DLE model would be taught language arts entirely in Spanish while English-dominant students would learn to read and write in English. However, beginning in second grade, all students would receive language arts instruction in both Spanish and English. The pamphlet also said that all students would learn math in English. However, science and social studies were to be taught entirely in Spanish for all students. The proposed DLE program did have some interesting twists. It incorporated something called language of the day. All communication and activities in the school outside of the content area teaching would alternate between Spanish and English every other day. David's parents attended a parent meeting for prospective students, and after listening to the questions and asking some themselves, they decided to send David to the DLE-model school.

Years later, Linda realized she had made the right decision. At the end of his elementary school years, David was not only bilingual but biliterate as well. That is, David could comprehend, speak, read, and write both English and Spanish proficiently. Linda's sister, however, regretted her decision of enrolling Timo in the all-English school. Not only had Timo struggled academically in his attempt to keep up with instruction that was not comprehensible to him, but he had eventually lost most of his ability to comprehend and speak Spanish. Timo was not comfortable communicating with his Spanish-speaking grandparents anymore. While Timo lost his native language, David continued to develop it and acquired a high level of English proficiency as well.

Conclusion

Research and theory show that students who receive adequate instruction in their first language learn English and achieve academically in English. Bilingual education, then, has been shown to be the best approach for helping ELLs succeed in school. Of the various bilingual models, dual language enrichment programs offer the best hope for adequately educating the growing numbers of ELLs in our country. Two-way DLE models bring the promise not just of *bilingualism* but of academic content *biliteracy* to ELL and English-dominant students alike. One-way DLE programs offer the strength of numbers since its student participants are mostly, if not all, ELLs. One-way DLE programs are often considered where there are large numbers of ELLs from one first-language group attending a school. Whether a DLE program is two way or one way, it will offer educators, parents, administrators, and students themselves one of the most effective enrichment programs in our nation's schools.

Applications

1. Review the sections that discuss the history of bilingual education and the major research studies that examine the effectiveness of bilingual programs. Draw a time line and plot the major events in the development of bilingual education. Insert also the major research studies. Reflect on how bilingual education in the United States has evolved over the years.

2. Susana is an ELL. She came to the United States from Mexico two years ago. She entered a bilingual program, but her parents requested placement in all-English instruction the following year because they wanted her to learn more English. She is in the fourth grade now. Susana is able to translate for her parents in various everyday situations. Nevertheless, Susana is struggling in school. Although she is passing math and science, Susana is having a very hard time in English language arts and social studies. Review the section that discusses the theory that supports bilingual education. With a partner, discuss the process of English language development that Susana has gone through. Hypothesize on why she is doing better in some subjects than in others. Discuss the type of instruction that Susana should have received to be successful in school.

3. Review the section that discusses the establishment of bilingual programs. Compose a checklist of all the requirements and steps that a school district must follow to provide equal educational opportunities to English language learners.

4. What is the difference between two-way and one-way DLE? Consider the population of ELLs in your area. Which of these two models would be most appropriate? Why?

Key Terms and Acronyms

additive bilingual program. Education model in which students develop their first language and add a second language.

basic interpersonal communication skills (BICS). Part of a theory of language proficiency developed by Jim Cummins, BICS is the basic language ability required for face-to-face communication that is highly contextualized and relatively undemanding.

bilingual education. An educational program in which two languages are used to provide content matter instruction.

Bilingual Education Act. Enacted in Congress in 1968 as Title VII of the Elementary and Secondary Education Act.

bilingualism. The ability to use two languages.

biliteracy. The ability to effectively communicate or understand thoughts and ideas through two languages' grammatical systems and vocabulary, using their written symbols.

cognitive academic language proficiency (CALP). Part of a theory of language proficiency developed by Jim Cummins, CALP is the language ability required for academic achievement in a context-reduced environment.

common underlying proficiency (CUP). Cummins' theory that, while the surface features of two languages differ for bilinguals, at a deeper level, the proficiencies developed in the two languages form one unified entity.

dual language enrichment (DLE). An additive model of bilingual education that promotes high levels of academic achievement as well as bilingualism and biliteracy for all participating students.

early-exit bilingual model. A subtractive model of bilingual education that has as its goal the acquisition of English in a short period of time.

Elementary and Secondary Education Act (ESEA). Legislation that established a discretionary competitive grant program to fund bilingual education programs for economically disadvantaged language-minority students.

English-only. A political movement to eliminate bilingual education, which has resulted in legislation in states such as California and Arizona forbidding the use of languages other than English for instruction.

isolationism. A government policy based on the belief that national interests are best served by avoiding economic and political alliances with other countries.

late-exit bilingual model. An additive model of bilingual education that attempts to maintain ELLs' first languages and cultures as they acquire English.

Office of Civil Rights (OCR). U.S. government agency that ensures, among other things, that English language learners have access to all instruction.

separate underlying proficiency (SUP). The false assumption that concepts learned in one language do not transfer or support learning in another language.

subtractive bilingual program. Model in which the second language and culture are intended to replace the first language and culture.

TEC. Texas Education Code.

Resources for Further Study

Stephen Krashen's website: www.sdkrashen.com/

Website on language policy: http://ourworld.compuserve.com/homepages/
jwcrawford

Office of Civil Rights policy:
www.ed.gov/print/about/offices/list/ocr/docs/lau1970.html;
www.ed.gov/print/about/offices/list/ocr/eeolep/index.html;
www.ed.gov/print/about/offices/list/ocr/docs/lau1990_and_1985.html

4

Effective Practices for Students with Disabilities in Inclusive Classrooms

Steve Chamberlain

Introduction

Students with disabilities represent a widely diverse group, both across and within disability categories. General education teachers often struggle when faced with the challenges of providing an appropriate and individualized education for these students. Key to student success in inclusive classrooms is a collaborative relationship with special educators, who are integral in identifying the *accommodations* and *modifications* that support students with disabilities in their efforts at success.

The legal mandate for serving students with disabilities in inclusive settings is discussed first in this chapter, followed by a description of the role of the general education teacher in identifying students with disabilities. Effective practices for students with disabilities, including appropriate accommodations as they apply to students with various needs, are discussed within the general framework of collaborative teaching environments. Finally, scenarios are presented to illustrate how general educators and special educators can work together to provide appropriate instruction for students with disabilities in inclusive classrooms.

Special Education Law: IDEA and Section 504

Two laws are especially pertinent to the education of students with disabilities: the *Individuals with Disabilities Education Act* (IDEA) and Section 504 of the Rehabilitation Act of 1973. IDEA is the law that established and maintains the current special education system in U.S. schools. Section 504, although not considered special education services, provides certain accommodations for students with disabilities who are not identified under IDEA.

IDEA

The Individuals with Disabilities Education Act, last reauthorized in 2004, was originally passed as the Education for All Handicapped Children Act (EHA) in 1975. This landmark piece of legislation followed on the heels of the civil rights legislation of the 1960s and paved the way for children with disabilities to be educated in neighborhood schools with their nondisabled peers. Congress reported that at the time of passage, one of every two children with disabilities received an inappropriate education, while one in eight were not in school at all. IDEA defines special education as "specially designed instruction, at no cost to parents, to meet the unique needs of a child with a disability" (U.S. Congress 2004, 12). A major purpose of EHA (hereafter referred to as IDEA) was to ensure that all students with disabilities received not only an education but an *appropriate* education. Several key components laid the foundation for the special education system of the last thirty years.

Disability categories • Thirteen disability categories are currently identified by IDEA 2004. The four categories with the highest incidence of students, approximately 90 percent of all students with disabilities, are the following:

- learning disabilities (an information-processing disorder that affects learning)
- mental retardation
- speech and language impairments
- emotional disturbance

The remaining nine low-incidence categories are

- orthopedic impairment (i.e., physical disabilities)
- other health impairment (e.g., attention deficit hyperactivity disorder [ADHD], asthma)

- traumatic brain injury
- visual impairment
- deafness
- hard of hearing
- multiple disability (usually a combination of a physical or sensory disability with mental retardation)
- deaf/blind

Of utmost importance when considering disability categories is to recognize the great diversity not only across different disability categories but also within different categories. For example, the difference between the educational needs of a student considered mildly mentally retarded and the needs of a student who is severely retarded is vast. The former may receive academic education in the general education classroom, while the latter is likely to need a functional *life-skills curriculum* that focuses on a variety of daily skills such as hygiene, grooming, toileting, and dressing at the elementary level and skills needed to transition into adulthood at the secondary level. Two students with cerebral palsy (CP) may also have extremely different characteristics and needs. A student who has one hand with slight motor impairment, a mild speech impairment, but no cognitive impairment will have vastly different educational needs from a student who is quadriplegic (i.e., has lost the use of all four limbs) and must use a wheelchair, has moderate to severe speech impairment, uses a communication board to communicate, and is moderately mentally retarded.

In fact, there are major differences in student characteristics and needs within each of the thirteen disability categories. For this reason, it is paramount to understand that categories can only give structure and definition to our understanding of a group of students identified within a specific category. To truly understand the unique characteristics and educational needs of any student with a disability, regardless of the category, educators must rely on accurate and comprehensive assessment results that describe strengths and weaknesses and indicate instructional implications for that student.

***Free and appropriate public education* (FAPE)** • IDEA specifies that students with disabilities are entitled to an appropriate education at no charge to the parents. However, there are no absolute criteria for what entails *appropriate*. In general, an appropriate education is one that meets the unique needs of a student with disabilities. Except in instances when arbitrators and courts make decisions about what is considered appropriate, *individualized education program (IEP) committees* make this judgment on a case-by-case basis. The nature and severity of the disability, the strengths and weaknesses of the student, and the preferences of both student and parents will all likely play a role in the kind of education considered appropriate by an IEP committee.

Least restrictive environment • Central to the discussion about what constitutes an appropriate education is the concept of *least restrictive environment* (LRE). IDEA states:

> To the maximum extent appropriate, children with disabilities . . . are educated with children who are not disabled, and special classes, separate schooling, or other removal of children with disabilities from the regular educational environment occurs only when the nature or severity of the disability of a child is such that education of the child with the use of supplementary aids and services cannot be achieved satisfactorily. (U.S. Congress 2004, 34)

Just as with FAPE, LRE is generally an IEP committee decision.

In most instances, people think of placement, or the kind of classroom, when they think of LRE. What is the most appropriate classroom setting in which a student should be served? Is it the general education classroom with *inclusion* support, the *resource room* (where a student receives services part-time in a pull-out, or separate, classroom), or a *self-contained classroom* (where students receive the majority of their services in a pullout classroom)? This model, where a range of services is offered to meet the unique needs of students with a variety of disabilities, is called the *continuum of services*. Offering a range of services recognizes that one size (i.e., kind of classroom) does not fit all. Placement options range from a variety of locations in the neighborhood school (e.g., general education classroom, resource room, self-contained classroom) to locations outside the neighborhood school (e.g., alternative placement centers, home, psychiatric institutions, hospitals, juvenile detention centers).

Closely tied to the concept of LRE is *inclusion*. This term means different things to different people. Some believe that the current special education system with the continuum of services and the LRE mandate is responsible inclusion that ensures an appropriate education for all students with disabilities. Others believe in the notion of full inclusion, where all students, regardless of the nature and severity of the disability, would be educated in the general education classroom with appropriate supports in that setting (Stainback and Stainback 1996). Those who argue for full inclusion believe that separate systems result in segregated classrooms and that all students can, in fact, be appropriately educated in the general education setting if they are given the proper supports in that setting.

In general, the LRE is the setting where a student can receive an appropriate education that is as normalized as possible (Taylor 2004). The general education classroom would be the least restrictive environment if a student can receive an appropriate education there. If not, then a resource classroom might be considered the LRE for that particular student. The more a student is educated with her nondisabled peers, the less restrictive the environment, as long as the student can receive an appropriate education that meets her needs.

Rueda, Gallego, and Moll (2000) suggest that LRE extends beyond the typical conception of placement and should be looked at based on the *context* of education. A key concept when discussing LRE is *access*. Certainly the physical placement or setting is concerned with access, but the idea of access extends to the broader concept of a quality education. Do students with disabilities have the same access to programs and opportunities for success? Do they have access to quality instruction that meets their individual needs? Rueda and his colleagues believe LRE should be considered at a broader level than just the physical setting.

Individualized education program • An *individualized education program* (IEP) is a plan agreed upon by the IEP committee (in Texas called the *admission, review, and dismissal [ARD] committee*) that indicates how a student will be served to meet her unique educational needs. Components of the IEP include the student's current levels of educational performance, annual goals and short-term instructional objectives, the specific special education and related services to be provided, the extent of participation in general education programs, accommodations and modifications for general education classrooms, projected dates for initiation, the anticipated duration of services, and appropriate evaluation procedures for measuring attainment of goals and objectives on at least an annual basis.

IDEA requires that IEP committee members include the students' parents, a special education teacher, a general education teacher (if the student is served in general education), a school district representative (usually a school administrator), an assessment professional (when assessment information is discussed in meetings, e.g., an educational diagnostician), and the student when it is considered appropriate (e.g., a high school student who is preparing for transition to adult life). Other individuals may also be members of the committee, such as providers of related services (e.g., physical therapist, transportation personnel), counselors, nurses, and parent or student advocates.

Due process procedures • *Due process procedures* were implemented to protect the rights of students with disabilities and their parents. Perhaps the most important protection has been to ensure full membership of parents on IEP committees. This allows parents to have an equal voice in the educational planning for their child. In addition, parents have the right to disagree with other members of the committee and can follow due process procedures if they have a grievance. These procedures include asking for mediation, a review before an arbitrator, and an appeal of the arbitrator's decision if they disagree with it. Parents also have the right of refusal for initial assessment for special education eligibility and initial placement for special education services, in addition to full access to their child's educational records.

Nondiscriminatory assessment • IDEA includes a number of stipulations to ensure that all students receive appropriate, *nondiscriminatory assessment* when being considered for special education eligibility. Such stipulations include requiring multiple measures when conducting an assessment for eligibility, use of tests that demonstrate technical adequacy for students from different cultural backgrounds, and, where feasible, use of tests in students' dominant language or primary mode of communication (e.g., sign language for deaf students). In addition, tests must be administered by trained personnel and evaluations must be made by a multi-disciplinary team (i.e., a team of professionals who can address different aspects of the student's needs).

Related services • Congress also recognized that students with disabilities may need services that cannot be delivered by educators. For example, a student with cerebral palsy may need the services of a physical therapist to help him stretch his muscles. A student with speech impairments will need the services of a speech or language pathologist. A student needing intermittent catheterization will need the services of the campus nurse. These services are integral to the well-being of students with certain kinds of disabilities. Providing these services in neighborhood schools allows students to be served in the least restrictive environment.

Transition services • *Transition*, as referred to in the special education literature, usually means transition from secondary school to adult life. The ultimate outcome for all students is to leave school prepared to be successful adults. Success, of course, will be defined differently for different individuals. For a student with severe cognitive impairment, transition outcomes may be to live in a group home with others with similar disabilities, to work part-time as a contributing member of society, and to learn certain activities for leisure and recreation. For a student with learning disabilities, transition outcomes may be to learn about specific resources and study skills that will help him be a successful college student.

IDEA requires that all IEP committees address transition no later than age sixteen, and by age fourteen where appropriate. Transition goals may focus on vocational skills, independent living skills, communication and social skills, functional academics, and community participation skills (e.g., using the transportation system, accessing necessary resources such as rehabilitation services). Oftentimes, members of community organizations, such as rehabilitation counselors, and business members who work with students in vocational programs will be involved in transition programs.

Paralleling the general education curriculum • A major focus of IDEA since its original passage has been on the inclusion of students with disabilities in the least restrictive environment. The 1997 and 2004 reauthorizations continued this emphasis by mandating that the curriculum used by students with disabilities should parallel the general education curriculum to the greatest extent possible. Students who are developmentally behind in certain areas are expected to follow the general education curriculum, even if they are following it at a lower grade level. The exception to this would be students with mental retardation (MR), whose curriculum is likely to be significantly altered in favor of a life-skills curriculum.

Inclusion in statewide and local accountability systems • IDEA 1997 and 2004 also placed emphasis on including students with disabilities in statewide and local accountability systems. Previously, students with disabilities were typically excluded from taking high-stakes tests for a variety of reasons, some focusing on the best interests of students, and others focusing on the best interests of school scores (Fielding 2004). From one perspective, given that high-stakes testing is a major mechanism for entering into greater affluence in U.S. society, this exclusion was akin to tracking students with disabilities at a very early age. IDEA recognizes that all students, including students with disabilities, deserve the opportunity to participate in such a system.

Section 504 of the Rehabilitation Act of 1973

One additional law especially pertains to students with disabilities. Section 504 of the Rehabilitation Act of 1973 states:

> No otherwise qualified individual with disabilities . . . shall solely by reason of his disability, be excluded from the participation in, be

denied the benefits of, or be subjected to discrimination under any program or activity receiving Federal financial assistance.

Section 504 is often employed when accommodations to the general education classroom alone are needed for a student with a disability to be successful in school, or if a disability is thought to be temporary. There is more flexibility in identifying students for 504 services and also for exiting them from services than there is with IDEA. If a student has asthma, accommodations such as limited physical exertion, use of an inhaler, and frequent rest periods may be all the student needs in order to be successful in the classroom. If, however, the asthma has previously caused the student to miss many class days during the year, qualification under the IDEA category "other health impairment" would allow this student to receive a wider variety of services and potential modifications to the student's curriculum. It is important to remember that when educators refer to special education, they are referring to services received under IDEA, not Section 504 services.

The General Education Teacher's Role in Identifying Students with Disabilities

The general education teacher plays a major role in the identification of students for special education services. It is the general education teacher who refers the struggling student to the educational diagnostician for a full and individualized evaluation (FIE) to determine if the student qualifies for special education services. Of note are two systemic safeguards implemented over the last thirty years to assist general educators in accurately discerning whether or not a referral is appropriate: *prereferral intervention* and *response to intervention*.

Prereferral Intervention

Prereferral intervention is a process required by IDEA that involves soliciting the help of other educators when a teacher has difficulty with a struggling student (García and Ortiz 2006). A team of campus educators (presumably the best teachers on a campus) will review the difficulties this teacher has experienced with her student and provide the teacher with best-practice strategies and interventions. The teacher then implements the strategies and collects data to determine if they are effective. If so, no further action is necessary. If not, the teacher will report back to the committee and the strategies will be modified or new strategies will be suggested. If these are not effective over time, the committee will likely recommend that the teacher refer the student for special education assessment.

Prereferral intervention is a general education process designed to provide teachers with assistance in teaching struggling students in an effort to keep these students in the general education classroom. It is also a response to the problem of *overrepresentation* and the misidentification of students from specific culturally and linguistically diverse groups in specific special education categories (García and Ortiz 2006).

Response to Intervention

More recently, response to intervention (RTI) has appeared as another systemic approach for maintaining struggling learners in the general education setting by providing them with supplemental and remedial instruction (Fuchs et al. 2003). RTI is typically enacted as a three-tier approach to reading instruction. Tier 1 instruction is typical instruction that all students receive in the general education classroom. Students who struggle with tier 1 instruction would be provided with additional explicit instruction in different areas of reading. The majority of these students are likely to find success with tier 2 assistance. However, those students who struggle with tier 2 instruction would be provided a third tier of modified instruction with a smaller student-to-teacher ratio.

Progress monitoring is key throughout this process, as is the use of research-based instructional practices. In this way, RTI is also seen as a potential assessment tool in identifying students who have the processing disorders associated with learning disabilities. Students who struggle with tier 3 instruction would likely be candidates for special education referral and assessment.

Responding to the Frustrated General Education Teacher

Although considerable progress has been made in ensuring that all students receive the best possible education, general education teachers may still feel frustrated as they attempt to meet the needs of special education students and at the same time meet the needs of all the other students in their class. These frustrations often boil over into comments like the following: "Why do we have to change how we teach those students? It's not fair to the other students who never get a break, it takes too much of our instructional time, and it teaches students with disabilities that it's OK to be lazy, someone will always help you out!"

Comments like these are typically rooted in teachers' frustration over having to adapt instruction for students with disabilities, one more addition to their myriad of tasks that seem never ending. While it is important to acknowledge such frustration, it is also important to challenge the myths embedded within such comments. An appropriate response to such complaints would be to point out that all students need supports to be successful. When implemented appropriately, accommodations and modifications are not an unfair advantage, but a necessary support for the student to be successful.

Success is the key. If the support does not create the conditions for success, then it would indeed be useless and a waste of time. The assumption should always be that students will be successful with such support. In addition, it is clear that nondisabled students are offered a variety of supports to help them achieve. Some have suggested that accommodations and modifications level the playing field to help students with disabilities cope with an unfair disadvantage that either they were born with or occurred after birth.

A further response to such comments would be to challenge the teacher's idea that appropriate use of accommodations leads to a learned helplessness response. When students are provided with unnecessary supports, held to low expectations, and unchallenged in the classroom, they *are* likely to learn to expect others to do things for them. However, when given the appropriate supports and instruction, students are capable of successful independent learning.

Finally, general education teachers who are frustrated with the expectation that they must adapt their classroom for students with disabilities are most probably frustrated because they do not know how to provide accommodations efficiently and effectively, so they are therefore not able to create an environment where all students will be successful. Given that a sixty-plus-hour work week is unacceptable for most of us, and that "sacrificing" the education of general education students to take the extra time to implement supports for students with disabilities is also unacceptable, there must be another solution.

The solution lies in *collaboration*. The special educator and general educator must work together, with the special educator offering her expertise in adapting instruction and materials and the general educator ensuring that the student is held to high standards of mastery of the curriculum. The general education teacher who feels overwhelmed at the prospect of being asked to address students' individual needs should be supported by other teachers and administrators who can help her find a solution so that all children in her classroom will be successful. This is much more likely to happen when all stakeholders share responsibility for the success of each student.

Effective Practices for Students with Disabilities Served in Inclusive Settings

Key in planning instruction for students with disabilities is to select approaches and strategies that meet the unique needs of these students. Teachers must have a repertoire of strategies from which to choose in order to differentiate instruction (Carolan and Guinn 2007). A variety of instructional approaches and strategies may be effectively utilized with students with disabilities. Choosing a particular strategy depends on a number of factors, including the nature and severity of the disability, the developmental level and grade level of students, and the individual and cultural differences and preferences of students (Chamberlain 2005). Some strategies may be unique to specific disability categories (e.g., use of Braille for students who are blind), while others may be useful with students who are identified under various categories (e.g., classroom organization, behavior management techniques, use of authentic assessments, use of visual aids such as graphic organizers). To the degree possible, teachers should select strategies that have been well researched and shown to be effective with students who share the characteristics of the teachers' students.

Teachers must also be cognizant that assessment and instruction are continually intertwined. Given the developmental lag typical for students with disabilities, continual assessment is essential if educators are to track the extent of mastery and the rate of growth for students in order to prepare instruction that is at the right level. Then, as teachers provide instruction, they constantly assess the effectiveness of their instruction for each student, which leads to future planning of instruction. An explanation of student supports in the general education classroom (i.e., accommodations, modifications, and *assistive technology*) will help illustrate how educators can respond to the needs of students with disabilities. Ensuring successful incorporation of these supports relies on effective collaboration between special and general educators.

Accommodations, Modifications, and Assistive Technology

All students need classroom supports to be successful in school. For some, those supports will be supplemental assignments that challenge students to reach their learning potential. For others, after-school tutoring and extra help from home will help students achieve in school. But for some, the supports must be more intensive and specialized if students are to succeed in the general education classroom. Most students with disabilities require some sort of accommodations, modifications, or assistive technology. Without these supports, these students are likely to underachieve in school. With these supports, the students are likely to be successful and even thrive in school.

Accommodations versus modifications • *Accommodations* refers to adaptations pertaining to how a student accesses information and demonstrates learning. *Modifications*, on the other hand, refers to significant changes in the curriculum (SchwabLearning.org Editorial Staff 2006). Modifications alter the instructional level (e.g., when a seventh-grade student with MR is given instruction at the third-grade level), the standards or expectations (e.g., providing a life-skills curriculum in place of the general education curriculum), and/or the performance criteria for students (e.g., lowering expectations for mastery, allowing students to submit assignments where the product is significantly altered from the product of nondisabled students).

Accommodations do not entail changes in the curriculum; they serve as supports so that students can participate in the general education curriculum. A variety of different categories of accommodations exist, including instructional, material, and assessment (which can include response mode, format, setting, and time). Accommodations in instruction include adjusting how students are grouped to better meet student needs, increasing the use of *direct instruction* (DI), teaching specific learning strategies, and implementing a variety of peer-assistance strategies (e.g., peer tutoring, peer reinforcing, peer note taking). Accommodations in materials can include highlighting texts, providing graphic and advance organizers, and increasing the font and spacing of text for students with vision or learning difficulties.

In regard to assessment, accommodations can be designed to alter how a student responds (e.g., having a student with severe speech problems point to an answer rather than respond orally) or how a test or assignment is formatted (e.g., putting only ten math problems on a page instead of thirty). The purpose of adapting assessments is to ensure that educators are actually assessing the knowledge or skills of a student, not the effects of his disability. For example, if a student does not have functional use of his hands in order to write an essay response, asking him to write such a response would not be a valid assessment of his composition skills, but an assessment of his ability to use his hands.

Assistive technology: A special kind of accommodation • According to the Assistive Technology Act of 1998, *assistive technology* (AT) (sometimes called adaptive technology) refers to "products, devices or equipment, whether acquired commercially, modified or customized, that are used to maintain, increase or improve the functional capabilities of individuals with disabilities" (U.S. Congress 1998, 6). Assistive technology is a kind of accommodation in that it is a support that will help create conditions for success in the classroom but will not change the nature of the curriculum. AT addresses a variety of student needs, including physical, communication, and cognitive and learning needs. Some AT is considered high-tech and generally expensive, such as computerized wheelchairs and speech synthesizers. Other AT is considered low-tech and inexpensive, such as foam wedges that help maintain posture for quadriplegic students, built-up spoons (i.e., foam attachments) that allow students to grasp spoons more easily, and reach-and-grasp instruments that allow students who use wheelchairs to grab objects from a distance.

Several assistive technology devices are specifically useful for students with sensory impairments. Beeper traffic signals allow blind students to know when the light has changed so they can safely walk across the street. The long cane is also used by the blind, and hearing aids are used by the hard of hearing. Assistive technology also exists for students with LD and MR, for example, calculators, pocket organizers, and computer programs that help students practice skills in different subject areas.

Collaboration and Consultation

Including students with special needs in the general education classroom with special education supports requires effective collaboration between special educators and general educators. *Collaboration* means to work together for a common goal. Characteristics of effective collaboration include effective communication skills, voluntary participation, shared goal setting, shared responsibility for key decisions, and shared accountability for outcomes (Kampwirth 2003). Collaboration assumes parity in the process; however, general educators and special educators will bring different strengths to the process that they can share with each other. In this way, each will serve as a *consultant* to the other. The special educator will have expertise in planning modifications and accommodations for students with special needs, while the general educator will likely have expertise in the curriculum and in a variety of instructional strategies such as cooperative learning and peer support systems.

Responding to Students with Mild Behavior Problems

Even with effective instruction, students with mild behavior problems, as many students with ADHD exhibit, often frustrate teachers, parents, and other students.

Although students identified under other disability categories also exhibit many of these behaviors, ADHD is used to illustrate how teachers can respond to mild behavior problems in the classroom.

The three major characteristics of students with ADHD are inattention (the inability to selectively focus), hyperactivity (the inability to control one's motor functions), and impulsivity (the tendency to act before thinking). Some students may be solely inattentive, but many have all three characteristics. Typically, teachers' frustrations come from a lack of skill in working with students who exhibit these characteristics. However, research suggests that there are many strategies teachers can utilize to create environments conducive to student success (Carbone 2001). These include

- creating highly structured learning environments
- using positive reinforcement
- engaging students in learning by making instruction meaningful and relevant
- breaking tasks into shorter time units
- varying the pace of instruction
- varying the kinds of instruction and activities within a given lesson
- giving clear and precise instructions
- giving one clear piece of instruction at a time
- providing active learning opportunities

Perry Green, a young adult with ADHD, stated in an interview (Chamberlain 2005) that the two most important accommodations offered to him as a student were (1) having an understanding teacher who engaged in dialogue about his ADHD and (2) being allowed to get up and move around in the classroom from time to time.

Many of these strategies can be used effectively with students with a variety of disabilities, but they should be especially useful for students who have difficulty with selective attention and poor impulse control. In general, behavior management strategies that focus on providing structured environments that help students know what to expect, and positive reinforcement that helps motivate students to stay focused on the task at hand, are useful with most students in the classroom. Social skills instruction is also especially important for students with ADHD but can also be useful with students with other kinds of disabilities. A systematic approach to teaching appropriate interaction skills, during which students are taught directly, given opportunities to role-play and give feedback to one another, and asked to generalize these skills by using them in real-life situations, has been found to be effective in helping students become more socially appropriate when interacting with others (McGinnis and Goldstein 1997).

Scenarios of Effective Instruction for Students with Special Needs

The following scenarios illustrate how special educators and general educators can collaborate to provide effective instruction that meets the needs of students with disabilities in mainstream classes. The first scenario describes a student with a high-incidence disability (learning disability), and the second scenario describes a student with a low-incidence disability (cerebral palsy).

Manuel, a Student with Learning Disabilities

Manuel is a seventh-grade student with learning disabilities who is reading and writing at a fourth-grade level. He receives the majority of his instruction in the general education classroom with inclusion support from a special education teacher in his content area classes (e.g., history, science). Manuel, who struggles to process new information on his own, receives instruction in reading and language arts in the resource room, where direct instruction is primarily used to teach him most new concepts and skills. DI is an instructional approach where learning tasks are broken into small increments and explicitly taught in sequence. When all steps are mastered in sequence, the whole task has been mastered. DI is well researched and proven to be effective in teaching students with learning disabilities (Magliaro, Lockee, and Burton 2005).

For Manuel to achieve success in his content area classes, his special education teacher, Mr. Saenz, and his general education teachers must collaborate with one another in order to provide the supports he needs for an appropriate education. For example, Ms. Flynn, Manuel's history teacher, needs assistance in helping Manuel learn grade-level material when he is reading at a lower level. Because learning disabilities involve certain difficulties in processing information, Manuel is also taught using a learning strategies approach that gives him tools to help him process new information. Mr. Saenz is likely to take the primary role in teaching Manuel these learning strategies in either the resource setting or in the inclusive setting. *Learning strategies* can be defined as "techniques, principles, or rules that enable a student to learn, to solve problems, and to complete tasks independently" (Mercer and Mercer 2005, 487). As students transition to the greater content emphasis of the secondary grades, strategies that teach students how to acquire knowledge and skills are necessary (Deshler and Shumaker 2006).

Mercer and Mercer (2005) differentiate learning strategies, content enhancements, and study skills but consider each essential in helping students learn, especially at the secondary level. An example of a learning strategy is *reciprocal teaching*, an interactive teaching and learning strategy that promotes both comprehension of text and comprehension monitoring through active participation in discussions of text (Klingner and Vaughn 1996). Reciprocal teaching utilizes a think-aloud approach and involves four strategies: predicting, questioning, summarizing, and clarifying. To teach the strategy, Mr. Saenz initially leads the dialogue and models the use of the four strategies while reading. Through guided practice, the responsibility for initiating and maintaining the dialogue is transferred to Manuel. Reciprocal teaching requires students to focus on the reading material and, at the same time, monitor for understanding.

Content enhancements also support Manuel in learning. Advance organizers (e.g., outlines, chapter previewing), visual displays (e.g., figures, graphs, diagrams, semantic maps), study guides, and mnemonic devices (e.g., acronyms, acrostics, visual imaging) are all examples of content enhancements that can act as supports for struggling learners (Mercer and Mercer 2005). An example of an advance organizer that is also a mnemonic device is the acronym *FORM* (Larkin and Ellis 1998), which is a tool used to introduce content area lessons.

Focus: What is the focus of the lesson?

Organization: What organizers will be used to make the lesson easier to learn?

Relationship: What have you learned before that will help you now, and how will what you learn now help you in the future?

Most Important Goal: What is the most important learning goal associated with this lesson?

Given that Manuel is reading at a fourth-grade level, he will not likely be successful if handed a seventh-grade textbook and asked to read it on his own without supports. To accommodate his needs, Mr. Saenz and Ms. Flynn might preview the text before asking him to read it. Previewing can involve the distribution of outlines, discussing important vocabulary and difficult-to-recognize words, or having Manuel skim the headings and predict the content of the text. Another accommodation might be to provide the text on audiotape so Manuel can listen while reading along or to pair him with a peer tutor. These accommodations will help Manuel comprehend his text even though his reading ability is not at grade level. The ultimate purpose behind the provision of accommodations and strategy-based instruction is to help students who struggle with learning tasks become more independent learners.

Although Mr. Saenz takes the primary responsibility in teaching learning strategies to Manuel and incorporating content enhancements into his educational program, Ms. Flynn also takes responsibility in assisting Manuel in using both. Together, they teach a number of study skill strategies to Manuel. Students can be taught study skills in a variety of areas, including textbook reading, test taking, test preparation, note taking, outlining, listening, oral presentation, and time management (Mercer and Mercer 2005).

Mr. Saenz might teach Manuel how to use a textbook by having him skim the major headings and formulate several questions for each heading. In regard to test-preparation skills, he might have Manuel divide the study material into equal amounts and devote a certain amount of time to each section of material. He might also teach Manuel the test-taking skill of eliminating obviously incorrect multiple-choice answers as a process of elimination. Study skill strategies are also designed to give students who struggle with learning greater ownership of their learning.

In addition to utilizing DI and strategy-based instruction with Manuel, Mr. Saenz recognizes another important element in instruction needed to engage students in the learning process: *contextualization of learning in relevant and meaningful ways*. This is essential for all learners, but perhaps most important for students whose cultural and linguistic background does not mirror the mainstream of America (Nieto 2004). Learning can be contextualized by making connections to students' background experiences and knowledge base, providing opportunities for students to share their backgrounds with others, and recognizing and validating the cultural and linguistic differences children bring to the classroom.

The more authentic, or real-life, classroom experiences are, the more relevant and meaningful they are likely to be (Jobling and Moni 2004). Moll (1991) studied the "funds of knowledge" of Latino children living in poverty in Arizona and found that children had a vast array of different kinds of knowledge and social networks. Drawing on these funds of knowledge, teachers can still employ direct instruction, but in ways that are not necessarily decontextualized (as, for example, many grammar textbook exercises are). For example, Ms. Flynn can utilize reading passages that are of interest to students, or use students' own writing, to teach specific grammar skills (e.g., insertion of commas to separate items in a list), thereby teaching the skills within a meaningful context for students.

Ashley, a Student with Cerebral Palsy

General education teachers can also expect to teach students with low-incidence disabilities in their classrooms. Ashley is a fourth-grade student with cerebral palsy who is quadriplegic, has moderate speech impairment, and has normal intelligence. Her IEP committee has decided that the least restrictive environment for Ashley is the general education classroom with appropriate special education supports. Ms. Davis, Ashley's primary special education teacher, and her general education teacher, Mr. Lerma, will collaborate to address Ashley's multiple needs and provide supports to meet those needs.

Before the beginning of the new school year, Ms. Davis and Mr. Lerma meet to discuss Ashley's IEP and her unique needs. Two major aspects of Ashley's education they need to discuss are *access* and *communication*. Because Ashley uses a wheelchair, access will involve entry into the classroom (e.g., Is there an appropriate ramp? Is the doorway wide enough?), maneuverability throughout the classroom, and time considerations for transitions (e.g., within-class transitions, between-class transitions). The classroom must be arranged so that Ashley can access all areas, including computers, materials and resources, and classroom centers. The teachers discuss these issues and brainstorm foreseen difficulties. Both teachers offer insight based on their previous experiences in arranging classrooms and in working with students who use wheelchairs.

Because Ashley has moderate speech impairments, communication is also a key aspect of her program that the teachers must discuss. The ability to communicate affects all developmental areas (e.g., language development, social development, cognitive development, emotional development). It will be essential that her teachers provide Ashley with the support she needs to communicate effectively in the classroom. A communication device may be incorporated into her program. If so, it will be important that her teachers understand how to use the device and also how to appropriately respond to Ashley. It will also be important that the teachers are prepared to create numerous opportunities for Ashley to achieve success in communicative interactions. This will involve encouraging not only Ashley, but her classmates, to communicate.

Ms. Davis suggests to Mr. Lerma that Ashley's classmates may be hesitant at first since they will likely struggle to understand Ashley. Given time, however, it is likely that they will develop the ability to understand and to communicate with her. Ms. Davis, given her experience, has more expertise in planning peer support activities, so she suggests a variety of peer-mediated supports, such as peer tutoring. Collaborating with the speech and language therapist will help both Ms. Davis and Mr. Lerma plan for these opportunities to encourage communication. As all educators (including Ashley's parents) collaborate to incorporate speech and language objectives into their daily interactions with Ashley, she will be much more likely to practice her communication skills.

Ashley's assistive technology will include a motorized wheelchair and a communication device. In previous times, the prognosis for a meaningful education for a student with quadriplegia would have been bleak. However, this need not be the case for Ashley. If she has motor control of her head, Ashley can use a laser light attached to a head band in order to operate a computer for communication. Speech synthesizers and computer programs allow students with speech and tactile difficulties to string together thoughts in meaningful communications. Even if Ashley cannot control her head movements, if she has control of her lips, she can operate a sip-and-puff blow stick (similar to sucking on a straw or blowing air through the straw) that will allow her to operate her wheelchair, her speech synthesizer, and her computer. Stephen Hawking, the Nobel-winning physicist, has interacted with the world in this way for more than twenty years and continues to contribute prolifically to his field. Given appropriate assistive technology and teachers who know how to use it, students with severe disabilities like Ashley can reach high levels of success in school.

Applications

1. Students with learning disabilities underachieve in school before being identified for special education services. In small groups, discuss with your classmates reasons other than a learning disability that students might underachieve in school. Why would teachers sometimes mistakenly refer an underachieving student for special education testing? What steps can teachers take to more accurately identify students who are suspected of having a learning disability?

2. It is not uncommon to hear frustrated teachers make flippant remarks about students with hyperactive tendencies. For example, one teacher was overheard saying, "Boy, do I have one who needs Ritalin!" In small groups, discuss with your classmates some alternative strategies for teachers who work with students with ADHD other than medication. How might you act as a change agent to counter negative attitudes some teachers have toward students with ADHD?

3. Select one of the nine low-incidence disability categories. Based on your knowledge about typical characteristics of your chosen category, brainstorm

with several of your classmates a number of accommodations that might be appropriate for students in this category.

4. Identify a special education teacher in a local school district. Interview this teacher about the different ways the teacher collaborates with others. Then identify one of the general education teachers with whom that special education teacher collaborates and interview that general education teacher about his experience collaborating with the special education teacher. What are some common elements of the collaborative experiences of the two teachers? Are there differences in their experiences?

5. Identify a parent of a child with a disability and interview the parent about her experiences with the IEP committee. Discuss how she has been involved with the committee and the degree to which she feels she is a full and equal member of the committee. What recommendations would she make to educators about how they can include parents in the IEP committee process?

Key Terms and Acronyms

accommodations. Supports that are deemed necessary for students with disabilities to receive an appropriate education. Accommodations do not change the nature of a student's curriculum but provide the student with an opportunity to demonstrate competence in the classroom. Examples include previewing content area text before having the student read a chapter, increased font size for text, allowing extended time on assignments and tests, and ensuring physical access in the classroom.

admission, review, and dismissal (ARD) committee (or meeting). In Texas, this is the name for the IEP committee or IEP meeting. See **individualized education program committee.**

assistive technology (AT). A special kind of accommodation that serves as a tool for a person with a disability. AT includes more expensive and complicated kinds of technology, such as motorized wheelchairs and computer-related hardware and software (e.g., speech synthesizers, voice-to-print programs, instructional programs), as well as less expensive and simpler kinds of technology, such as foam wedges that provide support for students who are quadriplegic and simple switches used with a communication board.

collaboration. The act of two or more people working together toward a common goal. Special educators typically collaborate with general educators, parents, students, related services personnel, administrators, community agencies, and other professionals in providing an appropriate education for children with disabilities.

consultant. One who shares professional expertise with others. Special educators have specialized training in working with children with disabilities and they consult with general educators, parents, and others to share that expertise.

continuum of services. A model for providing special education services to students with disabilities that is mandated by the Individuals with Disabilities Education Act (IDEA). The continuum includes a wide range of placements, from general education classrooms with different levels of special education support, to resource and self-contained classrooms, to services outside the neighborhood school, such as alternative placement centers, hospitals, mental health institutions, and homebound services.

direct instruction (DI). A bottom-up model of instruction that is teacher focused and involves teaching students how to perform tasks by breaking the tasks into component skills and explicitly teaching the steps in succession until the students can perform the entire task.

due process procedures. Procedures mandated by IDEA that protect the rights of parents and their children with disabilities. For example, parents are considered full members of the IEP team, have full access to their child's records, must be informed of their rights, can disagree with IEP committee decisions, can ask for mediation and arbitration, and can appeal an arbitrator's decision.

free and appropriate public education (FAPE). All students with disabilities have a right to a free and appropriate public education. Except in circumstances when courts have made FAPE determinations, the appropriateness of a student's education is generally determined by a student's IEP committee and should reflect the unique needs of the student.

inclusion. When students with disabilities are included in educational programs with their nondisabled peers. For some, inclusion means to follow the principles of least restrictive environment (via the continuum of services model), but for others, inclusion means fully integrating all students with disabilities, regardless of the nature or severity of the disability, in general education classrooms with appropriate supports.

individualized education program (IEP). Mandated by IDEA, the IEP is a written document that outlines the educational plan designed to provide an appropriate education that meets the unique needs of a student with disabilities. The IEP includes a statement about current levels of functioning, goals and objectives, specification of the percentage of time to be spent in special and general education, justification for the least restrictive environment, and accommodations and modifications.

individualized education program committee. Each student with a disability is served by an IEP committee (which includes the student's parents) that is responsible for that student's IEP. Meetings are held at least annually in order to discuss the student's IEP.

Individuals with Disabilities Education Act (IDEA). Originally passed as the Education for All Handicapped Children Act of 1975 (Public Law 94-142) and most recently reauthorized in 2004 (Public Law 108-446), IDEA laid the foundation for the special education system of the last thirty-two years. Among other things, the law establishes that all students with disabilities receive an appropriate education via an IEP in the least restrictive environment.

least restrictive environment (LRE). Mandated by IDEA, the LRE is a learning environment (typically referred to as a particular placement, e.g., general education classroom, resource room, self-contained classroom) where a student with disabilities can receive an appropriate education to the greatest extent possible with her nondisabled peers. Like FAPE, LRE is generally an IEP committee decision and is closely tied to the continuum of services delivery model.

life-skills curriculum. A curriculum generally used with students with cognitive impairments that focuses on a wide range of daily living skills such as self-care skills (e.g., hygiene, grooming, dressing, eating), social skills, communication skills, and functional academic skills.

modifications. Changes in the curriculum. For students with cognitive impairments, receiving a life-skills curriculum would be considered a modification. An alternate assessment such as a portfolio assessment or an IEP-based assessment (to take the place of a statewide assessment such as the Texas Assessment of Knowledge and Skills in Texas) would also be considered a modification to a student's program.

nondiscriminatory assessment. Assessment practices that take into account the cultural and linguistic backgrounds of students and lead to accurate interpretations and appropriate decision making for all students, regardless of their cultural or linguistic background.

overrepresentation. The phenomenon whereby students from specific cultural or linguistic groups represent a greater percentage of students in a particular disability category than would be expected when compared with the general population statistics. For example, African American students make up approximately 30 percent of students in the mild to moderate mental retardation category although they make up only approximately 14 percent of all students. A variety of explanations have been put forth for this phenomenon, including cultural bias with standardized assessments, culture clash between students (and their families) and educators, and educational systems that do not adequately address the educational needs of culturally and linguistically diverse students.

prereferral intervention. A systematic campus-based general education response to student underachievement designed to help teachers who struggle to find success with specific students. A team of educators, presumably the best teachers on a campus, provide instructional and behavioral recommendations to support teachers on their campus.

reciprocal teaching. A think-aloud strategy where teachers model new strategies by thinking out loud so that students can follow their reasoning. Four strategies are included: predicting, questioning, summarizing, and clarifying. Students then are asked to think out loud as they begin to use the new strategies, eventually learning the strategy to automaticity so that thinking out loud is no longer necessary.

resource room. One kind of placement for students with disabilities who require more specialized instruction than they are able to receive in the general education classroom for certain subject areas. The resource room is typically designed to serve small groups of students in the areas of reading, language arts, and math, and the teacher has received specialized training in working with struggling learners in these areas. Students who receive resource room instruction typically receive the majority of their instruction in the general education classroom.

response to intervention (RTI). An instructional model (to date used almost exclusively for reading instruction) that is designed to recognize learning difficulties early in students' education. When students struggle over time with typical instruction, they are provided with additional direct instruction that supports these students in the general education setting.

self-contained classroom. One kind of placement for students with disabilities who cannot receive an appropriate education in the general education classroom. Students with severe or profound levels of mental retardation, and in some locales, students with emotional disturbance, typically receive the majority of their instruction in the self-contained classroom.

Resources for Further Study

American Association of the Deaf-Blind (AADB): www.aadb.org/

American Association on Intellectual and Developmental Disabilities (AAIDD) (formerly American Association on Mental Retardation [AAMR]): www.aaidd.org/

American Foundation for the Blind (AFB): www.afb.org/

American Speech-Language-Hearing Association (ASHA): www.asha.org/default.htm

Asthma and Allergy Foundation of America: www.aafa.org/

Attention Deficit Disorder Association (ADDA): www.add.org/

Autism Society of America: www.autism-society.org/

Center for Effective Collaboration and Practice (CECP): http://cecp.air.org/

Children and Adults with Attention Deficit/Hyperactivity Disorder (CHADD): www.chadd.org/

Council for Children with Behavior Disorders (CCBD): www.ccbd.net/

Council for Exceptional Children: www.cec.sped.org/

Council for Learning Disabilities (CLD): www.cldinternational.org/

Epilepsy.com: www.epilepsy.com/

KidsHealth: www.kidshealth.org/

LD Online: http://ldonline.org/

Learning Disabilities Association of America (LDAA): www.ldaamerica.org/

National Association of the Deaf (NAD): www.nad.org/

National Center for Learning Disabilities (NCLD): www.ncld.org/

National Dissemination Center for Children with Disabilities (NICHCY): www.nichcy.org/

Office of Special Education and Rehabilitative Services (OSERS): www.ed.gov/about/offices/list/osers/index.html

Tourette Syndrome Association: www.tsa-usa.org/

Traumatic Brain Injury.com: http://traumaticbraininjury.com/

United Cerebral Palsy (UCP): www.ucp.org/

5

Personal Excellence

A New Paradigm for Gifted Education

Darwin Nelson

Introduction

Children are our nation's most valuable resource, and effective teachers help students learn and develop their full potential for personal and academic excellence. *Gifted and talented* (GT) *students* are a special population, and when teachers encounter them, they find the experience both exciting and challenging. According to the National Association of Gifted Children (*NAGC*), about 5 percent or three million children in the United States are considered gifted. Gifted students explore, compose, write, paint, develop theories, or do whatever else becomes a passion for them. Teachers recognize this drive as a need to know and to learn. This drive for achievement and mastery often leads the gifted student to high levels of achievement that are recognized and valued by others.

Giftedness creates energy or drive in students and is often associated with feelings of excitement when these students succeed, feelings referred to in the field of gifted education as *flow* (Csikszentmihalyi 1990). Teachers need to be able to recognize gifted students and know how to support and engage them. These students are varied and representative of the many diverse students in the regular school population. In this chapter, I first describe myths about gifted and talented students. I then present dimensions of giftedness and talk about how to recognize gifted and talented students.

I conclude the chapter with a practical example of how a teacher introduces and teaches the concept of *emotional intelligence* (*EI*) to a class of gifted Hispanic students. The teaching strategy illustrated is student centered and an example of *transformative emotional learning*. The example is built around the theme of personal excellence and emphasizes the importance of emotional intelligence skills in the development of personal, academic, and career excellence.

Defining Giftedness

What is a gifted student? How are GT students different from their age mates? Do they really need special education programs? What does it mean to be gifted? How do we define giftedness? At the most basic level, gifted children excel in some way when compared with other children of the same age.

There is no universally agreed upon definition of giftedness. Giftedness, intelligence, and talent are fluid concepts and differ by context and culture. One definition refers to giftedness as advanced cognitive abilities and heightened intensity, which combine to create inner experiences and awareness that are qualitatively different from the norm (Columbus Group 1991). Gagne (1995) sees giftedness as the possession and use of untrained and spontaneously expressed natural abilities. Renzulli (1978) defines giftedness as the interaction among three basic clusters of human traits, above average general or specific aptitudes, high levels of task commitment or motivation, and high levels of creativity.

The United States Office of Educational Research and Improvement (OERI 1993) dropped the term *gifted* and began using the term *outstanding talent*. In their report, *National Excellence and Developing Talent* (1993), OERI concluded with "Outstanding talents are present in children and youth from all cultural groups, across all economic strata, and in all areas of human endeavor" (20). In schools across our country, there is a wide range of personal beliefs about the word *gifted*, and educational programs for gifted students vary from school to school.

Myths and Misconceptions About Giftedness

Other than the generally accepted fact that gifted students excel at a level that is beyond that of their age mates, there is little agreement about how giftedness should be defined (Gallagher and Gallagher 1994). Some might say, for example, that a student identified with emotional or reading problems could never qualify for identification as a gifted student. This, as readers will see, is not the case. It is essential for teachers to recognize myths and misconceptions about giftedness and develop an understanding that is based on research and best practices.

Myth 1: GT students must do well on IQ and other tests • Many teachers, parents, and students think that a person is gifted if she scores above a certain level on intelligence tests or standardized tests given in schools. A high *IQ* is only one indication of one kind of giftedness. The myth that a high IQ is the major indicator of giftedness still exists, but IQ is inadequate as a sole criterion for identifying gifted students. High standardized test scores are not necessarily an indication of giftedness either. García (1994) points out that standardized tests provide a very limited understanding of a child's abilities and that the assessment of gifted students must be multidimensional.

Myth 2: GT students do not need a special program • Another myth related to gifted children is that they really do not need help or special programming and that they will do fine in a regular classroom learning environment or that all children are, after all, gifted. As teachers, we want to see the potential and unique gifts of each child and work to help them all develop their full potential. Students with exceptional academic gifts, however, have special needs that differ from their same-age classmates. The role of the teacher in gifted education is critical, and teachers play an important role in identifying, nurturing, and engaging gifted students in meaningful and challenging learning. Without special training in gifted education, most teachers are not aware of the needs of gifted students and do not know how to best serve them in the classroom. The National Research Center on Gifted and Talented (*NRC/GT*) found that 61 percent of classroom teachers had no training in teaching gifted students. Academically gifted students need positive support, affirmation, and trained teachers to help them develop excellence in cognitive, affective, and behavioral domains.

Myth 3: GT students suffer socially if advanced too soon • Myths abound around areas like acceleration options, early entrance, grade skipping, and early graduation. Teachers, parents, and program administrators often see these practices as socially harmful to gifted students. Academically gifted students often feel bored, frustrated, and out of place with their age peers. Research studies have shown that many gifted students are happier with older students who share their interest than they are with students the same age.

Myth 4: GT programs are elitist • Another misconception is that gifted education programs are elitist and offer special privileges for a select few. The main focus of effective gifted education is meeting individual student needs. Gifted and talented students come from all cultures, ethnic backgrounds, and socioeconomic groups. The proper identification and education of gifted students from minority cultures and backgrounds of poverty require specific knowledge and skill. In our society, an expanded view and definition of giftedness is a necessity and must address the cultural and linguistic diversity of our children.

Myth 5: All GT students are happy and well adjusted • The myth that gifted students are happy, popular, well adjusted, and self-sufficient in the school environment finds little support in the research literature or in the personal experience of successful teachers of gifted and talented students. In its excellent summary of myths and truths about giftedness, the National Association of Gifted Children (NAGG) states that 20 to 25 percent of gifted children have social and emotional difficulties, about twice as many as in the general population of students.

The discussion of the myths and misconceptions about gifted students should challenge teachers to formulate a personal definition of giftedness that is supported by research and best practices in gifted education. It is important to understand that a simplistic definition of giftedness and thinking that is flawed by myths have created serious problems for gifted students, who are often overlooked and inappropriately served by current educational programs.

We must expand our definition of giftedness and realize the importance of the affective domain in the development of the full potential of the gifted student. Achieving personal excellence should be a goal. Personal excellence is a self-defined and self-valued process that involves building potential from within (Nelson and Low 2003) and is a reflection of emotional intelligence. *Emotional intelligence* (EI) is a new and expanded view of intelligence and emphasizes the importance of affective development in academic achievement, personal well-being, and career and life effectiveness. Giftedness has multiple dimensions, and it is important for teachers to become aware of how students' gifts and talents are reflected.

Dimensions and Reflections of Giftedness

Giftedness is complex and multidimensional rather than a specific or easily defined construct, and it is important to understand the dimensions and reflections of giftedness in order to best meet the needs of these students. Figure 5.1 describes the five dimensions of GT students (Nelson and Low 2003).

UNDERSTANDING SPECIAL POPULATIONS

Dimension I: Emotional Intelligence

- ability to think constructively and reflectively
- unique and creative thinking
- original oral and written expression
- creative problem solving
- invents and improvises
- nonhostile sense of humor
- advanced self-management skills
- listens and acts independently
- demonstrates wisdom in judgments and behaviors

Dimension II: Visual and Performing Arts

- senses and understands spatial relationships
- outstanding ability to express unique feelings through dance, art, drama, music, and poetry
- creates rather than emulates
- excellent motor coordination
- keen observer

Dimension III: Intellectual Ability

- thinks and formulates ideas abstractly
- complex information processing
- excited by new ideas
- challenged by difficult tasks
- extensive vocabulary
- curious
- understands complex relationships

Dimension IV: Academic Achievement

- easily memorizes information
- quick and advanced comprehension
- reads widely with in-depth understanding
- absorbed and committed to personal interests
- outstanding achievement in personal interest areas
- self-motivated to complete assignments and projects

Dimension V: Personal Excellence

- high aspirations and personal standards
- goal-directed intentional behavior
- accepts personal responsibility
- assertive communicator
- good decision maker and problem solver
- pursues challenging projects
- excellent time management skills
- builds healthy and effective relationships

figure 5.1 Dimensions and Reflections of Giftedness

Dimension I: Emotional intelligence • Dimension I, emotional intelligence, is the key to personal, academic, and career excellence and involves the affective component of the cognitive abilities that gifted and talented students display. A simple definition of EI is the learned ability to think constructively and behave wisely. Emotionally intelligent behavior requires a harmony of constructive thoughts and emotions that are expressed productively. The thoughts, emotional expressions, and actions of healthy and high-achieving gifted students are clear reflections of emotional intelligence. Teaching strategies and gifted education programs in the twenty-first century need to be directed at both the cognitive and affective development of gifted students (Low and Nelson 2005).

Dimension II: Visual and performing arts • The second dimension presents ways gifted students express their individual talents though movement, dance, music, art, and poetry. Gifted students are creative in thought and also in the ways they express their special talents. Invention and original expression are clear reflections of giftedness. The drive and energy generated by giftedness push the student toward high standards of performance or artistic perfection. This intense commitment to internal standards of perfection can produce works of art that can be admired and appreciated by others. On the other hand, the emotional intensity of this commitment also produces extreme levels of stress for the gifted student.

Dimension III: Intellectual ability • The extraordinary thinking and information-processing abilities of gifted students is reflected in dimension III, intellectual ability. Although high levels of intelligence are a sign that giftedness may exist, the redefined and expanded definition of *intelligence* now includes multiple dimensions such as curiosity, excitement with learning, and willingness to engage in challenging tasks. The research of Gardner, Mayer, and Sternberg (1997) describes how intelligence can be expressed in both academic and practical ways.

Dimension IV: High academic achievement • Gifted students often have the ability to learn, memorize, and comprehend at amazing speeds. These behaviors are the reflections of giftedness displayed in dimension IV, high academic achievement. However, since gifted students may become totally focused on areas of personal interest that are idiosyncratic and novel, high academic achievement may not be evident in all subject areas. Many gifted students are recognized for outstanding achievement, especially in mathematics and the sciences. Regardless of the area of high achievement, gifted students demonstrate remarkable levels of self-motivation, drive, and commitment to master a subject or discipline.

Dimension V: Personal excellence • Dimension V, personal excellence, includes intrapersonal, interpersonal, and self-management skills that are cognitive, affective, and behavioral reflections of giftedness. Healthy and high-achieving gifted students are often leaders and are well liked and accepted by their peers. Personal excellence is observable when people are self-directed, value themselves and their talents, and are able to build quality from within (Nelson and Low 2003). Self-confidence, or positive self-efficacy, and the ability to establish and maintain healthy and effective interpersonal relationships by developing rapport and empathy skills are also signs of a person gifted in the area of personal excellence. In addition, people who have a clear and direct communication style, are assertive, and achieve their goals show evidence of dimension V. The gifted and talented student often also possesses skills in self-management, time management, and stress management and shows personal responsibility. The drive for mastery and excellence seems to push the gifted to extremely high levels of personal achievement and leadership.

Identification of Gifted Students

Just as schools vary in their perception of what a gifted and talented child is, the identification of these students also varies. The foundational definitions of giftedness clearly indicate that a student's giftedness should not be confused with the means by which giftedness is observed or assessed. Parent, teacher, or student recommendations, a high score on an examination, or a high IQ score is not giftedness; it may be a signal that giftedness exists (NAGC 2007). In addition, it is important to note that a student gifted in some areas may even, at the same time, be considered to have a learning challenge in other areas. For example, a student labeled by some measures as having dyslexia or as being ADHD might also be very gifted in dimensions such as the visual and performing arts or intellectual ability.

Each state, if it has a state mandate for GT, has its own criteria for nominating GT students. In Texas, it is the district that determines the criteria. With that said, Texas has moved to district norms because using the national norms tends to keep special populations including ELL students out of GT programs. Texas, as well as most of the country, has an overidentification of white middle- to upper-class representation in its GT programs. A gifted education programs needs to be inclusive and representative of the general school population.

Identifying Gifted Students from Diverse Backgrounds

The proper and accurate identification of gifted students from diverse linguistic, cultural, and socioeconomic backgrounds requires specific knowledge and skills as well as a keen awareness and appreciation of individual differences and special student needs. An identification of a child as gifted must consider the influences of language, culture, family, and socioeconomic background. Giftedness has many faces and is often masked and hidden from the eyes of educators who employ ethnocentric and superficial criteria in the identification and selection of students for gifted education (Callahan 2005; Bernal 2003). Frank (2007), in her dissertation on migrant education and gifted children, interviewed teachers of gifted and talented students. She found that most of the teachers displayed automatic dismissal of children who did not speak English proficiently or were from homes of poverty. These teachers did not understand second language acquisition theory and expected students who were gifted to be able to speak English proficiently within a few short months. Many automatically dismissed migrant children for gifted programs because of their home situations and their need to move constantly. In some cases, it was clear that teachers interviewed also gave minimal consideration to children of color when they were identifying students for gifted programs. These underlying prejudices, then, might help explain the lower numbers of gifted and talented students among English learners, children of color, and children in lower socioeconomic neighborhoods.

Multiple Criteria for Identifying Gifted and Talented Students

There are several important considerations for the identification of gifted students from diverse backgrounds. Since giftedness is reflected in many dimensions, the identification of gifted students must be based on a broad and multidimensional definition of giftedness that recognizes multiple forms of intelligence, including emotional intelligence as a positive model for affective development. Giftedness includes high task commitment and the ability to see a project through to its successful conclusion, and this ability is a central component of giftedness along with high ability and high creativity (Renzulli and Reis 1985).

At the observational level, Sternberg and Zhang (1995) suggest five criteria for judging whether someone exhibits giftedness:

1. Excellence: The individual must be superior to the peer group in one or more specific dimensions of performance.

2. Rarity: Very few members of the peer group exhibit the characteristic or characteristics.

3. Demonstrability: The person must be able to actually exhibit the excellent and rare ability through some type of valid assessment.

4. Productivity: The person's performance must lead to or have the potential to lead to producing something.

5. Value: The person's performance is highly valued by society.

In addition to this consensual and intuitive definition of giftedness, additional criteria are needed in the identification of gifted students.

Both quantitative and qualitative selection criteria are needed in the accurate identification of a gifted student. Other criteria that can be used to identify gifted students include authentic assessments, portfolios, and culture-specific assessments of language, family, and environmental factors. Clasen, Middleton, and Connel (1994) suggest a multidimensional culturally fair assessment strategy. Accurate and equitable identification of gifted students demands multiple assessment criteria and an awareness and understanding of the child's language, culture, family, and environment.

Special Needs and Common Problems of Gifted Students

The basic needs of gifted students do not differ from the basic needs of all children, including acceptance, love, respect, understanding, and encouragement to develop excellence as a person and as a student, guidance, support, and security. In addition to these basic needs, however, gifted students have special needs that correspond to their special gifts and talents. Some of the special needs of gifted students involve the need for a flexible academic program that involves higher cognitive concepts and processes and freedom from structured requirements and limited time frames. Gifted students need diverse learning resources and opportunities for brainstorming and creative problem solving. Collaborative learning opportunities with other gifted and talented students and involvement in in-depth cultural experiences are also special needs.

Gifted students need assistance in the recognition and acceptance of their gifts and talents and the time and freedom to explore subjects and projects of individual interest. The joy and rewards of giftedness are a source of pride for students and parents. At the same time, they sometimes experience pain, isolation, and extreme levels of stress because they do not fit in with their peers and they have extremely high expectations for themselves.

Freedman and Jensen (2006) have identified some of the most common problems of gifted children as being (1) isolation, (2) perfectionism, (3) establishing and maintaining healthy and effective relationships, (4) interpersonal communication, and (5) excessive levels of stress. Gifted adults report that the social skills that would help them interact with and connect to family, friends, and the larger world were missing from their lives.

Recent research—Gardner and Sternberg (1997), Goleman (1995), and Nelson and Low (2003)—suggests that the development of emotional intelligence is the key to academic, personal, and career success. Developing emotional intelligence requires experience-based learning as well as cognitive learning. The emotional intelligence unit presented later in the chapter illustrates how a teacher introduces and teaches the construct of emotional intelligence in a class of gifted, bilingual Hispanic children.

Successfully Teaching Gifted Students

There are certain characteristics of successful teachers in gifted education. Specific guidelines were developed and recommended by the Center for Talented Youth (CTY) at the John Hopkins University. Teachers in gifted education must have a deep knowledge of the subject matter and handle the content with confidence. In addition, teachers must have mental flexibility and help students make connections among the various disciplines. Students must be encouraged to question and critique, and teachers should never stifle questioning even when they may not be able to answer all the students' questions.

Teachers of gifted and talented students must be both interested and interesting. While teachers are usually the first among equals, teachers must be able to learn from their gifted students. The creation of a community of learners is essential in a GT classroom, and teachers are responsible for creating this risk-free community. Part of this community building comes from teachers' abilities to use different strategies and respond to their students' various learning styles.

In a classroom of gifted students, teachers must be friendly without becoming students' friends. They must maintain a sense of humor and like to teach the students. Most of all, teaching GT students is exhausting, so teachers must have physical stamina. Because of the demands of constantly working with these challenging students, gifted and talented teachers are constantly growing professionally as educators. These roles and characteristics indicate important factors in successfully teaching gifted students. Gifted students can and do teach valuable lessons to teachers. Visit the website of the National Association for Gifted Children at www.nagc.org/ for an in-depth explanation of the standards for gifted education. NAGC provides excellent resources for teachers of gifted students and is the most important current source of new research and best practices in gifted education.

Giftedness and Limited English Proficiency

Teachers working with gifted students who are limited in English proficiency need to develop an awareness and understanding of the special challenges these students often face in the school environment. Frasier (1995) has pointed out the barriers that English language learners (ELLs) face when they first enter school as being (1) an environment that is dissimilar to any of their past experiences, (2) a disconnection between home and life outside the home, (3) a curriculum that seems irrelevant to their lives, (4) instruction that is often irrelevant to their needs, (5) a sense of alienation, and (6) an assumption that because they are limited in English proficiency, they are less capable. In particular, gifted Hispanic students with limited English proficiency often feel alienated and tend to get lost in remedial programs before their giftedness is recognized and affirmed by appropriate educational services. Culture and family systems affect the attitudes and behaviors of gifted students of limited English language proficiency. All gifted learners are entitled to the best of educational services to nurture their gifts and develop their talents.

Emotional Intelligence

Emotional development is the most overlooked dimension of giftedness. The cognitive abilities and the energy and drive of gifted students are observable and more evident than their emotional needs. Emotional intelligence is the learned ability to think constructively and act wisely (Nelson and Low 2003). High levels of intelligence and cognitive abilities do not guarantee effective or wise behaviors.

The cognitive complexity of the thinking patterns of gifted students poses challenging problems for the gifted students as well as their teachers, parents, and peers. The role of emotional intelligence in personal, academic, and career excellence has been described by Nelson and Low (2003). The emotional skill characteristics of healthy and high-achieving gifted students may vary. These students are, for example, often motivated and excited by work that is personally meaningful. They are persistent in finishing tasks and are often self-directed. GT students who have high emotional skills creatively solve problems that are difficult.

In addition, these students have a strongly developed sense of right and wrong. They appreciate their own skills and expect a lot of themselves and others. Their communication style is direct and honest, and they usually establish healthy and effective interpersonal skills. These students have the ability to multitask because they plan and organize, accept responsibility for their actions, and are excellent leaders. The concept of emotional intelligence and the affective needs of gifted students are a prime consideration for parents and teachers. Often school programs are oriented only to the cognitive and intellectual needs of gifted students, and the affective domain is not considered.

The theory and research of Seymour Epstein (1998) indicates that constructive thinking is the key to emotional intelligence. How gifted students think rather than what they think is the most important consideration in developing emotional intelligence. In the scenario that follows, a teacher of gifted bilingual students presents a unit on emotional intelligence. The teaching strategy used is student centered and transformative. The goal of the teacher is to respect the individual perceptions of the students and to engage them in exploring, identifying, understanding, learning, and applying emotional intelligence skills that are essential to achieving personal, academic, and career excellence. The unit highlights the importance of affective skill development in gifted education.

Emotional Intelligence Unit

Jaime is an experienced teacher with a graduate degree and specialized training in gifted education. Jaime is a gifted person and shares the language and cultural traditions of his students. His experiences as a gifted student in a small rural school in South Texas have increased his awareness and understanding of his students' special needs and challenges. He is genuinely interested in the success of his students and enjoys the opportunity to teach and mentor high-achieving students. Within his class he has a great deal of diversity. Many of his Hispanic students were migrant students in their early years. Many of his students would be considered to have low socioeconomic status and were recipients of free lunches throughout their schooling.

Jaime's students are high-achieving, gifted, Hispanic students who are high school seniors. Many of them have received academic scholarships at leading universities in different parts of the country and will be leaving home for the first time. Jaime is aware of the levels of stress that his students are feeling as they plan to leave their families and transition to new and unfamiliar areas of the country. Despite their high levels of academic achievement and the well-developed cognitive abilities of the students, Jaime is aware of their problems in areas such as self-confidence, interpersonal communication, and self-management skills. In fact, a few students struggled throughout their schooling with ADHD.

Jaime has worked hard to develop an affective curriculum for his gifted students. He bases his teaching on research-derived theories of emotional intelligence and emotional learning strategies that have demonstrated effectiveness for improving academic achievement and personal well-being. He uses an expanded definition of intelligence that emphasizes the multidimensional nature of giftedness and teaches his students both critical and constructive thinking skills. The theme of personal excellence and the unit on emotional intelligence are integrated with the content emphasis in his senior English class for gifted students.

The students have read and discussed two books that present research-derived theories of emotional intelligence, *Constructive Thinking: The Key to Emotional Intelligence* (Epstein 1998) and *Emotional Intelligence: Achieving Academic and Career Excellence* (Nelson and Low 2003). In addition to reading and discussing the two books, the students have completed Epstein's Constructive Thinking Inventory and the Emotional Skills Assessment Process (Low and Nelson 2005). The two EI instruments are positive self-assessments that the students have used to identify their current levels of constructive thinking and emotional intelligence skills.

The emotional intelligence unit focuses on the practical applications and specific skills that students can use to improve academic achievement, personal well-being, and career success. Jaime has prepared individual profiles of his students' constructive thinking patterns and emotional intelligence skills so each student has a personal awareness of his current strengths and each student has identified one or two skills to learn and develop. Once the students received their profiles, Jaime challenged the students to develop a class profile of strengths and areas for development. The students worked in groups to list both strengths and needs and then made a whole-group profile, which Jaime displayed in the room. The group profile of the class showed the students' current strengths in goal achievement, time management, and commitment ethic. As a class, the students identified self-confidence, assertive communication, and stress management as the three emotional intelligence skills that they needed to learn and further develop.

Every day, Jaime welcomes each student with a handshake and a smile as the students file in for class. He uses an electronic slideshow presentation to guide the learning activities for the unit on emotional intelligence. He begins with a practical definition of emotional intelligence and the class profile illustrating the students' perceptions of their thinking patterns and emotional intelligence skills. Jaime defines emotional intelligence as the learned ability to think constructively and behave effectively and wisely. He explains that our human brains have two primary information-processing systems. One system is rational and one system is experiential. The rational system is the one we use for logical reasoning and critical thinking. The experiential system is emotionally oriented and responds to images, metaphors, and narratives. The experiential system influences our beliefs about ourselves, affects how we communicate with others, and reacts quickly and automatically when we experience strong feelings.

Jaime engages the students by asking for their personal definitions of intelligence and wisdom. He asks, "What does it mean when we say a person is intelligent? What does it mean when we say a person is wise? Think about the difference between intelligence and wisdom." Jaime emphasizes that a person can be both intelligent and wise, but a person can be intelligent and not behave wisely. He explains that emotional intelligence involves learning to think constructively and creatively so our behaviors are intentional and effective rather than automatic and determined by feelings.

Jaime refers to the class profile and points out that the emotional skill that the majority of students have identified as most important to learn is assertive communication. He discloses his own experience with this behavior and his hesitancy and difficulty with telling his own parents that he had chosen to attend a college two thousand miles away from his home. He explains the importance of assertion in communicating with professors, in clarifying academic assignments, in finding a mentor to help him develop research skills, and in asking for help when he needed it.

Assertive communication is a learned emotional skill that is influenced by family systems, language, and cultural factors. Jaime knows how polite his students are and how hesitant they are to ask directly for what they need and want. He challenges them to think of this skill as a learned behavior by saying, "En español, ¿cómo se dice la palabra *assertion*?" His students seem blank and unable to respond to this request. A few respond with Spanish words that are similar in meaning. The students cannot come up with an exact or equivalent word.

Words are used to communicate meaning. If one does not have a word in one's vocabulary, it may be difficult or confusing to express that behavior. Since *assertive* is not part of his students' vocabulary, it is hard for Jaime's students to exhibit the behavior. Jaime explains, "If we want to become more honest and direct in our communication, we will have to learn and practice assertive communication in our relationships with others. Assertion is one of the most important academic skills for you, as Hispanic students, to learn and apply in a college learning environment."

Personal Excellence

The previous scenario emphasizes the importance of affective skill development in gifted education. Teachers and counselors of gifted students need to take a holistic view of the learner and expand their definitions of giftedness to include the development of emotional intelligence as an important component of gifted education. In order to achieve excellence in academic, personal, and career dimensions, gifted students must be given the opportunity to develop emotional intelligence skills that are essential to career and life effectiveness. Excellence is much more than high achievement, and personal excellence involves intrapersonal, interpersonal, and self-management skills that help students develop their full human potential.

Applications

1. The National Association of Gifted Children estimates that about 5 percent of U.S. children, or about three million children, are considered gifted. Investigate the gifted programs offered in a district near you. What percentage of the school population has been identified as gifted? How are these students nominated and selected? Are the gifted programs inclusive and representative of the general school population?

2. This chapter presents myths and misconceptions about gifted students. What was your opinion about gifted students before reading the myths? Now, what is your personal definition of giftedness? Discuss this in a group.

3. The chapter discusses methods of identifying gifted students. Review the ways for identifying and selecting students for gifted education. Explain to a partner the importance of multidimensional assessment and of both quantitative and qualitative assessment procedures.

4. Gifted children have special needs and problems as well as special gifts and talents. Expand your knowledge about the special needs and problems of gifted students by exploring recent research and best practices using the online resources listed at the end of the chapter.

5. Review the important characteristics of teachers in gifted education. Which of these characteristics are descriptive of you? Do you think you would like to teach gifted and talented children? Explain.

6. Gifted students with limited English proficiency from backgrounds of poverty are often overlooked and not included in gifted education programs. Explore and identify the specific procedures employed in your school for the selection of bilingual minority children for gifted education programs.

7. The chapter emphasizes the importance of the social and emotional needs of gifted students and the role of emotional intelligence in achieving personal, academic, and career excellence. Identify emotional intelligence skills that are important to academic achievement and career effectiveness.

Key Terms and Acronyms

emotional intelligence (EI). EI is displayed by self-management skills, the ability to listen and act independently, and demonstration of wise judgment and behavior.

flow. Feelings of excitement created when students succeed.

gifted and talented (GT) students. Students who excel in some way when compared with others their age. The federal Elementary and Secondary Education Act defines gifted and talented students as "students, children, or youth who give evidence of high achievement capability in areas such as intellectual, creative, artistic, or leadership capacity, or in specific academic fields, and who need services and activities not ordinarily provided by the school in order to fully develop those capacities."

intelligence. The ability to learn, reason, and problem solve. Debate revolves around the nature of intelligence as to whether it is an innate quality or something that is developed as a result of interacting with the environment. Many researchers believe that it is a combination of the two and now include multiple dimensions in the definition.

IQ. Intelligence quotient. A numerical representation of intelligence. IQ is derived from dividing mental age (result from an intelligence test) by the chronological age times one hundred. Traditionally, an average IQ is considered to be 100.

NAGC. National Association of Gifted Children.

NRC/GT. National Research Center on Gifted and Talented.

transformative emotional learning. An approach to teaching that helps students develop emotional intelligence.

Resources for Further Study

Online Resources

Center for Gifted Education Policy, American Psychological Association: www.apa.org/ed/cgep.html

The Center for Talented Youth at the John Hopkins University: http://cty.jhu.edu/

Duke University Talent Identification Program: www.tip.duke.edu/

Jacob K. Javits Gifted and Talented Education Program: www.ed.gov/programs/javits/

National Association of Gifted Children: www.nagc.org/

National Excellence: www.ed.gov/pubs/DevTalent/toc.html

Print Resources on Emotional Intelligence

Epstein, Seymour. 1998. *Constructive Thinking: The Key to Emotional Intelligence.* Westport, CT: Praeger.

———. 2001. *Constructive Thinking Inventory Professional Manual.* Lutz, FL: Psychological Assessment Resources.

Gardner, Howard. 1993. *Multiple Intelligences: The Theory in Practice.* New York: Basic.

Goleman, Daniel. 1995. *Emotional Intelligence: Why It Can Matter More than IQ.* New York: Bantam.

Low, Gary R., and Darwin B. Nelson. 2005. "Emotional Intelligence: The Role of Transformative Learning in Academic Excellence." *Texas Study of Secondary Education* 14 (2): 41–44.

Mayer, John D., Peter Salovey, and David K. Caruso. 2000. "Emotional Intelligence as Zeitgeist, as Personality, and as a Mental Ability." In *The Handbook of Emotional Intelligence: Theory Development, Assessment, and Application at Home, School, and in the Workplace*, ed. R. Baron and J. D. A. Parker, 92–117. San Francisco: Jossey-Bass.

Nelson, Darwin B., and Gary R. Low. 2003. *Emotional Intelligence: Achieving Academic and Career Excellence.* Upper Saddle River, NJ: Prentice Hall.

2

Meeting the Needs of Diverse Learners

Drawing on Multiple Intelligences to Teach Special Populations

Kathy Bussert-Webb

Introduction

All students, including English language learners and students identified for special education or gifted and talented services, benefit when teachers develop lessons that draw on *multiple intelligences*. School curricula often limit students to just two intelligences, *linguistic* and *logical-mathematical*, but many learners often respond well to a multiple intelligences (MI) approach. This chapter describes MI theory and research, how the eight intelligences are related, and why they help diverse learners. It gives examples of how to integrate each into the curriculum and provides an extended classroom scenario.

Theory of Multiple Intelligences

Gardner (1986), a cognitive psychologist from Harvard, created MI theory from studies of child prodigies, gifted and "normal" children and adults, people from diverse cultures, experts in various fields, and *idiot savants*, people who have severe mental retardation but who can perform difficult tasks with music, puzzles, or numbers. Because he was interested in identifying regions of the brain responsible for certain mental tasks, he studied brain-damaged patients. For instance, a person who has a severe stroke will have her linguistic ability compromised (Gardner 1986). Part of the reason for Gardner's theory was to prevent interventions that harmed children's development. He believed schools attended to reading, writing, and arithmetic, or the linguistic and mathematical intelligences, to the detriment of diverse students. Additionally, he wanted educators to identify young students' *proclivities*, or preferences, and then draw upon the results to enhance their curricular and extracurricular experiences.

Gardner (1986) defined intelligence as a problem-solving ability or a skill to create something of worth. He decided not to call these talents because he sought to challenge *psychometricians*, whose jobs are to study the intelligences of children and adults through intelligence quotient (IQ) tests. Gardner believed he could get these testing professionals to question their own practices in labeling the intelligence of others. Also, Gardner questioned Piaget's concepts of cognitive development by arguing that a person does not go through the same mental stage in all subjects. For example, it is possible for a child to perform only up to *concrete operations* in math, but up to *formal operations*, the highest Piagetian stage, in language arts. Piaget and many psychometricians believed intelligences hung together, but Gardner posited that someone could be normal in math, struggling in reading and writing, and gifted in sports.

Being gifted in sports is important throughout the world. Indeed, having a special value across cultures is one of Gardner's eight prerequisites for intelligence. For example, cooking is not included in Gardner's list, even though cooking without recipes or measurements and guessing ingredients as one is eating require special talents. However, Gardner (1983) wrote that cooking and baking abilities do not have much value in certain groups. Other factors to determine intelligence are whether a skill or talent originates from a specific part of the brain and associated core operations; for instance, the linguistic intelligence involves acquiring and applying meaning, word order, vocabulary, and sounds to diverse contexts to communicate meaning.

In *Intelligence Reframed*, Gardner (1999) discussed the possibility of existential and *moral intelligences*, but he could not verify them because they do not fit all of his criteria. For example, existential and moral capabilities do not appear to originate from specific parts of the brain, and also their cognitive components are not defined clearly. In 1999, Gardner added an eighth intelligence, *naturalist*, to his 1983 list. He stated no one would ever agree on one final set of intelligences because we have different goals and types of analysis. "There will never be a master list of three, seven, or three hundred intelligences which can be endorsed by all" (Gardner 1983, 60).

Gardner believed intelligences can be honed through one's experience in a culture. He was not presenting a *nature versus nurture*, or *genetics versus environment*, dichotomy. "We cannot . . . neatly factor culture out of this equation, because culture influences every individual" (Gardner 1983, 57). Also, Gardner emphasized that there is no hierarchy of intelligences agreed upon throughout the world. In some cultures, for instance, the naturalist intelligence is regarded more favorably, and hence, is more advanced. In highly industrialized countries, such as the United States, the linguistic and mathematical intelligences are highlighted.

Some confuse *learning styles* with intelligences. Learning styles focus on how humans process and remember information, while MI theory relates to assessing, understanding, and developing human intelligences. According to Dunn (1993), learning styles are auditory, visual, tactile, kinesthetic, group oriented, individual oriented, field dependent, and field independent. Someone with a field-dependent learning style requires group work, constant scaffolding, and extrinsic motivation, while someone with a field-independent learning style has an intrinsic desire to work alone without much guidance or outside motivation.

Some educators have criticized Gardner's MI theory. A few say it is difficult to develop a valid MI assessment. However, Shearer (2004, 2006) developed a valid and reliable multiple intelligence survey (the *MIDAS*), which Gardner himself endorsed. Others argue that Gardner's theories have not been tested empirically to determine if these constructs really exist (Fasko 2001). Yet experts in education and child development contend that we should measure theories by the contributions they make, not necessarily by experimental tests. Clearly, MI theory has helped to change understandings and practices in education (Chen 2004). Because of MI theory, educators realize that a "collective capacity" of people with diverse intelligences is more powerful than people who share the same intelligence (Chapman 2007, 9). Furthermore, schools and corporations throughout the world have adopted MI approaches (Shearer 2006).

An example of MI theory into practice comes from Greenhawk (1997), who reported a 20 percent increase in students' scores on the Maryland state test after just one year of implementing MI across the elementary school's curriculum. Subjects learned how to assess and use their own MI strengths and demonstrated their knowledge through the use of many of the intelligences. Similarly, in a pilot study by Carlson, Gray, and Hoffman (2004), third graders made statistically significant gains on sight word recognition and comprehension after twenty-three weeks of music intervention.

Explanations of the Eight Intelligences

The eight multiple intelligences are *bodily-kinesthetic, spatial, musical, intrapersonal, interpersonal,* linguistic, logical-mathematical, and naturalist. Figure 6.1 contains

Name	Description	Examples
Bodily-kinesthetic	Fine and gross motor skills; body smart	Quick reaction time; sports; dancing; acting; balancing; and proficient use of one's hands to make or repair anything, such as art, machines, fabric, or wood
Spatial	Interpreting and creating visuals; space smart	Maps; visual memory; board games; coordinating clothes and colors; two- and three-dimensional art; choreography; carpentry; and auto mechanics
Musical	Interpreting and creating music; music smart	Singing; playing instruments; remembering songs, rhythms, or melodies; ability to connect music to one's mood and memories; and using music to relax or work
Intrapersonal	Accepting oneself; self-smart	High self-esteem; enjoying solitude; ability to reflect and grow from a negative experience or criticism; and awareness of one's facial expressions or tone of voice
Interpersonal	Interacting with others; group smart	Persuasive; leader; outgoing; dealing well with conflict; quick at learning cross-cultural norms; hosting parties; and sensitivity to others' expressions and moods
Linguistic	Language; word smart	Learning languages quickly; reading, writing, speaking, or listening well; enjoying school lectures or churh sermons; word games; persuasiveness; remembering language; and research
Logical-mathematical	Logic and patterns; math smart	Math; remembering numbers; handling money; computers; chess; understanding patterns and relationships; debate; logic or reasoning; and developing and testing hypotheses
Naturalist	Plants; animals; weather; earth; nature smart	Identifying and caring for plants and animals; collecting or classifying natural things; passion for recycling and reducing waste; fishing; and a love for the outdoors

figure 6.1 The Eight Intelligences Explicated

descriptions and examples of the eight multiple intelligences. These ideas are from a combination of my original research (Bussert-Webb 2001, 2005), as well from Gardner (1983, 1986, 1999), Shearer (2004, 2006), and D'Youville College (no date).

Relationships Between Intelligences

We all have the eight multiple intelligences within us to varying degrees. In fact, it is unusual for someone to be strong in one intelligence but extremely weak in the other seven. Perhaps this is because the intelligences interact with one another. For example, an experienced chess player will have strong logical-mathematical and spatial intelligences. She must consider how her move will affect the game, which demonstrates logic. She must be able to scan the entire board and to see the relationships between all of the pieces, showing spatial intelligence. Similarly, if a person has a high self-esteem and a strong intrapersonal intelligence, chances are his positive feelings about himself will affect his relationship with family members, significant others, friends, and acquaintances. Yet perhaps manifestations of the multiple intelligences are interrelated because very little in nature is truly dichotomous or binary. An MI mosaic, like the faces of our students, appears before us—interconnected yet different (Nieto 2004).

Why Multiple Intelligences Help Diverse Learners

Teachers who use an MI approach can support students with divergent needs and passions; some may excel in art, while others may achieve in sports. An MI curriculum can help diverse learners to construct meaning and can inspire them to excel because of the focus on their strengths.

Gifted and Talented

For students identified as gifted and talented (GT), an MI approach may challenge them in their strong areas and may help them to further develop their weaker intelligences. Even if students are gifted, it does not mean they do well in all subjects. In fact, gifted students may not find a traditional curriculum challenging. Some teachers mistakenly try to remedy the boredom of gifted students by giving them more worksheets and traditional projects, but what these students really need are novel, challenging, creative, and interesting activities and assignments that engage them in ways that activate their multiple intelligences.

Reid and Romanoff (1997) discuss a novel, challenging curriculum for the gifted in North Carolina, where schools implemented an MI approach through problem-solving critical and creative thinking activities and assessments. Second- through fifth-grade gifted students in the program scored 17 to 20 percent higher on standardized math and reading exams than students referred for, but not participating in, the program. Sternberg and Grigorenko (2004) corroborated this finding with their own studies of students identified as gifted. They found that gifted students learn better when they can apply creative, critical, and practical thinking skills.

Special Needs

Teachers must modify instruction and evaluation to fit students' individualized education programs (IEPs). Some of these modifications relate to the multiple intelligences. For example, students with special needs may have math tests read to them, which involves the linguistic intelligence. Also, students identified as special needs may learn better from lesson modifications incorporating their stronger intelligences, including spatial, bodily-kinesthetic, and musical intelligences (Chen 2004). Students labeled special needs may have other intelligences to be celebrated when we move away from a sole focus on texts or a text-centric curriculum (Conquergood 2002). MI theory into practice helps students with special needs to highlight their talents, versus their deficits, in a classroom.

Wagmeister and Shifrin (2000) describe how teachers put MI theory into practice at their Los Angeles school for students with language-based learning disabilities. Teachers in grades 2–12 use the results of brain research to incorporate activities to stimulate and connect different parts of the brain. Students explore topics through thematic, hands-on MI curricula. For example, the elementary students created a rain forest through music, sound effects, and humidifiers. They also explored the topic through in-school field trips, the Internet, and *text sets*, which are collections of books organized around a specific topic (Harste, Short, and Burke 1995). Also, an entomologist brought in exotic insects and arachnids to stimulate learning, and a high school student cotaught with the teachers. Besides thematic units such as these, students at the school learn to sew and cook, and they also produce daily news broadcasts, complete with text, sounds, and graphics.

Katz, Mirenda, and Auerbach (2002) studied these types of MI approaches for students with special needs. Participants, ages seven to ten, were able to speak but had autism, Down syndrome, and intellectual disabilities. The researchers examined the social interactions and engaged behavior of the participants in the treatment group using an MI curriculum and the control group using a traditional curriculum. They found that MI participants were twice as active in creative, hands-on tasks than were control group participants, and that the MI participants spent more time with on-task discussions with peers than the control group.

English Language Learners

An MI approach helps English language learners (ELLs) also. In an action research study of 650 K–12 students and 23 English as a second language and foreign language teachers from eight states and three countries, Haley (2004) found that participants in MI classrooms outperformed students in the control groups, measured by pre- and postgrades. Moreover, student evaluations of MI classrooms demonstrated enthusiasm toward the target language, the lessons, and assessments.

Researchers have given several reasons that MI supports the learning of ELLs. First, the entire brain is used to process creative and artistic activities, as well as language and logic. "Whenever the focus is on something other than correct language production, such as gently mixing colorful paints, conversations develop" (Gonzalez-Jensen and Gara-Weiner 2000, 56). When ELLs use alternative *sign systems*, such as drama, art, and music (Leland, Harste, and Smith 2005), they feel more at ease and content. This comfort level and enjoyment help to lower their affective filters so greater learning can take place. (See Chapter 2.)

How Teachers Can Incorporate the Intelligences

To remember all eight intelligences when designing lessons and evaluation strategies, it is helpful to incorporate these four learning domains:

- sensorimotor
- cognitive
- affective
- social

The *sensorimotor domain* relates to the spatial and bodily-kinesthetic intelligences. Classroom examples of activities that represent this domain include skits, charades, student-created art, and tasks that use the five senses (Dettmer 2006). While the sensorimotor domain deals with fine and gross motor skills and spatial interactions, the *cognitive domain* focuses on imagination, creativity, and providing mentally challenging, but not frustrating experiences (Dettmer 2006). In Chapter 2, this is referred to as i+1, input plus one, or instruction a little above the learners' current ability. Being aware of i+1, or the input hypothesis, helps teachers to scaffold through the use of role-plays and visuals and to involve the group and body domains. The input hypothesis also suggests the use of mini-lessons, which are short lessons to teach a point, versus lecturing for more than fifteen minutes at a time (Fountas and Pinnell 2001).

The affective domain refers to providing fun, meaningful, and engaging learning experiences for students, as well as "internalization, wonder, and risk-taking" (Dettmer 2006, 70). MI approaches try to weave the affective domain into all instruction and assessment. The next domain, the *social domain*, relates mostly to the interpersonal intelligence. It includes teamwork, building friendships, respect, manners, feelings, and helping others; Dettmer created this fourth domain because of the necessity for people to interact successfully in and out of school.

Acquisition and learning are more than likely going on when all four domains are connected in a lesson because more students' predispositions can be reached. If one could imagine a four-leaf clover, the head (cognitive domain), the heart (affective domain), the body (sensorimotor domain), and the group (social domain) all touch as in a Venn diagram. The center represents learning, which is where the clover blooms as a tiny yellow flower. It is important to include all four domains in any lesson (see Figure 6.2). Naturally, using the four domains involves at least four intelligences—spatial, bodily-kinesthetic, linguistic, and interpersonal—to help diverse learners.

Gifted Students

Teachers could have gifted learners assist students who are struggling; this could be done as partner work or in small groups. In buddy math, for example, the teacher demonstrates the steps in solving a certain type of problem. The teacher goes through the steps, applies them to a specific problem, and then pairs the students heterogeneously, that is, puts a student more capable in math with a student who is less skilled. The more experienced math student demonstrates aloud to his partner how to solve the new problem, using the teacher's same steps. Next, the less knowledgeable mathematician uses the same steps, supported by the more capable peer, with a similar problem.

Furthermore, students identified as gifted would benefit from doing additional research in curricular areas that interest them the most and that follow state standards. In math, for instance, learners could write the formulas and calculations used to determine the total quantity and costs of materials for their dream homes. Part of their representations could be visual. For the same math project, students could make three-dimensional representations of their houses.

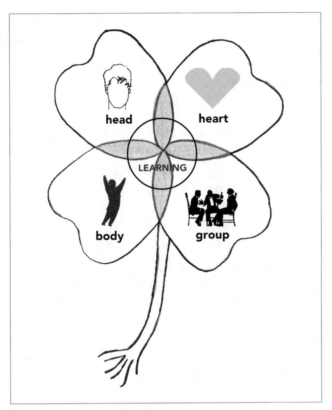

figure 6.2 The Four Learning Domains

Booth Olson's *Saturation Research* (2007) challenges students labeled as gifted to use their creativity and ingenuity. For instance, gifted upper-elementary and secondary learners can write research reports from the perspective of what they investigate. As part of their assessment, students can choose from the sign, or communication, systems of art, dance, music, language, and drama to teach the class about their topics of investigation (Leland, Harste, and Smith 2005). For example, students in a high school English class can represent their research projects in collages, posters, mobiles, songs, and sculptures. With modification, saturation research and alternative representations of learning can work in all content areas and grade levels. For instance, an upper-elementary student studying circumference could demonstrate himself as the circumference by having class members stand in a circle as he walks around them. A middle school history student studying a famous person could write a report as if she were that person, and dress up and talk like that person in a role play. Also, if a high school student in a biology class researched the liver, she could personify this organ and quote and cite sources, as in the following example: "I weigh about three pounds and I process the blood coming from the stomach and intestines" (Lucile Packard Children's Hospital 2006).

Students with Special Needs

Students identified as special needs benefit when teachers tap into the interpersonal intelligences through group work. This allows learners to work on answers together instead of having to answer individually. For example, teachers can do a buzz-with-your-partner activity in which students work with partners to reach consensus on questions and then report back to the whole group for further discussion.

The computer can be an important tool to support students with special needs, also. Specifically, the use of technology to synthesize and represent learning helps children labeled dysgraphic and dyslexic to move away from a focus on isolated skills, such as handwriting and spelling. Learning keyboarding skills liberates a child who has struggled with handwriting, just as learning how to use spell check helps a child who has problems spelling. Last, when students with special needs design and give technological presentations, making and sharing meaning extend beyond language to also include art and music. This increases the learning potential for students who learn differently.

Students with special needs can also listen to books on tape as they read silently. Many companies have software that allows learners to type in text and then listen as each letter, word, sentence, or paragraph is read back to them aloud. One software program allows students to scan pages from their favorite books; the computer program then reads the text aloud (Wagmeister and Shifrin 2000). These uses of technology can dramatically enhance learning for those who need extra support; see also Chapter 7, on technology for diverse learners, as well as www.texthelp.com/page.asp and www.donjohnston.com/.

English Language Learners

Educators can incorporate pictures and other *realia* to teach ELLs about new concepts to provide *visual scaffolding*. *Realia*, or real-life objects connected to the lesson, help students to experience the language as they see, hear, smell, touch, or taste. *Manipulatives*, such as geometric shapes and math chips that students move and manipulate, help students to understand concepts in the target language. Teachers can also have a class of recent immigrants act out commands using total physical response (TPR). Incorporating these MI strategies helps to make learning more comprehensible for ELLs, described in Chapter 2.

Hands-on classroom activities relate to context-embedded language, which helps to scaffold instruction for ELLs. An illustration of context-embedded language might involve small groups taking turns to act out different rights from the Bill of Rights while other students guess which right each skit represents. This involves the linguistic, interpersonal, spatial, and bodily-kinesthetic intelligences. Another context-embedded example is a math lesson on negative and positive numbers followed by an activity in which students move along a grid taped to the floor to show understanding. This incorporates the linguistic, logical-mathematical, spatial, interpersonal, and bodily-kinesthetic intelligences. Conversely, examples of context-reduced language would be teacher lectures with no visuals and multiple-choice exams, which involve mostly the linguistic intelligence.

For teachers to use an MI approach, they must change not only the way they teach but also the way they assess students (Stanford 2003) because multiple-choice, true-or-false, short-answer, and essay tests limit students' demonstration of skills and knowledge. One powerful tool to assess ELLs, as well as young children and students with special needs, is an interest inventory. Kronowitz (2007) developed an easy-to-understand picture inventory for these learners to complete alone, with partners, or with the teacher. Learners can make a smiley face at each icon on the inventory representing an area in which they feel competent, for example, a paintbrush with palette (spatial intelligence), a pen with an essay in the background (linguistic intelligence), a math expression like 3 + 3 (logical-mathematic intelligence), a child playing soccer (bodily-kinesthetic), a child playing with others (interpersonal intelligence), a child singing (musical intelligence), and so on. A teacher could create her own icons of the multiple intelligences and leave space for the students to draw activities they prefer. Having students complete this, other multiple intelligences surveys, or interest inventories during the first week of class can help a teacher to learn the gifts that her students bring to the classroom, which may benefit instruction and assessment throughout the year.

Strategies for All Learners

Some people believe certain strategies are only for ELLs, only for students with special needs, or only for gifted learners. However, some diverse students qualify for more than one special service. ELLs can also be identified as gifted and talented, just as gifted students can be identified as special needs. It is even possible for a student to qualify for all three special services. Moreover, a good strategy can benefit regular students because we all have more-developed intelligences.

For instance, an English-dominant student who does not qualify for any special service may learn more effectively in his English class when a teacher uses realia, manipulatives, and visual scaffolding. These strategies may be modified for different grade levels, subjects, and contexts. Thus, it is essential to emphasize MI theory is not a set program or fixed techniques, but rather an attitude toward teaching, learning, and assessment (Stanford 2003). This flexibility is the beauty of MI theory. It is up to each teacher to adapt it creatively to the teaching context.

The following scenario demonstrates how a teacher incorporates multiple intelligences with diverse students in a way that inspires and challenges all of his students—gifted, special needs, ELLs, and those who fit none of those classifications. This teacher, Carlos Gómez, embraces MI theory as a way to challenge and scaffold for Claudia, an ELL; Belinda, labeled gifted; Ana, identified as learning disabled; Andy, who is wheelchair bound; Joe, a student who does not qualify for any special service; as well as others in this class who are mainstream students. Carlos received IEPs in his box at the beginning of the semester about students' required modifications.

Count of Monte Cristo Unit

Carlos teaches ninth-grade English in a South Texas high school of two thousand students. This school is one of five in the district with a student population of at least eighteen hundred. Although 90 percent of Carlos' students are Mexican American, they are diverse in their gifts, language backgrounds, and experiences. Some have been in the United States for only a year, while others grew up here. Even though there is pressure for Carlos to teach to the state-mandated test under No Child Left Behind (NCLB), he has managed to follow his MI beliefs. Carlos has "gotten away with having fun," as he puts it, because his students score well on the state reading and writing tests. This is partly because he has high expectations, has a master's degree as a reading specialist, and has learned how to use an MI approach to cover the test objectives.

Now, in his fourth year of teaching, Carlos has learned to cover objectives without the practice passages and ensuing comprehension questions. For this thematic unit, he chose a *graphic novel* version of *The Count of Monte Cristo* (Grant 1990). At first glance, Carlos' choice of a French novel, set in the 1800s, may seem out of place in this South Texas school. However, for the previous six weeks, Carlos focused on Latino literature. His students read *Brownsville: Stories* (Casares 2003) and *The House on Mango Street* (Cisneros 1984). Carlos believed that *The Count of Monte Cristo* novel would cover state standards concerning culturally diverse texts and the genre of historical fiction; he chose to use the graphic novel version because the plot was closest to the original French novel and because he thought the visuals would support students with special needs, ELLs, and reluctant readers.

Also, Carlos tied the novel into unjust arrests and civil rights; he arranged for a campus security officer to do a mock arrest of an honor student at the beginning of the unit (Bird et al. 2002). He did this to draw a parallel to the unjust arrest of Edmond, the story's protagonist, who had committed no crime, when the novel begins. As a *culminating experience* (Bird et al. 2002), Carlos' students plan to prepare and conduct a mock trial of Edmond, who seeks revenge on those responsible for his imprisonment.

Today a vice principal new to the school comes by Carlos' room for a walk-through. "Look," he says, "I see your students are engaged in learning, but I just did a walk-through in Mrs. Bentacourt's class, and she's having her students read practice passages. I could hear your stereo in her otherwise quiet classroom. Can you turn it down?"

"Sure, no problem. Sorry," Carlos says as he lowers the volume of the Tejano music playing in the background.

The appraiser continues, "I've heard your students do well on the Texas Assessment of Knowledge and Skills [TAKS]. But you know the pressure we get from the district to raise our scores. So how does this activity relate to state-tested standards?"

Carlos explains, "Students are doing a vocabulary activity called community words" (Bussert-Webb 2006). "They are monitoring their comprehension when deciding which words they don't understand in context and when hypothesizing definitions. But they're not just hypothesizing. They have to check hypotheses with reference materials, and they're learning how to use the dictionary effectively. Each pair has to read the entire dictionary definition, find the one definition fitting their sentence, and then draw a picture of it to synthesize it.

"Next, they are learning grammar, like parts of speech, from the same dictionaries. They have to write if the word is a noun, a verb, an adjective, or an adverb. On their six-week test, they will have to write original sentences in which they change nouns into verbs and so forth so they become flexible language users. This is also a writing skill. Last, they have to present the words to the class, which involves the standards of listening and speaking."

"Which aren't on the test," counters the administrator.

"Yes, you're right," says Carlos, "but oral language skills are part of the state standards for language arts."

"Today the students are continuing with the comic book version of *The Count of Monte Cristo*," Carlos continues.

"Comic book?" the appraiser asks.

"Well," says Carlos, "let's look at some of the words from this graphic novel, which are on the board with page numbers. We have *betrothal*, page 25; *blackmail*, page 38; *perverse*, page 38; *privations*, page 41; *atone*, page 44; and so forth. Even the *Spider-Man* booklet from the Sunday paper has really hard words."

"Yeah, but the TAKS doesn't have the pictures," the vice principal counters. "Aren't the pictures a crutch?"

"That's what educators thought in the sixties," Carlos states. "Now researchers have found that art accompanying text helps students to enjoy reading and to comprehend better. Visuals help ELLs and students with special needs by providing more context and scaffolding. Anyway, viewing and representing are part of the standards because of the many graphics and icons in our lives."

"I'm impressed. Just hold down the noise a little bit for your neighbors," the administrator says as he shakes Carlos' hand. The vice principal leaves, and Carlos begins to walk around the room again, checking on student progress, observing, and assisting. He watches and listens to Joe, an English-dominant student, and Claudia, a Spanish-dominant student: "'Presume quiere decir presumida, como uno que cree que es lo mejor de todos.' *Presume* means presumptuous, like someone who's conceited or boastful," Claudia tells Joe. Joe writes down Claudia's hypothesis. Next, they check the dictionary definitions to decide which one best fits into the sentence in the *Monte Cristo* novel. They look at the context and work together to try to choose the best meaning.

Carlos continues circulating and assisting when needed. He sees Belinda and Ana draw a picture of their word, *omnipotent*. As Carlos squats down beside the pair, Belinda says, "Our word's *omnipotent*, so we drew God looking down from the clouds!"

"Excellent," Carlos says, smiling. The students put their butcher block papers on a wall area designated for their period. Carlos turns off the music so each pair can present its words, definitions, contexts, parts of speech, and pictures. Those who are not presenting take notes; they will have to use these words in new contexts as part of the six-week test on the *Count of Monte Cristo* unit. Before the test, they will create role-plays and play games to synthesize the words; synthesis is a higher-order aspect of *Bloom's taxonomy* and is necessary for students to create new contexts for the words.

Carlos has incorporated several multiple intelligences in these activities. Drawing pictures to represent the words and decorating each word involves the spatial intelligence. Working in pairs involves the interpersonal intelligence. Allowing music of the students' choice to play in the background involves the musical intelligence. His students use the linguistic intelligence when they select words from the short story they read the previous day, as well as when they hypothesize word meanings, use dictionaries, and write the information.

Carlos also includes the bodily-kinesthetic intelligence. Instead of sitting at their desks and receiving information, students are on mats and pillows on the floor. Also, they move to get markers and dictionaries and to hang up the butcher paper. Andy is physically disabled, so Carlos has him pull his wheelchair to a table, where Andy and his partner have access to markers, butcher block paper, the text, and a dictionary. As each pair presents, others take notes of the words, parts of speech, and definitions. The next day, they will play charades with these words, as well as other words Carlos has drawn from the *Count of Monte Cristo* unit. Describing words through pantomime, like charades, involves facial expressions and body movements as well as teamwork and vocabulary knowledge, or the bodily-kinesthetic, spatial, interpersonal, and linguistic intelligences.

Conclusion

Multiple intelligences theory, which is supported by research, identifies eight intelligences that students possess in varying degrees. As Carlos has demonstrated, teachers can incorporate an MI approach into lessons and assessments to help all students succeed, including ELLs, those with special needs, and gifted students, even in a school that focuses on high-stakes tests.

Applications

1. Go online to http://ddl.dyc.edu/~hsa/learningstylesmar7.htm. Print and take the MI test for yourself. Score it by adding up each question you answered *true*. What are your strongest to weakest intelligences? How can you use your strongest intelligences more when studying and doing projects? How can you develop your weaker intelligences? Include the completed test with the answers to these questions.

2. How were your intelligences addressed in English, reading, social studies, science, and math classes in your K–12 schooling? If they were not addressed, describe in detail what you did in those classes and what knowledge and skills you remember from them. Describe any class in your entire educational career, including college, that was similar to Carlos' class.

3. Select at least four family members—grandparents, aunts, uncles, cousins, parents, and so on. Give examples of how at least two of these family members use their multiple intelligences on a regular basis, either for work or outside of the workplace.

4. Name and explain each of your stronger multiple intelligences. Also explain how you developed them inside and outside of school. What in both environments helped you to refine these intelligences—for example, family members, school clubs, teachers, religious services?

5. This chapter suggests ways an MI approach helps students with special needs, gifted students, and ELLs. Outline a lesson that uses several of the multiple intelligences; describe how the lesson helps meet the needs of diverse learners.

6. Download at least two songs with sound and lyrics or two art pieces that would complement your future content area and grade-level certification. Describe how you will use the music or art to fit your content area and grade level and how it will help your students identified as gifted, ELL, and special needs. Be prepared to share with the class.

7. Using the example of Carlos Gómez, the high school English teacher in the scenario, include at least five multiple intelligences in a weeklong thematic unit that is tied to state standards for your subject and grade level.

Key Terms and Acronyms

Bloom's taxonomy. A classification of skills and objectives that teachers set for learners; the three domains for Bloom's taxonomy are affective, psychomotor, and cognitive. See *cognitive domain*.

bodily-kinesthetic intelligence. A proclivity, ability, and skill in movement, as in sports, dance, or other physical activities.

cognitive domain. This hierarchical taxonomy of thinking has six levels, from easiest to hardest: knowledge, comprehension, application, analysis, synthesis, and evaluation.

concrete operations. A Piagetian stage in which a child, usually seven to eleven years old, realizes things can be compared, seriated, classified, and reversed; however, at this stage a child is not supposed to be able to think abstractly.

culminating experience. A classroom engagement at the completion of students' projects or thematic units to synthesize and extend learning.

formal operations. The fourth and most advanced Piagetian stage, starting at age eleven and continuing to adulthood, which involves one's capacity to reason abstractly and to understand complex concepts as well as nuances.

graphic novel. A thick comic book for teens and adults that develops a complex story with complex characters.

idiot savant. Someone with mental retardation who can perform cognitively difficult tasks, usually in math or music.

interpersonal intelligence. A proclivity, ability, and skill necessary to get along well with others and to be a positive leader.

intrapersonal intelligence. A proclivity, ability, and skill necessary to know and like oneself and to accept one's own shortcomings and attributes.

learning style. The way someone learns, processes, and remembers information.

linguistic intelligence. A proclivity, ability, and skill necessary for reading, writing, speaking, and listening in one or more languages.

logical-mathematical intelligence. A proclivity, ability, and skill in numbers and logic.

manipulatives. Objects that students use and handle to increase learning during a lesson.

MIDAS. Multiple Intelligences Development Assessment Scales. A valid and reliable multiple intelligences test to determine in which intelligences one is strongest.

moral intelligence. Considered and then rejected by Gardner for the ninth intelligence, this refers to personal character and consistent empathetic behavior; it also means ability to assess and make decisions in terms of high standards in ethics, morals, or religion.

multiple intelligences (MI). A theory to assess, understand, and develop human intelligences.

musical intelligence. A proclivity, ability, and skill in using instruments, including the voice; aesthetic sensitivity to music.

naturalist intelligence. A proclivity, ability, and skill in nature, especially in botany, zoology, or geology.

nature versus nurture/genetics versus environment argument. An argument about whether people are the way they are because of something innate in them or because of their surroundings and experiences.

proclivities. Natural tendencies to behave and achieve in particular ways.

psychometricians. People who assess the intelligence of others using a variety of paper and pencil tests.

Realia. Real-life objects used to help students to learn through their senses; things students can hear, touch, feel, and smell that relate to the lesson.

saturation research. Writing reports or research papers from the perspective of who or what is investigated.

sensorimotor domain. Formerly called the *psychomotor domain*; fine and gross motor skills.

sign system. A way to make and share meaning through art, dance, drama, language, music, and math.

social domain. A domain related to the effective interaction with others.

spatial intelligence. Proclivity, ability, and skill to interpret and respond to visual information related to location.

text set. A group of materials at different reading levels organized around a similar theme.

visual scaffolding. Helping students to learn by supplying related visuals during a lesson.

Resources for Further Study

Howard Gardner: www.howardgardner.com/

Key Learning Community, a public MI school: www.616.ips.k12.in.us/

MI modification products for students with special needs: www.donjohnston.com/

MI modifications for students with special needs: www.texthelp.com/page.asp

MI school for special needs: www.westmarkschool.org/

Website for adults to assess MI strengths: http://ddl.dyc.edu/~hsa/learningstylesmar7.htm

Website for children and adults to assess MI strengths: www.businessballs.com/howardgardnermultipleintelligences.htm

7

Using Technology to Teach Diverse Populations

Janice Wilson Butler

It is late November and the fifth-grade students are shivering as a cold front blows frosty air into the city. Today is José's first day in the United States and his first day in a new school. He smiles shyly at Ms. Contreras, wondering if any students will be able to understand him when he speaks his native language. He struggles to understand what everyone else is talking about, since he has only recently started learning English. Sandra walks by wearing a headset, but her nose is also buried in a novel about a girl who solves mysteries. She has struggled with reading all year, but her teacher found a fantastic book for her about solving crimes (Sandra wants to work for the FBI). She listens to the book on her iPod and follows along as it is read. Andrew sits at his desk immersed in the latest math challenge. He helps everyone in the class with math, but he struggles with writing and avoids any activity that requires writing. Jonathon walks up to the teacher's desk and hands Ms. Contreras his individualized education plan. He needs her signature before he can turn it in to his content mastery teacher. He doesn't see much use for school and wonders if his mother will let him stay home the next day. Ms. Contreras looks out at eighteen different students, diverse in their needs, interests, and skills. Although it will be a challenge, she is determined to engage each child, molding them into enthusiastic learners by the end of the school year. Her eyes wander to the window and she watches the wind whipping the leaves across the playground. Then, glancing at the four computers in the back of the room, she smiles brightly, excited about her idea for reaching out to each student in her class.

Introduction

The convergence of several factors, precipitated largely by the explosive advances in technology, offers the potential to change vastly the face of education just as it has changed the world in which we live. New legislative demands for accountability in technology standards created by the No Child Left Behind Act of 2001, the skills required of the twenty-first-century workforce, the rapidly expanding global economy, students with diverse needs, and a young population with no knowledge of a world without computers or the Internet create a challenging environment in which the modern educator must work. At the same time, technology offers great potential for enabling educators to meet the diverse needs of all learners.

This chapter discusses a constructivist, student-centered approach to learning that addresses the varied needs of learners in the modern technology-enhanced classroom and differentiates the content, process, and product of the curriculum as it relates to technology integration. It also presents a broad overview of technology-infused strategies, including project-based learning, and provides examples of a variety of social networking tools now available in the Web 2.0 environment. (At the end of the chapter are detailed descriptions and links to technology tools and resources.)

Theoretical Foundation

Dewey (1897) described formal education as a social process and schools as the social community in which students learn how to be productive citizens. Without students' processing the world through social activities, Dewey (1916) stated that "formal instruction [would] be merely the subject matter of the schools, isolated from the subject matter of life-experience" (131). This philosophy of education is more relevant to students now than ever before. Today, students are not only members of the local community or society but are also joined through technology to a global community. This global community requires students to use higher-order thinking skills in solving complicated and multifaceted real-world problems.

Indeed, in today's world, "solving complex problems are [sic] no longer left to the few; all individuals whether they are working on an assembly line, or in a corporate think tank, need problem solving skills" (Newby et al. 2000, 6). In order to address the multifaceted educational needs, leaders in the fields of education, business, and government identified six elements that will prepare students to be successful in work and life in this century (Partnership for 21st Century Skills 2002). They stated that in order to foster learning, it is imperative that schools "emphasize core content, emphasize learning skills, use 21st century tools to develop learning skills, teach and learn in a 21st century context, teach and learn 21st century content, [and] use 21st century assessments that measure 21st century skills" (7). Students need to develop information and communications skills, thinking and problem-solving skills, and interpersonal and self-directional skills. In addition, students need to study the three emerging content areas of global awareness, financial literacy, and civic literacy. While these three areas are not yet part of the traditional curriculum, teachers are able to use technology tools to embed these emerging content areas into the language arts, reading, mathematics, and social studies curricula. Thus, global awareness is reinforced as teachers and students in one country collaborate with teachers and students in another part of the world. Financial literacy can be taught using social collaboration tools that allow students to share in the development of spreadsheets using data that are collected at their school or in their community. Civic literacy can be woven into a project that addresses community, state, national, and even world issues, such as global warming.

To foster the ability to solve complex problems, teachers use a constructivist approach in which students construct their own knowledge based on prior learning and experiences. From this perspective, "learning is determined by the complex interplay among students' existing knowledge, the social context, and the problem to be solved" (Newby et al. 2000, 34). Learning in contexts and learning through interactions with others are two critical components that allow students to construct their own knowledge. Constructivist teachers develop instruction that provides opportunities for learning in contexts that are personally meaningful to the individual, collaborative activities that provide opportunities for students to combine knowledge and share solutions to problems, and opportunities to construct new knowledge while looking for solutions to problems (Newby et al. 2000).

While the constructivist perspective is not new, the availability of a vast array of technology tools facilitates the introduction of real-world problems to challenge all learners in today's diverse classrooms. Indeed, the integration of technology into the "ongoing educational process can play a significant role in creating educational environments that reflect the way people interact with the real world, sharing representational and computational task burdens" (Norton and Wiburg 2003, 34).

Ms. Contreras stays after school a few hours to prepare the learning centers for the next morning. She has already spent the first part of the year preparing students to be self-directed in their learning. Using inquiry-based strategies, she taught them to look for their own answers and to be just as excited about the hunt as the answers to their questions. She often uses both inductive and deductive lessons, finding that her students learn better when they construct the answers to questions based on their prior learning. Ms. Contreras has been using these information-processing teaching models throughout the year because "they emphasize ways of enhancing the human being's innate drive to make sense of the world by acquiring and organizing data, sensing problems and generating solutions to them, and developing concepts and language for conveying them" (Joyce et al. 2000, 17). Connections to prior learning are reinforced as students seek to understand and make sense of the new materials.

In addition to teaching students about learning, she has also ensured that students who are not proficient on the computer have learned requisite skills for completing the activities. She found at the beginning of the year that some students were adept in using technology while others had little experience. Having assessed her students' knowledge of technology, she now makes sure each student team includes at least one "techie." Each techie is responsible for bringing others in the group up to speed with each type of technology tool. (Although Ms. Contreras is quite proficient with technology, she's found that students generally learn faster from other students.)

Now that the students have the requisite skills for developing a project-based learning lesson, she is ready to nudge them toward being more responsible for their own learning.

She is freezing cold and exhausted as she walks out the door, but she can hardly wait for the next day.

Overview of Project-Based Learning (PBL)

One approach to curriculum that is consistent with a constructivist view of learning is project-based learning, also called problem based-learning. In this teaching model, students construct knowledge through a long-term, real-world project. The Buck Institute of Education (BIE) has developed a model of project-based learning based on creating standards-focused projects that include performance-based assessments. The BIE "defines standards-focused [project-based] learning as a systematic teaching method that engages students in learning knowledge and skills through an extended inquiry process structured around complex, authentic questions and carefully designed products and tasks" (Markham et al. 2003, 4).

Projects can be brief, lasting a couple of weeks, or can run much longer, sometimes becoming the guiding theme for an entire school year. With project-based learning, students are engaged in their learning, often determining the content that they will learn during the course of the project while solving real-world problems. Because they are developing an authentic product that is relevant to them, students become engaged in the activities. In the project-based classroom teachers interact closely with students, becoming "coaches, facilitators, and co-learners throughout the process" (Markham et al. 2003, 4).

The BIE lists the following components for outstanding projects (Markham et al. 2003, 4–5):

Develop learner-centered lessons, recognizing that students want to learn and want to be taken seriously as learners.

Ensure that students are learning the central concepts and principles of a discipline so that learning can be extended beyond the scope of the project.

Choose issues that are significant at the time and encourage students to delve deeply into the real-world issues.

Include the essential tools and skills, including technology, for learning how to plan and organize in-depth studies into a project.

Require products that solve a problem or answer a question developed through rigorous research and reasoning.

Require several products that will permit feedback, thus encouraging students to "go back to the drawing board" and learn more.

Use performance-based assessments incorporating high expectations that necessitate using a range of skills and knowledge.

Include a collaborative component in the project.

Research suggests that project-based learning is often more popular with students than traditional methods of teaching (Thomas 2000). In addition, project-based learning seems to be equivalent to or slightly better than other models of instruction in producing gains in general academic achievement. Students develop skills in problem solving, organization, collaboration, and decision making. Project-based learning works well in diverse classrooms, because the unique abilities, talents, and preferences of each student are highlighted and emphasized (Thomas 2000). Since standards are a critical component of the BIE project-based learning model, it becomes a powerful method for helping students develop the knowledge and skills they need to be successful in school.

The next morning the students rush into Ms. Contreras' room talking about the snow that fell the night before. It doesn't usually snow in this area, but this year they have already had several major snow storms. When Sandra raises her hand asking why it is so cold this year, Ms. Contreras invites the students to suggest ideas—it is the perfect beginning for the lesson she planned. Several students start talking about global warming. Jonathon interrupts, "But it is getting colder, not hotter. How can that be global warming?"

Sandra is excited about what the others are saying. It sounds a lot like they are trying to solve a mystery, just like in the book she has been reading. She walks over to the Smart Board saying, "OK, you guys, let's start brainstorming ideas about why it's so cold." She opens the concept mapping software and begins adding information as the students offer many suggestions. Andrew walks up to the Smart Board and asks the others in the class for suggestions on setting up categories for the problem they decide to study. Ms. Contreras stands at the back of the room, occasionally making suggestions as the students begin developing a plan for investigating changes in weather and global warming.

Differentiating Instruction Using Technology

According to Tomlinson (2005), "differentiated instruction provides multiple approaches to content, process, and product" (4). In addition, it is student-centered, assessment-based, and blends whole-class, group, and individual instruction (5). In differentiating content, teachers can either adapt what they teach or adapt the access to content. Technology can be helpful in differentiating content by offering a variety of ways to access learning. Instead of reading a book, English language learners and struggling readers can listen to the book on an iPod. Students can be challenged to learn vocabulary through an online game or can create a vocabulary game for other students.

Differentiating process involves "sense-making . . . [the] opportunity for learners to process the content or ideas and skills to which they have been introduced" (Tomlinson 2005, 79). Processing content provides critical connections for students from which they can more effectively grasp a new idea. Classroom activities that provide the best opportunity for students to make sense of new materials are interesting, encourage students to think critically, and "cause the students to use a key skill(s) to understand a key idea(s)" (Tomlinson 2005, 79). Technology can be helpful in differentiating process by offering a variety of tools that help students make sense of new ideas. Using technology to create and share concept maps allows students to clarify their own connections to the new knowledge. Developing a blog—a personal online diary—about a new idea can provide a way for students to sound out their ideas as they are processing knowledge.

Differentiating products is an excellent way to assess student knowledge, understanding, and skills. In some instances, tests may be eliminated as an assessment and a product used instead. While a product can be fun for the students to develop, its primary purpose is to "cause students to think about, apply, and even expand on all the key understandings and skills of the learning span it represents" (Tomlinson 2005, 85). With the variety of technology tools available today, differentiating products can take many forms, in some cases determined by the students themselves.

Technology Tools for Enhancing Learning

The variety of technology tools available today can enable teachers to provide students with access to a world beyond the classroom. Today's students consider these technology tools as ubiquitous as the previous generation considers television. Prensky (2001) calls this new generation of students *digital natives*, a generation that has "spent their entire lives surrounded by and using computers, videogames, digital music players, video cams, cell phones, and all the other toys and tools of the digital age" (3). In addition, students today can, with seemingly lightning speed, assimilate a new technology, dumping the old one when it becomes no longer essential to their daily lives. In a matter of months, reading email became outdated as text messaging became the preferred mode of communication. Online social collaboration tools such as MySpace and Facebook connect students with others across the world, allowing them to obtain information from experts in the same field. Second Life and other multiuser virtual environments connect individuals from across the world as they meet virtually to play games, topple empires, collaborate on a project, or attend class. *Google* has now become a verb that means *to look for*, and individuals google topics for information more than 2.7 billion times per month (Sullivan n.d.).

Teachers who use new technology tools in the classroom have found that students are more interested in what they must learn when it is presented in the language they understand. Social collaboration tools such as blogs, wikis, virtual worlds, and web conferencing; media tools such as MP3 players and podcasts; and freely available software for concept mapping, desktop publishing, and data analysis provide opportunities to make diverse classrooms rich in content as well as appealing to the digital native.

The students have decided that they will divide tasks up and develop a time line for completing the project on climate change and global warming. Ms. Contreras shares an article she read the night before about a "carbon footprint." The article described a carbon footprint as the effect an individual has on the environment based on his or her carbon dioxide emissions each year (www.carbonfootprint.com /carbonfootprint.html). After discussing the article for several minutes, the students decide that they want to learn more about a carbon footprint. It sounds to them as though they can really make a difference in the climate by making changes in their school and in their community. José still knows many people in El Salvador. He decides to send his uncle, who is a teacher, an email asking him if he would be interested in his students' collaborating with José's class in the United States. Using Google Maps, José shows the rest of the class where he used to live. Several other students think it is exciting to talk to others so far away and are curious whether global warming has also affected El Salvador. They decide to join José's group and hope they can also find ways to make a difference so far away. José volunteers to translate emails from the class in El Salvador if anyone does not understand them.

Andrew wants to look at weather data from the last hundred years to see if there really has been a change in weather patterns. He teams up with others interested in data collection and analysis, and they begin googling sites that contain archived weather data. Their focus is on their town and the town that José comes from; they want to develop charts that are easy to manipulate so they can graphically show any changes in weather. Andrew creates a Google spreadsheet so that students in El Salvador can also enter data about their town's weather changes over the last hundred years. He also sets up a spreadsheet to start categorizing all the activities that affect the carbon footprint—both positively and negatively.

Sandra has heard her father talking about An Inconvenient Truth and wants to send an email to former vice president Gore asking him to visit their class virtually through videoconferencing tools. Ms. Contreras is not sure Gore will respond and encourages Sandra to find other sources for guest speakers. While Sandra begins drafting a letter asking experts to speak virtually to the class, the students in her group google other experts in the field of global warming.

Jonathon is excited about the plan and feels as though he can finally make a real difference. He begins sketching out a graphic logo for their project and asks if he can set up a page on a wiki for the students in both classes to use for sharing information. It is the first time that Ms. Contreras has seen Jonathon excited about an assignment this year.

Web 2.0 Connections

The students in Ms. Contreras' fifth-grade class use a number of technology tools that have become available with the development of what is termed Web 2.0.

While there is not a single, easily-grasped definition of Web 2.0, Warlick, an educator, author, and consultant for more than thirty years, describes it this way:

> Web 2.0 encompasses a range of emerging web-based applications that are, more than anything else, about conversation. Most often listed are blogging, podcasting, and wikis along with other more specific tools such as VoiceThread. They are each about content building, but each also has the ability to discuss or converse embedded in the application.
>
> These content conversations are subterranean, meaning that participants often do not know who the conversant is, and almost never work face to face. As a result, people participate/collaborate with each other without the baggage of position in the class, perceived biases, or other prejudices. It is empowering to the learner, because it gives voice to what they are learning (D. Warlick, personal communication, December 21, 2007).

Indeed, people do participate and collaborate with others in a way that was virtually unheard of several years ago. For example, for this chapter, I contacted Warlick through his blog site and asked if he would be willing to provide a definition of Web 2.0. He responded almost immediately with an explanation that was focused not only on defining the term, but also on the educational benefits of Web 2.0. This immediate accessibility to experts in the field offers more real-world contact for both teachers and students.

In addition, many of the web-based applications appeal to students who are already knowledgeable about and skilled in using the tools. Thus, the tools have received a great deal of attention in the world of K–12 education. Individuals in the field loosely agree that Web 2.0 encompasses "a more socially connected Web where everyone is able to add to and edit the information space" (Anderson 2007, 3). If one had to come up with a single word to describe this new generation, the word would probably be *connected*. Students today are connected to their peers, to teachers, to role models, to information, to games, to the world. Using the web-based applications inherent in Web 2.0 has become a highly effective method of engaging all students in the learning process.

Ms. Contreras is quite excited about the students' work on the global warming project. She has been able to embed science, math, data analysis, health, history, reading, and writing into the project. In language arts, for example, Texas students in the fifth grade are expected to be able to "frame questions to direct research, organize prior knowledge about a topic in a variety of ways such as by producing a graphic organizer, and take notes from relevant and authoritative sources such as guest speakers, periodicals, or on-line searches" (Texas Essential Knowledge and Skills—Fifth Grade, n.d., 7). Students in Ms. Contreras' class have the opportunity to conduct primary research and plan strategies for gathering information and making interpretations of the effects of global warming. A variety of additional standards are being addressed throughout the project and offer a more realistic environment in which students can bridge the content with prior learning because they are gathering and analyzing data with real-world significance.

Andrew is teaching students to use spreadsheet software to graph changes in weather over the past century. The students have been using a Google spreadsheet so that his team and the team in El Salvador can add information and collaborate on methods of presenting the results. All students in Ms. Contreras' class now have a good grasp of ratios and percentages, since they are looking at real changes in weather across large time periods. In creating and analyzing spreadsheets containing data students have collected during the project, mathematics standards such as describing "the relationship between sets of data in graphic organizers such as lists, tables, charts, and diagrams; and [solving] problems involving changes in temperature" (Texas Essential Knowledge and Skills—Fifth Grade, n.d., 13) have been covered.

Sandra is not able to get former vice president Gore to speak to the class virtually, but she does receive a response from a NASA scientist and a professor from MIT specializing in climate change, both of whom come to class virtually to share information with the United States and El Salvador students.

After hearing them speak, Sandra wonders if some weather changes could have been the result of changes in the world. Her team begins investigating historical events that may have had an impact on the climate and discover some links to coal mining and deforestation that may have correlated to changes in temperature over the years.

Jonathon sends an email (that Sandra helped him write) to the mayor. He wants to share the class wiki with the members of the city council and see whether they will proclaim May 15 to be Carbon Footprint Day. The mayor has been working on setting up recycling centers and is interested in the environment, so he enthusiastically agrees to come to talk to the class in person. When he sees the wiki that Jonathon developed and the logo for the class project, the mayor asks the city web designer to place a link on the city's web page.

Ms. Contreras has given José an iPod so that he can listen to lectures at home and hear the English language spoken at night. He is rapidly learning English. In addition to learning English, he is learning about different types of animals through the iPod videos that Ms. Contreras downloads from United Streaming and YouTube. He is excited about the topics because he hopes one day to become a zoologist. José is quite popular with the other students, since he is able to help in communicating with stu-

dents in El Salvador. After posting photos on the wiki that Jonathon built, students in both classes learn that they share many things in common. For José, the world becomes a smaller place, and his new country, warm and welcoming.

Web 2.0 Tools in the Educational Environment

In Ms. Contreras' class, students use various technology tools as they complete their projects. Below are brief descriptions of some of the tools that are available to teachers.

Blogs • *Blog* is the portmanteau of web log, an online publishing application that allows individuals to post personal thoughts and insights for those with similar interests to read and comment on. Others can sign up for the blog and receive notice when new information becomes available, thus bringing together individuals with like interests in an online forum. A form of blogging that is becoming popular in schools is for teachers to post student work and invite the students' peers to comment on the writing in this authentic and real-world environment. Since many K–12 schools have been hesitant to allow the use of blogs because of safety concerns, blog sites such as Warlick's blogmeister offer a controlled environment in which students can safely post and communicate. For more information, google *blogs in education, educational uses for blogs, blogging, blogmeister.*

Wikis • A *wiki* is a web-based application that can be viewed by all and edited/modified by anyone with editing privileges. Wikis offer tremendous potential for developing collaborative content by users who do not live and/or work in the same location. Wikis generally have a WYSIWYG (what you see is what you get) interface that enables users who are not familiar with writing programming code to build relatively sophisticated web pages. Wikis can incorporate sound, videos, photos, spreadsheets, tables, and charts into the pages and are cross platform friendly (can be used by anyone who has access to the Internet) regardless of computer operating system or browser used. Because wikis can be edited from any Internet connection, educators who are not physically present in the classroom can still maintain contact with their students (Educause 2005). In addition, the wiki stores a history of who made contributions and what individuals add or delete, making them a valuable resource for collaborative projects. For more information, google *wikis, wikis in education, K–12 education, educational uses of wikis.*

Social Bookmarking (Tagging and Tag Clouds) • *Social bookmarking* is a way to maintain favorite online sites that can be accessed with a single click. In addition, social bookmarks "enable powerful cross-referencing between bookmark owners, providing opportunities to share and [collaborate on] through the web content that is important" (Warlick n.d., 1) to individuals with shared interests. Thus, one person not only can look at his or her favorite locations, but can also see what others with like interests are bookmarking, harnessing the power of multiple individuals working together. One of the most popular sites for social bookmarking is del.icio.us. After joining the free service, individuals can use social bookmarking the same as they do favorites in a browser. Individuals create a tag— a one-word descriptor for a hyperlink. Multiple tags can be assigned to one site and can be edited at any point. Each person can build a storehouse of related information driven by personal interests. A tag cloud includes a list of all tags, with the largest number of tags (most popular) highlighted either by size or by color. For more information, google *tags, tag clouds, social bookmarking in education, del.icio.us, technorati.*

Podcasting • *Podcasting* is a portmanteau of iPod broadcasting. With podcasts, individuals can publish audio and/or video broadcasts online, allowing users to view or listen whenever and wherever it is convenient. While podcasts do not require an iPod for listening, a defining feature of podcasts is access through a subscription feed, called Really Simple Syndication (RSS). Many school districts are using iPods and podcasting to reach their English language learners after school hours; iPods are distributed to ELL students and uploaded with content from classes using teacher lectures, PowerPoint presentations about a subject, or movies from United Streaming, YouTube, TeacherTube or other video-sharing websites. In the evening, students can review lessons and hear English spoken, playing the podcasts repeatedly if needed. Students are also able to record and then listen to their own voice, which is helpful for those who are first learning a new language. For more information, google *podcasting, iPods and ELL, iTunes, podcasting and special populations, uses of podcasting in education, video podcasting, vodcasts, educational podcasts.*

Twitter • Although it is quite new, twittering may prove to be a useful tool for educators. Twitter is a free online service that became operational in March 2007 and enables someone to broadcast short messages—140 characters or less—to a general audience or to a designated group of individuals. Twitter will relay messages via the Internet or through cell phones. Educators who have experimented with Twitter have used it to get class information quickly to students or parents. For more information, google *twitter, twitter and education*.

RSS feeds • RSS stands for Rich Site Summary or Real Simple Syndication. The RSS icon on a blog, wiki, or other content site allows readers to subscribe to and view content without having to go to the site. Instead of having to visit a multitude of individual sites each day to view relevant and interesting information, individuals can use an aggregator or news-feed collector that places the new content into a single folder. An RSS allows individuals to easily subscribe to and aggregate information into a single location. Each individual controls the content by subscribing or unsubscribing to sites based entirely on personal preferences and interests. RSS feeds are beginning to be used extensively in education (Richardson 2005). For more information, google *RSS feeds*.

YouTube • YouTube is a video sharing website that allows users to upload videos and view videos by others. While some think that YouTube is filled with inappropriate movies and absurd rubbish, an incredible number of teachers and students are using this site for educational purposes. Appropriate movies are uploaded for students to view or can be downloaded and then shown to students in class without an Internet connection. YouTube has entered the mainstream as a favorite spot for presidential debates and political commercials. The ease of creating home movies using free or inexpensive video editing software has allowed virtually anyone the opportunity to become a star or director. While YouTube is still generally considered the gold standard in video sharing websites, a number of other companies now offer similar services. For more information, google *YouTube, YouTube in education, TeacherTube, video sharing websites*.

Web conferencing (Skype) • While the tools mentioned previously are generally considered to be asynchronous (users can collaborate without having to be online at the same time), web conferencing tools offer incredible opportunities for teachers and students to meet synchronously. Previously, meeting online for a conference required expensive equipment for connecting and communicating. Today, having a conference online merely requires a computer, headset with microphone, and an Internet connection. Free web conferencing tools, such as Skype and dimdim, which use VoIP technology, allow multiple users to meet via computer at the same time using a combination of text, audio, and video. In this environment, applications, movies, websites, interactive white boards, and other tools can be shared and modified collaboratively. Several commercial web conferencing tools allow for recording or archiving the conference. Some web conferencing tools, such as Wimba Live Classroom and eLuminate, do charge a fee. Web conferencing offers perhaps unprecedented opportunity for educators: guest speakers from across the world can meet with the class from any location; students from around the world can collaborate, sharing languages, photos, or cultural artifacts, virtually; teachers can collaborate with other teachers and professionals worldwide; students who are homebound can attend class virtually and interact with other students in the class. For more information, google *Skype, dimdim, web conferencing, webconferencing, vyew, Horizon Wimba, eLuminate.*

Creative Commons • One of the most exciting developments for educators is the advent of the Creative Commons copyright license, a movement to allow artists more freedom to determine how their works can be used. Started in December 2002, "Creative Commons defines the spectrum of possibilities between full copyright—*all rights reserved*—and the public domain—*no rights reserved*" (Creative Commons n.d., 1) Creative Commons' licenses allow artists to maintain copyrights to works while encouraging others to copy, distribute, display, and perform, remix, and mashup. "Creative Commons provides free tools that let authors, scientists, artists, and educators easily mark their creative work with the freedoms they want it to carry. [Individuals] can use CC to change . . . copyright terms from 'All Rights Reserved' to 'Some Rights Reserved'" (Creative Commons n.d., 1). Educators are able to find and safely use graphics, photos, music, lesson plans, and more with Creative Commons licensing. For more information, google *Creative Commons, ccmixter, flikr, freesound project.*

Google apps • Google offers a wide array of free online tools for educators, thousands of whom are currently using the tools and blogging about them extensively. One has to search a bit to find all the tools, but the effort yields extensive rewards. On the Google home page, in the upper left corner, click on *More* and then *Even more* to see the list of current tools. Some notable tools are blog search, a tool to find blogs that are of interest; desktop, a program that allows users to search their computers and return results in the same format as Google web results; notebook, a program that allows users to clip and collect information as they surf the web; and blogger, a program that one can use to create a personal or a class blog.

The following tools allow students to collaborate across platforms around the world: Google docs, spreadsheets, and presentations allow students to create and share content online anytime, anywhere; Picasa, an online photo editing and sharing program; SketchUp, a program for building 3D models that can then be added to Google Earth; Custom Search, which allows teachers to build a search engine that permits students to search only on specific sites (fantastic for ensuring they have reliable and safe sources). Google Earth is a free, downloadable application that "combines the power of Google Search with satellite imagery, maps, terrain, and 3D buildings to put the world's geographic information at [educators' and students'] fingertips" (Google Earth n.d., 1). Also, Google Labs' Experimental Search provides an inside look at what is in development and gives individuals an opportunity to try tools out before they are released to the general public. For more information, google *google labs, google experimental labs, google docs, google timeline, google maps, google earth, google apps, google education, google body.*

Digital storytelling • Porter (2006) explains that a person who uses digital storytelling takes "the ancient art of oral storytelling and engages a palette of technical tools to weave personal tales using images, graphics, music, and sound mixed together with the author's own story voice" (1). She further describes it as an emerging art form that enables individuals to "reclaim their personal cultures while exploring their artistic creativity" (1). In addition, the technology component of digital storytelling enables individuals to go outside the realm of traditional linear oral stories.

Digital stories are powerful tools for diverse learners. English language learners become involved in creating digital stories and are more willing to practice oral language skills. Easy to use and free, digital storytelling software is accessible for special education students and offers features that make it challenging for the most gifted students. This fun-to-use software captures the imagination of students and adults alike and becomes a powerful tool for learning content. Because they can be uploaded and saved onto a computer, stories created by students can be easily shared. For more information, google *digital storytelling, Photo Story 3, Movie Maker, Digitales, digital storytelling for educational purposes.*

Trends to watch • The Horizon Report, released annually (the 2007 report is available at www.educause.edu/ir/library/pdf/CSD4781.pdf), focuses on trends that have one year or less, two to three years, and four to five years until they are broadly adopted. For later or earlier reports, google *Horizon Report* and the year. Below are few of particular interest:

http://en.citizendium.org/wiki/Main_Page

Citizendium is a new open wiki encyclopedia project that is aimed at credibility and quality.

www.ibm.com/developerworks/library/x-mashups.html

Mashups are interactive web applications that combine media content from a number of sources to create something new.

http://scratch.mit.edu/

Scratch is a free programming language developed at the MIT Media Lab. Geared for young people, ages eight and older, Scratch helps students learn mathematical and computational skills while developing enjoyable projects.

www.pachyderm.org/

Pachyderm is a multimedia authoring tool accessed through a web browser that allows users to create interactive, Flash-based multimedia presentations.

http://secondlife.com/

Second Life is a 3D virtual world in which residents interact and live a second life. It is a commercial entity. Residents of Second Life spend roughly $1 million US dollars per day. Businesses and higher education institutions purchase virtual land and conduct business as well as hold classes in this virtual world.

www.whyville.net/smmk/nice

Whyville is a virtual world for children. Boys and girls from around the world go to Whyville to chat, play, and learn together. Unlike Second Life, the site has an obvious educational slant.

At the end of the project, Ms. Contreras found that her students were energized and enthusiastic about learning and were willing to work harder than they had for many of the traditional assignments she had given them in the past. Because accountability was extremely important at her school, Ms. Contreras ensured that activities and products reflected the standards-based components necessary for doing well on the end-of-year assessments. One way that she did this was by having students create assessment instruments in the form of games to test critical concepts. She also had each student produce four pages in the wiki and then use the writing process and peer editing to improve their product. Ms. Contreras found that students wanted to rewrite and edit their papers more extensively than they normally did because the wiki would be read and used by members of the community instead of just the teacher.

On May 15, the city celebrated Carbon Footprint Day. The students in Ms. Contreras' class were the experts who provided information to the city council as well as to other adults and students who attended the ceremony. Using Skype, a web camera, a computer, a multimedia projector, and a microphone, students in Ms. Contreras' class and the city council members were able to talk live with students in El Salvador during Carbon Footprint Day. Through the student-prepared activities developed during the project, the city council members became more aware of global warming and its impact on the world. They decided to maintain the link to the class wiki on the city website in hopes that citizens would become more conscious of their energy consumption and maintain May 15 as Carbon Footprint Day in the community.

Sandra enjoyed the research component of the project and liked working to solve a mystery. She decided a career in the FBI would definitely be interesting to her and asked Ms. Contreras what else she could do to improve her reading ability. Sandra knew she would have to be a strong reader if she was going to have a career in the FBI. Andrew liked teaching the other students how to create charts and graphs and manipulate data with spreadsheets. He thought he would consider becoming a math teacher. All the students in class agreed that he could tutor them once they got to middle school. Jonathon was able to work closely with the mayor during the project and found something in which he excelled. He continued with the class wiki and agreed to provide some training for the city council members. The mayor told Jonathon that they were really behind in technology and needed some help catching up. Jonathon set up an additional wiki for the city council and was looking forward to teaching adults for a change. José learned more English throughout the year and gained great self-esteem by serving as the interpreter for students in the United States and El Salvador. He wanted to continue learning English and thought he might like a career as an interpreter.

While it had been a long semester and everyone was tired, the students and Ms. Contreras agreed that they had never had more fun learning. In addition to being fun, the project-based learning activity offered each student an opportunity to excel in a variety of ways. Ms. Contreras decided to continue developing project-based learning activities, since she now understood their power in reaching the diverse needs of each student.

Conclusion

Students today will emerge from their K–12 educational experiences into a highly competitive global community. For success in this global community, students must be strong academically as well as skilled in higher-order thinking and problem solving. In addition, they must have the ability to work effectively with others around the globe in a technology-driven world. While using technology in isolation has not been shown to be effective in improving learning outcomes, technology integrated into the core curriculum offers a powerful tool for enhancing learning and differentiating instructional content, product, and process. In addition, the use of a variety of technology tools offers educators a way in which to address the unique needs and strengths of each student while significantly contributing to the learning process for all.

Applications

1. Think back to when you were in elementary or secondary school and the projects you can still remember. What were the characteristics of the projects and what did you like the most about them? How were they similar to and different from the project-based learning activities described in this chapter?

2. Go to www.edutopia.org and view a movie about one of the project-based learning activities on the site. You can choose something from an elementary school or a secondary school. What did you like about this project? How could you adapt the activity for your classroom? What are some of the challenges you can foresee in attempting this type of activity?

3. Discuss differentiating instruction through content, through process, and through product. How can instruction be differentiated using content, process, and product and maintain rigor and relevance in diverse classrooms? Give an example of each kind of differentiation.

4. Choose four different technology tools and develop a brief outline of a lesson that integrates the selected tools into the instruction.

Web Resources

Wikis

The following wikis offer free services as well as being advertisement free for educators:

http://pbwiki.com

http://wikispaces.com

www.wetpaint.com This wiki does not offer HTML editing, but has more templates to choose from than the others.

Social Bookmarking

http://del.icio.us This social bookmarking service allows you to keep all your bookmarks organized by popularity or most frequent use.

http://technorati.com/ One of the oldest social bookmarking sites.

www.citeulike.org A social bookmarking service for scholars that extracts citation details and stores them for access anywhere.

www.dig.com Digg is a popular website that emphasizes technology and science content but has recently moved toward more generic content pulling from blogs, videos, and images on the net.

Podcasts

www.apple.com/itunes/ iTunes is a free digital music site that allows you to download, organize, and play music.

www.epnweb.org The Education Podcast Network, podcasts by and for educators.

www.podcastalley.com/podcast_genres.php?pod_genre_id=7 Podcast Alley provides links to a variety of educational podcasts.

RSS Feeds

www.weblogg-ed.com/wp-content/uploads/2006/05/RSSFAQ4.pdf RSS: A Quick Guide for Educators

Video Sharing/Editing Websites

http://eduscapes.com/hightech/tools/video/video2.pdf Great article with information on video editing and video sharing websites.

www.youtube.com Video sharing. No rating; so be careful when using with students.

www.teachertube.com/ Specifically for educators; students and teachers can post and use videos.

www.schooltube.com/default.aspx More ads than Teacher Tube, but primarily geared to schools.

http://eyespot.com Free video editing and remixing.

www.jumpcut.com You can upload photos, edit, create slideshows, and then share for free.

Web Conferencing

www.skype.com Call computer to computer anytime, anywhere, free.

www.dimdim.com/ Free open source web conferencing service.

http://vyew.com/content/ Free web conferencing service with limited features; can archive sessions.

www.wimba.com/ Not free, but has powerful features specializing in the education market.

Creative Commons

www.creativecommons.org

Google Apps

www.google.com

Digital Storytelling

www.coe.uh.edu/digital-storytelling/ Comprehensive site on educational uses of digital storytelling.

www.storycenter.org/ Center for Digital Storytelling

Project-Based Learning

www.pbl-online.org/pathway2.html Designing Your Project: Design Principles for Effective Project Based Learning. An online guide that will help you design a project-based learning lesson.

http://edutopia.org Site established by the George Lucas foundation contains much information and videos on project-based learning.

8

Diversity in Early Childhood

Georgianna Duarte

Introduction

The early years, from the prenatal period to age six, are rapid and dramatic and shape long-term outcomes. During this critical period, children's learning, development, health, and well-being depend on their circumstances as individuals, as members of their families and communities, and as members within society as a whole. It is also during these early years that young children's literacy development, academic achievement, and development of prosocial skills are developed in schools (Sadowski 2006). This chapter discusses theory and research related to early childhood education (ECE) and *developmentally appropriate practices* (DAPs). While the *early childhood years* are defined as birth through age eight (National Association for the Education of Young Children [*NAEYC*] 1996), this chapter will focus on preschool through third grade.

Who Are the Children?

Nearly 13 million American children live in families with incomes below the federal poverty level. The number increased by more than 11 percent between 2000 and 2005, meaning that 1.3 million more children live in poverty today than in 2000. Children living in poverty have complicated lives. They often suffer from a lack of food, security, safe housing, and stability (National Center for Children in Poverty [NCCP] 2006). These factors clearly impact school readiness. The children most affected are from the African American, Latino, and American Indian communities. In fact, black and Latino children are more than twice as likely as white children to experience economic hardships that directly affect their schooling.

Children in early childhood classrooms come from complex cultural, racial, ethnic, and language backgrounds. As Smith and Murillo point out in Chapter 1, the ways in which children are raised, socialized, and educated are important in understanding how we can best meet their needs. We know that 40 percent of young children entering school belong to a minority racial or ethnic group, and oftentimes, the classroom teacher does not reflect the same background. It has been predicted that by the year 2010, one of every three Americans will be either African American, Hispanic American, or Asian American (Diaz-Rico and Weed 2006). Many of the children from these groups come to school speaking a language other than English (see Chapter 2).

Research evidence indicates that high-quality child care is the most effective force in improving educational outcomes and providing disadvantaged children with a chance to start school on a more equal footing with children from more advantaged backgrounds (Raver and Knitzer 2002). Minority children, particularly Latinos, are less likely than majority children to attend an early childhood program prior to public school. It has also been found that to be effective, child care does not have to be all day or all year, but it must be high-quality (National Task Force on Early Childhood Education for Hispanics 2007). Given these critical economic realities, early childhood educators are challenged in their professional lives to better understand and meet those needs (National Task Force on Early Childhood Education for Hispanics 2007).

Changing Families

Families are as diverse as the children who enter our classrooms (Banks 1993). As diverse children enter the classroom, we need to learn about the backgrounds of our learners, their parents or caregivers, where they were born, where they are living and have lived, and for how long. In an effort to meet the instructional and developmental needs of the young child, it is vital to understand the context of the family.

The family structure looks very different than it has in the past. Families of children in schools are increasingly diverse. The number of children who are adopted or live in blended households is increasing because of the high divorce rate. Children may be living with grandparents or extended family members, be in foster care, or even be homeless. Similarly, there are many children of same-gender parents, and this family structure is frequently not recognized and respected. With this diversity in mind, it is critical that early childhood programs reflect a sensitivity to and understanding of the students and families they serve.

Family-Responsive Programs

As Chapter 1 points out, programs for children need to be more responsive to families. Head Start (HS) is an example of a family-responsive program, and the services are primarily for preschool, infant, and toddler children who come from low-income households. The focus of Head Start is to assist children and families of low income in holistic ways and includes comprehensive education, health, nutrition, and parent involvement services. As of late 2005, Head Start provided services to some 905,000 children, 57 percent of whom were four years old or older, and 43 percent of whom were three years old or younger.

The goal of Head Start is to provide a high-quality program to ensure that children are ready to begin formal public school. The National Performance Standards for Head Start have become the benchmark of high quality for other preschool programs. They reflect a commitment to a family's heritage and experiences. A critical cornerstone of the program is family and community partnerships, where parent education, involvement, and empowerment are present at all levels of the service delivery system.

All Head Start programs screen the children to evaluate their overall health, including dental care, and provide regular checkups. The instructional program also includes oral health, hygiene, nutrition, personal care, and safety. For more than thirty-eight years, the HS program has been committed to an early intervention and prevention model and provided full services to all the children in the program including those with disabilities.

Early childhood programs strive to increase parental involvement but are challenged by differences in languages and cultures of the families. Quality home-school relations require clear and respectful communication. Access to information is a serious matter to diverse families, who need information for their children's success and survival. Many families need support through the use of a translator and policies that support the home language and materials in their languages. Young children are not translators and should not be used to communicate with the parents.

Effective HS practice is challenged by the current political climate, which emphasizes English over the first language children bring to school with them. The HS Child Outcomes framework encourages and supports English acquisition and stresses early readiness for children. As a result, the home language of the many English language learners in the programs is ignored, especially in states with English-only policies, such as California and Arizona. The children in these programs are at risk of losing not only their home language but also an important bond with family.

A culturally appropriate program responds to diverse families in systematic ways. For example, a classroom with all printed materials in the languages of the families provides a foundation of respect and equity. Similarly, the classroom should have materials, books, and artifacts that represent the families and their life situations in realistic ways (Gestwicki 2006). Parents and children alike need to feel welcomed to HS centers, which have a formal learning environment they are not used to. In addition, parents need opportunities to be involved in activities that are responsive to their needs, schedules, abilities, talents, and interests.

Developmentally Appropriate Practice

Effective practice (Wortham 2006) shows that for children to thrive, they need quality early learning experiences. The concept of developmentally appropriate practice has three major dimensions. The first is age appropriateness. This means that curriculum decisions are based on knowledge of the typical development of children. The second, social and cultural appropriateness, means that instruction provides relevant, respectful, and meaningful experiences for children. The final dimension is individual appropriateness. This means that teachers must individualize their instruction to meet the needs of each child. The decisions they make should be based on an understanding of individual children's growth patterns, strengths, interests, and experiences. DAP is based on the theories of Dewey, Vygotsky, Piaget, and Erikson. The term reflects an interactive, constructivist view of learning (Bredekamp and Copple 1997).

Play Is Essential

An integral part of developmentally appropriate practice is children's spontaneous *play*, and this is fostered through diverse concrete experiences and hands-on activities that are integral parts of the curriculum. Frost (2007) states that play is the chief vehicle for the development of imagination and intelligence, language, social skills, and perceptual motor abilities in infants and young children. While children play, they explore, act out, and engage during a focused period of time (Raver and Knitzer 2002). We know that a variety of play activities help children to develop new skills, master their environment, and more importantly begin the process of self-regulation and abstract thought. Through play, children have opportunities to use language and develop both imagination and creativity.

When we think of play, we typically think of children using simply gross and fine motor skills. However, when children play, they engage in conversations, self-talk, and make-believe discussions and use extensive language to negotiate new ideas, friendships, and situations. The work of people like Piaget (1962) and Johnson, Christie, and Wardle (2005) demonstrates that children's cognitive structures function best during play. When we watch children play, it is clear that they explore many different behaviors, and it is for this reason that play is a very effective vehicle for learning.

Basing their work on Vygotsky's view that learning is social, researchers have determined that children's mental skills are at a higher level in the zone of proximal development during play. Young children do not learn language in a vacuum. They learn it by interacting with each other through play. Given the diversity that children bring with them to school, play offers a form of expression for all children to help them understand the world they live in. A play-based curriculum offers rich opportunities, diverse learning materials, *learning centers*, and inviting spaces for social and linguistic interaction.

Learning Is Active

Developmentally appropriate practice involves active and meaningful learning experiences. Active learning requires materials, objects, equipment, and learning centers that are age and developmentally appropriate for the children in the classroom. Hands-on activities that encourage children to work directly with learning materials provide them with room for tailoring a task to their own style and pace of learning. A classroom with a variety of manipulatives that are inviting, safe, relevant, and interesting encourages and supports active learning. Diverse learners need activities that have connections to the home, other people, and the outside world. In the same way, active learning involves a schedule that is flexible and has blocks of time for projects, involved play, and conversation.

Equally important is the organization of physical space in a classroom. Active children need room. An effective learning space includes rugs, tables, trays, easels, and a mixture of furniture for projects and collaboration. The walls should be covered with visuals paired with print to foster children's emergent literacy skills and encourage oral language development.

Meaningful learning experiences in early childhood classrooms are those that address the interests, developmental needs, and skills of all learners in the classroom and are culturally responsive. Effective teaching builds on children's motivation to explore and experiment during their learning experiences. An important principle of DAP is for the teacher to make learning meaningful for the individual child by using a variety of practices that respond to the age, development, and needs of the child. For example, a cooking activity may build on previous cooking experiences in the home, but it also involves math, literacy, language, and science concepts. With the enormous variety of cultures and languages in classrooms, teachers have opportunities draw on their children's backgrounds and make connections to the family. Developmentally appropriate practices position the teacher as an intentional guide and facilitator (Hyson 2006; Novick 1996).

Research on brain development (Jensen 2000; Shonkoff and Phillips 2000) has also contributed much to our understanding of how children learn, and shows that young learners are complex humans with a variety of thoughts, emotions, imaginations, and predispositions. Children are not blank slates, or empty receptacles, but rather interesting, inquisitive humans. Developmentally appropriate practice involves the whole child and addresses all four components of learning identified by Katz and Chard (2005): knowledge, skills, dispositions, and feelings. While the very definition of DAP includes language and culture, the diversity of young children continues to challenge teachers. Therefore, the following section focuses on these areas more carefully.

Curriculum Is Culturally Responsive

Just as it is important to be sensitive to young children's diverse families and their needs, it is critical to offer culturally and linguistically responsive instruction. Young children come from diverse language backgrounds and cultures. Teaching these children is complex, and it requires instructional strategies and environments that focus on the individual needs, strengths, and abilities of the child. Not all Hispanic children are the same, nor do all Chinese children process information the same way. It is vital for teachers to listen carefully in the classroom to understand differences on a deeper level. For example, large-group gatherings of children are an important time to discuss differences as assets and to help children understand unique differences in their peers. These gathering times open the door for more meaningful discussions and help broaden children's understanding of and attitude toward others. Effective activities such as artwork, dramatic play, and emergent writing provide opportunities for validating the unique characteristics of each child (NAEYC 1996). Responsive teachers are sometimes referred to as intentional teachers who engage in routines, activities, and practices that build trust and a positive relationship with children and families (Gay 2000). Diverse children need instructional strategies that recognize their different learning styles. Culturally responsive instruction validates children's uniqueness, worth, culture, and heritage.

Effective Classroom Practices

In early childhood classrooms, effective practice involves a balance of activities that are initiated by the children or the teacher and involve individual, small-group, and large-group activities. These might include classroom routines such as weather, calendar, menu, and literacy activities. A balance of activities provides extensive opportunities for the child and teacher to learn together. There should also be ample opportunity for children to interact with each other. The curriculum should include collaborative projects, math centers, and time at the computer. Centers are especially important. Centers offer a wide variety of choices where children can freely play and manipulate materials and equipment as they develop language and concepts. For the young diverse learner, these opportunities are critical in building social relationships.

Teachers make a variety of choices in planning their instruction, but using a variety of strategies is effective in working with young children. As Murillo and Smith point out in Chapter 1, no one instructional strategy meets the needs or styles of all children entering the classroom. Strategies may include skill instruction, guided reading, modeled writing, cooperative learning, independent learning activities, free play, guided play, thematic instruction, projects, learning centers, problem-based learning, and literature-based instruction (Hyson 2006; Katz 2006). Research shows that competent teachers are also caring, observant teachers (Darling-Hammond 1996). Diverse strategies need to be developed that are based on the systematic observation of the children. With careful observation of the children, teachers can more effectively plan for the needs and abilities of their students.

Cooperative Learning

Cooperative learning is an instructional strategy that should also be reflected in the classroom routines, such as when children problem solve in centers.

Cooperative learning activities have many benefits for diverse learners in early childhood classrooms. Cooperative learning ensures rich language interaction and promotes positive race relations. It encourages the development of social skills and helps young children feel secure and comfortable in the classroom. Cooperative learning helps build children's self-esteem. Working together fosters an appreciation for and acceptance of similarities and differences and improves respect for diversity. Young children need to feel a sense of belonging, a sense of community, and cooperative learning can help create this security.

Integrated Curriculum: A Project Approach

An *integrated curriculum*, where content is taught by connecting ideas around a theme, is very important for young learners because they can more easily understand the content if ideas that are being taught are all related. Freeman and Freeman list the reasons to teach language through integrated content and its benefits for English language learners in Chapter 2. Teachers recognize that meaningful learning happens most effectively when children transfer their learning from one experience to another. For example, when children study native birds, they might do a variety of literature and art projects, study nests in science, count birds for math, and learn about why birds live in certain places and why they migrate. In this case, all of their curriculum is connected to birds. In an integrated curriculum, students always know what the topic is, and much of the vocabulary is repeated as they do each of their projects. An integrated approach, then, promotes skill development in areas such as literacy, language, mathematics, the arts, science.

Integrated curriculum is often realized through a *project approach*. A project is an in-depth investigation of a topic worth learning more about (Katz and Chard 2005). A project offers children a variety of concrete opportunities. As DAP explains, children learn primarily through projects, learning centers, and playful activities that reflect the current interests of the children and integrate opportunities for social and emotional development (Hyson 2004; Epstein 1998; Bredekamp and Copple 1997).

In an integrated project approach the curriculum is organized around core concepts and essential questions such as "What do birds need to live?" An investigation is a project conducted by the children and can be undertaken by a small group, a large group, or an individual child. It is a research effort deliberately focused on finding answers to questions that are posed by the children, the teacher, or the teacher working with the children. The goal of a project is to learn more about a topic of interest rather than to seek right answers to questions posed by the teacher.

A project does more than introduce subject matter; it builds on children's knowledge and previous experiences (Helm and Katz 2001). For example, a project might ask a question such as "What do plants need to grow?" Migrant children can talk about the crops their families work with in different parts of the country and bring in their knowledge of plant growth as well as other places and other climates. This validates the experiences of their families and their lives. Freeman and Freeman discuss organizing curriculum around big-question themes in Chapter 2.

Language Experience Approach

Another quality practice in the early childhood setting is the *language experience approach*, where children tell a story, retell a personal event, or share dreams or feelings, and the teacher writes their words down. When young language learners try to express themselves by telling a story from their own lives, it can be a powerful learning experience because it allows students to develop oral language and reading. As the children share their narratives, the teacher writes. He then reads them back to the children, so they can edit or change their stories. Language experience activities reinforce that sounds can be transcribed into specific symbols, and that those symbols can be used to re-create ideas expressed orally. The produced text provides many opportunities for children to learn vocabulary, grammar, writing conventions, structure, and personal voice. The writing is meaningful because the text comes from the children and it reflects what the children are interested in and what they are learning. While the literacy benefits are enormous for such an approach, there are many social-emotional bonuses for using such an approach as well (National Research Council 2001) as children interact and share their experiences and those experiences are written down and read and reread.

Children's Literature

Frequently, books can be used as a foundation for planning units or shared projects. Teachers using literature as a foundation in the curriculum report numerous benefits for both language and literacy development (*Early Learning Standards* 2002). Nonfiction books are also important and become a powerful foundation for conversations with both adults and peers. Vocabulary growth is supported by reading as children connect their prior knowledge and experiences to what is read. When reading is coupled with hands-on activities, students develop even more language. Listening comprehension is fostered as children listen to the teacher read aloud and as they then talk about the books they have heard (Englebright-Fox 2006).

Telling a traditional story or reading a variety of culturally relevant literature is a chance to bring the language and culture of diverse students into the classroom in relevant ways (see Chapter 2). There is much children's literature that celebrates diversity of all kinds, and early childhood classrooms should be filled with literature in which children can see themselves reflected. Retelling a story provides children an opportunity to express themselves, share their literacy experience, and clarify their own ideas about the story. Providing time and space for telling and retelling stories gives language learners opportunities to develop their language fluency. An instructional environment with literature integrated across the classroom supports all areas of literacy.

Classroom Environments

Classroom environments have a profound effect on what children learn, how they think, and what they value. Environments for young children need to not only reflect the knowledge and skills to be learned in the curriculum but also respond to how we believe children learn. Environments should also show important connections to family. When an early childhood classroom is cozy, inviting, and engaging, children explore, feel safe, and approach learning with a sense of wonder and curiosity (Curtis and Carter 2006). For children to learn, we need to create learning environments that support and promote their development and learning in all areas of the curriculum. DAP environments are inclusive settings where all children are valued and supported in their learning and development.

Certainly, many schools are limited by financial and other constraints, but teachers have an important and exciting opportunity to create environments that respond to and support diverse language learners. Basic ingredients for a quality environment include physical and emotional safety. Accommodations for special needs are part of a quality indoor classroom design. Effective room arrangements accommodate for walkers, wheelchairs, and also zones where children can have privacy and can carry out individual tasks.

The environment should promote the social-emotional development of the children and embrace the diversity of children. Evidence around the room of the various languages, cultures, unique characteristics, and special needs of the children fosters trust, rapport, and emotional well-being. The inclusion of children's photographs and their families validates their lives and unique backgrounds. An inviting, personalized classroom displays names and photographs of the children. This kind of print-rich environment fosters language and literacy learning and can extend to labeling furniture, materials, areas of the classroom, and personal areas. Arranging classroom space carefully and providing a print-rich environment are important aspects of creating a quality classroom environment and planning curriculum. Learning centers are part of the early childhood classroom environment and are key to the curriculum.

Learning Centers

Learning centers are well-defined areas in a classroom where children can go to engage in a learning activity. Learning centers can be diverse, because they vary in content and materials. Each center is thematic, carefully designed, and organized with appropriate materials, equipment, visuals, and space. Individual children choose a center, the amount of time they want to spend in the area, and the materials they plan to use. Centers provide opportunities for children to strengthen existing skills, learn new skills, and develop independence. For all children, including those with special needs, they are spaces for extensive language use and socialization. The open-ended activities in these centers allow the child to successfully play and learn at whatever skill level the child happens to be. Learning centers offer children a time to be independent and responsible for their own learning. This responsibility is the foundation for lifelong learning.

Outdoor Learning Environment

Just as teachers design indoor environments to meet the developmental needs and abilities of young children, it is important to plan carefully for the outdoor environment. Frequently, we think of outdoor environments for gross motor development where children can run, swing, roll down hills, or chase peers. However, outdoor environments can offer much more and in all areas of development. Time outdoors gives teachers diverse opportunities to individualize instruction with children. The outdoor learning environments provide children a chance to expand and develop social skills and to become more independent and more observant of their natural world. Likewise, outdoor spaces that foster language use provide children with opportunities to engage in more complex schemes of play, which promotes expansion of vocabulary. While the physical benefits are numerous for large and small motor skill development, early childhood researchers are now learning more about the richness of opportunities for social and language development in outdoor learning environments.

Integrated Project: Houses and Families

The following scenario provides an example of how one kindergarten teacher has incorporated developmentally appropriate practices in her classroom of diverse learners. Ms. Alvarez teaches kindergarten in a community in southern Texas that borders on Mexico. She planned her thematic project with her assistant, the children in her classroom, and input from several of the parents. The parents expressed concern that their children were losing their cultural identity and did not understand their home language. Ms. Alvarez planned the project to respond to state and national standards of early learning (Gronlund 2006). She planned a unit about community to help the children develop important concepts about community, family, and housing. The children, parents, and teachers collaboratively contributed to the project.

The project began with an art activity where the children transformed the classroom into a river community like their own, close to the border of Mexico. She engaged all the children in a massive collaborative painting project: A floor mural of greens and blues represented the river that children saw daily, the Rio Grande, and stretched the length of the classroom floor. Children chose a variety of paints, chalks, and colors to reflect the changing river. As they created the river, they shared materials and ideas. While children painted, conversations were rich with the children's experiences and observations. These included the color of the river, the cleanliness of the river, and incidents on the bridges, with traffic, and when visiting Grandma or shopping in Mexico.

During circle time, the teacher read the story *La gran casa azul* (Banks 2005). A discussion followed where children talked about their homes, where they were located, and who lived with them. Then the teacher asked the children open-ended questions about their houses. This helped children talk about concepts such as roofs, walls, windows, porches, patios, two-story and one-story homes, and duplexes. The discussion led to stories of family members. The teacher followed the interests of the children and posed questions about grandparents and extended family members living together. The teacher provided time for a discussion where they shared stories of their grandparents, some of whom lived on the other side of the river. These stories were written on large story cards by the instructional assistant and a parent. Here, concepts of community, family, and home were discussed with respect to the story. Prior knowledge and experiences were shared and webbed on a large sheet of paper.

Ms. Alvarez planned for a variety of instructional formats. Following the large-group read-aloud, she encouraged the children to work in pairs to share a variety of books about family and community. She planned carefully to ensure that

Altman, L. 1994. *Amelia's Road*. New York: Lee and Low.
Anzaldu, G. 2002. *Friends from the Other Side: Amigos del otro lado*. San Francisco: Children's Books.
Banks, A. 2005. *La gran casa azul*. Mexico: Juventud.
Barton, B. 2005. *Building a House*. New York: Mulberry.
Carling, A. 1998. *Mama and Papa Have a Store*. New York: Penguin Putman.
Garza, C. 1996. *En mi familia*. San Francisco: Children's Books.
Legnazzi, C. 2001. *Yo tengo una casa*. Mexico: Fondo de cultura economica.
Lowell, S. 2004. *The Three Little Javelinas*. Flagstaff, AZ: Northland.
Slavin, B. 1994. *El gato volvio*. New York: Scholastic.
Spier, P. 1980. *People*. New York: Trumpet Club.
Wing, N. 1996. *Jalapeno Bagels*. New York: Atheneum.

figure 8.1 Bibliography for Community Unit

books were integrated across all centers and displayed for easy access. The books represented a wide range of skill levels to meet the individual cognitive levels in her classroom. Through communication with families, Mrs. Alvarez included recommended selections from parents. Figure 8.1 is a bibliography of the books Ms. Alvarez used in her project.

To meet the various levels of emergent literacy in her class, Ms. Alvarez intentionally placed photographs of the children's houses, posters of houses, and pictures of various rooms across the classroom. Labels in Spanish and English, sentence strips in both languages, and bilingual stories accompanied these visuals. When finished, the room was filled with visuals including photographs, line drawings, children's creations, and vocabulary cards next to photographs.

Ms. Alvarez planned to meet early childhood standards as she engaged children in art and construction projects focused on home building. She individualized instruction as she planned the various center activities to support developing skills. To ensure quality interaction, she varied the number of children in each of the learning centers. Following large-group instruction, the children made independent choices, usually selecting a friend to join them in a center.

The children were encouraged to work collaboratively in pairs to foster language and social-emotional development. The children talked to each other as they used milk cartons and other recycled materials to construct houses and then wrote sentences with the teacher describing their houses. Following the completion of their houses, they placed their projects on either side of the painted river to represent where family members lived in the community. The concepts of form, number, object correspondence, design, and spatial relationships were supported through the identification of doors, windows, and rooms. The teacher initiated small-group discussions, and as the children discussed, she wrote what they said using the language experience approach. She recorded the individual characteristics of the houses they described.

Ms. Alvarez believed it was important to respond to individual differences, and she carefully planned activities in the block area in addition to the art and reading and writing activities. She read *Building a House* (Barton 2005) and encouraged the children to look at the book as they worked on their own buildings using blocks. First, the children described various home structures, and Ms. Alvarez listed the types of houses on a large chart. Next, the teacher provided an assortment of boxes and blocks so the students could build their own homes. In another center, the teacher posted vocabulary words printed on cards. Words such as *roof, window, door, bedroom, living room, stairs, upstairs,* and *downstairs* were matched with pictures as the children worked in small groups. Once the children in the block area had finished their constructions, they were encouraged to describe what they had built to the teacher and any other interested peer.

In response to various literacy initiatives in the district, Ms. Alvarez continued with her emphasis on families and homes by helping the children create journals, write lists of family members, and assemble story cards for display. She also had students listen to stories on tape and talk about photographs of their homes and families to further develop their oral language and listening skills. The book *En mi familia* (Garza 1996) was especially useful for fostering language because in this book, Garza includes drawings of events typical of Mexican Americans in Texas including the outside birthday barbecue and making tamales. Students enthusiastically shared their experiences with events shown in the book and chose to enact the outside dance in the drama center, complete with the instruments the band in the book played.

The teacher also read *The Three Little Javelinas* (Lowell 2004) and *People* (Spier 1980) to the students, which promoted further discussion. *The Three Little Javelinas*, a Texan takeoff on the traditional *Three Little Pigs*, encouraged discussion of types of houses. *People* brought out differences in people, their homes, their families, and their customs and fascinated the children so much that they enjoyed looking through the pages in pairs or small groups.

A culminating activity for the project was taking two neighborhood walks. Parents and grandparents were invited. As they all walked, the teacher pointed out various construction materials and types of houses and encouraged the children to share a digital camera to photograph buildings of interest. During the walk, the children in teams collected various natural materials, including fallen branches and rocks, for their classroom river construction project. Back in the classroom, the students described what they had seen and placed their constructed homes and materials gathered from the walks on either side of the river.

Through open-ended projects and learning centers, Ms. Alvarez encouraged the children to focus on similarities and differences in homes and families. To foster the home-school connection, and build relevant partnerships, Ms. Alvarez invited parents and family members to participate throughout the project. Parents and grandparents were invited for the walks, participated as storytellers, and observed literacy activities.

Through intentional planning, the children were involved in meaningful oral language and reading and writing activities as they developed both language and concepts. To evaluate their learning, Mrs. Alvarez used a variety of holistic assessment instruments including anecdotal records and collected work samples. Students in Mrs. Alvarez's kindergarten were fortunate to be involved in a series of integrated, developmentally appropriate activities that will ensure them school success in the future.

Conclusion

Developmentally appropriate practice includes culturally relevant teaching. It is grounded in human development, individualized instruction, and diverse teaching approaches. Early childhood professionals are facing a population of children of diverse cultures, languages, and families. Yet the current population of teachers does not match this increasing diversity. National studies show that more than 80 percent of ECE teachers are white, non-Hispanic educators (National Center for Early Development and Learning [NCEDL] 2000). As teachers, we are challenged by a nation of children living in poverty who have limited access to health care and quality early childhood programs. Many young children are entering schools speaking languages other than English. Clearly, today's children lack extensive support systems that will help them be ready for school. One could also strongly argue that schools are not ready for our children. Today's schools are not ready for the complex needs and backgrounds of an increasingly diverse population of learners. For early childhood professionals to effectively teach, it is imperative to respond to the complexity of children and families in holistic ways and to use a variety of strategies to address diversity. It is vital to create meaningful learning experiences and establish strong family, school, and community partnerships based on respect and understanding.

Applications

1. Observe two young children in a kindergarten. How do they interact in play and in the centers, and how do they use the materials? Take notes and be prepared to share with classmates about your observations.

2. Young children from diverse backgrounds enter early childhood programs that look very different than their homes. The classroom environment needs to reflect the various cultures, characteristics, and languages the children bring to school. Examine an early childhood classroom to determine if individual characteristics of the children are reflected in the visuals, artifacts, instructional charts, and materials. List the things you see that reflect the diversity of the children in the class.

3. This chapter discusses the importance of learning centers and effective environmental elements. Examine an ECE classroom and identify the learning centers. Do the centers have a clear purpose? Are the materials diverse, organized, and appropriate? Are the activities relevant to the learner and the teaching objectives?

4. Interview an administrator to find out about support services in a school for early childhood students and families. Do these services match the needs of children and families? Be prepared to share what you have learned with the class.

5. Locate the classroom schedule for an ECE classroom and examine it to see if there are opportunities for both large-group and small-group activities as well as individual choice times and collaborative learning. How much time do children have for exploration or independent choices? How much time is spent in large group? In small group? In transitions?

6. Instructional strategies are effective when they respond to individual developmental and learning needs. Observe a first-grade classroom and list the different ways the teacher responds to individual needs of diverse students.

Key Terms and Acronyms

developmentally appropriate practice (DAP). Planning that is based on knowledge of how children learn, age appropriateness, individual appropriateness, and social and cultural appropriateness.

early childhood years. Birth through age eight.

integrated curriculum. A curriculum where children broadly explore knowledge in various subjects related to a common topic or theme.

language experience approach. An approach to reading instruction based on activities and stories developed from the personal experiences of the learner. The stories about personal experiences are written down by a teacher and read together until the learner associates the written form of the word with the spoken form.

learning centers. Specific areas where children interact with materials, objects, and equipment.

play. A behavior that is intrinsically motivated, freely chosen, process oriented, and pleasurable.

project approach. An in-depth study of a topic investigated by children.

Resources for Further Study

Annie E. Casey Foundation: www.aecf.org/

Association for Childhood Education International: www.acei.org/

Center on the Social and Emotional Foundations for Early Learning: www.csefel.uiuc.edu/

Culturally and Linguistically Appropriate Services: www.clas.uiuc.edu/

Intercultural Development Research Association: www.idra.org/

International Play Association USA: www.ipausa.org/

Kids Count data report: www.kidscount.org/

National Association for the Education of Young Children: www.naeyc.org/

National Association of Child Care Resource and Referral Agencies: www.naccrra.org/

National Head Start Association: www.nhsa.org/

Parent and Educator Partnership: www.pepartnership.org/

Teaching for Change: www.teachingforchange.org/

United States Census Bureau: www.census.gov/

Zero to Three: www.zerotothree.org/

9

Teaching Middle School Mathematics for All

James A. Telese

Introduction

"Ugh, I hate math." This comment is often heard among children and adults. Whenever I tell someone what I do for a living, which is preparing mathematics teachers for grades 6–12, they often respond with similar comments, along with "Oh, I never was any good at math." Perhaps you have made similar comments to your friends, and you may have heard other adults say how much they dislike math. Is there something about mathematics, or is it how it is taught that makes people feel that way? A popular musician recently titled a song "Math Sucks." It is a challenge to overcome these negative attitudes.

Ask elementary students if they like mathematics, and many of them will say that they do. But something happens in middle school, and students begin to dislike mathematics. By the time they finish eighth grade, they try to avoid taking mathematics and dread facing future math classes. How can these attitudes be changed? The answer to that question is through teaching mathematics in an inspiring, motivational fashion that builds on student curiosity and creativity.

All students should have the best chance to succeed at mathematics, including students who are labeled special education or English language learners. Mathematics lends itself to teaching in a variety of ways so that every student can foster positive beliefs about himself and mathematics. A deep understanding of middle school mathematics provides students a strong foundation that allows them to be confident in their approach to learning algebra in high school or in the eighth grade. Mathematics educator Robert Moses (1995), an African American who leads an organization for improving the teaching of algebra, calls the subject "a new civil right." Hence, understanding mathematics is also a new civil right.

Principles of Effective Mathematics Teaching

The *National Council of Teachers of Mathematics* (NCTM), a professional association whose members consist of teachers who teach math from elementary through high school, supervisors of mathematics teachers, and mathematics teacher educators, has published a document titled *Principles and Standards for School Mathematics* (2000). Standards are presented for teaching content related to algebra, geometry, measurement, data analysis, and probability for grades pre-K–2, 3–5, 6–8, and 9–12. Coupled with the content standards for each grade level are standards for problem solving, *reasoning* and proof, communication, connections, and representations. For greater detail related to these standards, visit the website www.nctm.org/.

The document contains six principles:

- the equity principle
- the curriculum principle
- the teaching principle
- the assessment principle
- the technology principle
- the learning principle

Of importance for this chapter are the equity principle, teaching principle, and learning principle. The equity principle highlights the idea that excellent mathematics education requires setting high expectations and providing strong support for all students. Students who are poor, speak a language other than English, have disabilities, or are nonwhite are more likely than their peers in other demographic groups to have low expectations set for them. It is crucial for math teachers to set high expectations for all students regardless of their cultural or personal characteristics or handicaps. An equitable mathematics program supports "their learning and is responsive to their prior knowledge, intellectual strengths, and personal interests" (NCTM 2000, 13).

The teaching principle highlights the idea that teachers should have an understanding of what students know and need to learn and should challenge them to learn it well in a supportive environment. Two features of a supportive classroom environment are to know how students learn and to use effective pedagogical strategies. Teaching mathematics requires having what could be considered a box of *tools*, including strategies and techniques for teaching mathematics. Eventually knowledge of how to use the tools will develop with experience, but instructional planning also plays a critical role in use and knowledge of tools and strategies for the classroom.

The learning principle features the idea that students need to develop a deep understanding of the content. Teachers can help students develop a thorough understanding by building new knowledge on students' prior knowledge. There are at least two types of mathematical knowledge, according to Skemp (1976): instrumental learning and relational learning. Instrumental learning focuses on learning through memorization and lots of practice. Some basic mathematics concepts, such as the multiplication table, need to be memorized.

Relational learning connects topics to each other and provides a context for the use of a mathematical procedure, such as learning how to solve a linear equation through problem solving. A balance between practice and teaching concepts is critical. Students need to know both basic facts and how to use them to solve real-world problems. Some have argued that too much drill and kill hinders problem solving and too much problem solving hinders the learning of basic facts. Consequently, NCTM argues for the use of standards-based instructional practices reflecting what is considered to be best practices for all students.

Learning Theories That Support the Principles

Two theories of learning support the principles for effective mathematics teaching. These are constructivist theory and sociocultural mathematics learning theory.

Constructivist Theory

A discussion about the teaching of mathematics should include learning theories related to mathematics. One very broad theory, *constructivism*, has been used in mathematics teaching at various grade levels. Constructivism has many varieties, but generally, it is a cognitive learning theory that has several roots, ranging from Piaget's (1952, 1977) developmental learning theory, which points to the importance of learners' receiving instruction at the appropriate level for their age, to social cognitive theory and information-processing learning theory.

The major tenet in constructivism is that humans learn by constructing their knowledge. They connect new ideas to previously learned information. Piaget explains that learning involves assimilating new ideas. In this process, previous knowledge may need to be modified to accommodate the new information. Through assimilation and accommodation, people build up mental structures called schemata. Schemata are like scripts or video clips that run in our heads and represent the knowledge we have constructed on a topic. When new knowledge is not easily assimilated and accommodated into existing structures, students become confused and disequilibrium occurs because they have to enlarge or create a new structure or schema in order for mental equilibrium to return.

Teachers should recognize that students come to a learning situation with knowledge obtained from previous experiences, and this prior knowledge influences how the new knowledge will be constructed during the learning process (Bruner 1960, 1996). For example, an English language learner newly arrived from Russia might experience disequilibrium if the math teacher shows her how to multiply numbers using a method familiar to most students in the United States but quite different from the method used in Russian schools. The Russian student would need to assimilate the new information and add it to her previous knowledge of how to carry out multiplication. In the process, her schema for multiplication would need to be modified.

The process of constructing one's own knowledge by building on previous knowledge is vastly different than the traditional behaviorist view of learning, where learners parrot back what the teacher has told them. Learning mathematics requires constructing knowledge, instead of passive reception, through interaction with mathematical objects and a mathematical community (Davis, Maher, and Noddings 1990). The mathematics classroom is often viewed as the learners' mathematical community. When the classroom is viewed as a mathematical community, mathematics learning becomes a process whereby students actively construct knowledge through enculturation into practices of the mathematics community. This means that through repeated exposure, students realize what is to be learned, how it is to be learned, and how to act within accepted classroom norms. For example, if students are encouraged to make *conjectures* without fear of criticism, then they will be more likely to continue to think critically and participate in discussions.

Consequently, the teacher's role becomes that of a facilitator rather than a lecturer standing in front of a class, behind a podium. Facilitators guide students and support them through careful planning and questioning and using worthwhile mathematical tasks.

What does it mean for a teacher to teach in a way that is consistent with constructivist principles? The answer is that teachers should take into consideration students' past experiences and knowledge. They should offer situations that foster learning by meeting individual needs with activities that are important to each student. This can be a big challenge for teachers, especially in classrooms with diverse learners who come from different social and cultural backgrounds and who come with different levels of mathematical ability.

Sociocultural Mathematics Learning Theory

The National Science Foundation (NSF 2006) has recently recognized the importance of the sociocultural context in learning. Sociocultural mathematics learning theory goes further than the constructivist view centered on the individual constructing knowledge. This theory recognizes the role that the social environment plays in learning. Not all children have been socialized to learn in the same way.

There are two kinds of meanings identified by Russian psychologist Leont'ev (1975): cultural and personal. Cultural meaning develops from a culturally historic past that forms generalized knowledge and skills. The role of symbols transmitted mainly through language helps individuals to get along in the world. The result is an understanding of how to use knowledge in particular domains of human activity. For example, when students enter middle school, they may experience an adjustment phase because they enter a new cultural situation with each teacher, although there is an overall school culture. Students experience various classroom cultures in relation to the number of teachers they have assigned to them. The mathematics classroom, along with their other classes, becomes a new cultural experience. New rules of behavior and interaction have to be learned for each teacher.

Personal meanings arise from cultural meanings, whereby values are attached to actions and goals derived from an activity (van Oers 1996). This implies that mathematics instruction should have relevance to the students and build on their cultural experiences. Racial, ethnic, and linguistic minorities have been shown to make educational gains when teachers capitalize on their cultural and linguistic experiences (NSF 2006). However, teachers need to be careful to avoid operating on stereotypes. For example, not all Latinos are the same. Individual students have had different experiences and have developed different learning styles.

Language plays an important role in the development of personal meaning through cultural experiences. Students should have opportunities to explain their thinking and express their reasoning through dialogue with other students and between themselves and the teacher. This results in a discussion where the negotiation of meaning occurs (van Oers 1996). It is important to realize that students develop their own meanings through discussion with others and that their understanding may not necessarily mesh with the teacher's intended meaning. Therefore, through careful listening, the teacher gains an understanding of student meanings and, when necessary, can offer insights into the negotiation of meanings (van Oers 1996). This process allows for students to know what are acceptable meanings and the teacher to know what meanings students have developed during the course of instruction.

Teaching Mathematics for Understanding

Application of the mathematics learning theory previously described can lead to the development of mathematical understanding. Teaching for understanding is important because students will be able to apply knowledge from previous learning to new topics and solve new and unfamiliar problems (Carpenter and Lehrer 1999). Without understanding, students look at mathematics as a collection of isolated skills. They have difficulty applying what they have learned to new situations and to real-world problems.

Understanding is developed through five mental activities:

- constructing relationships
- extending and applying mathematical knowledge
- reflecting on learning experiences
- articulating knowledge
- personal involvement in the construction of knowledge

The first mental activity involves constructing relationships where formal mathematical concepts, operations, and symbols are related to earlier intuitions and ideas. For example, middle school students intuitively solve linear equations when they shop for video games. The second is extending and applying mathematical knowledge, where a network of structured knowledge is formed consisting of new information connected to existing understandings. The third activity is reflecting on learning experiences so that students come to realize how the new knowledge is related to what they already understand. The fourth requires articulating knowledge either verbally, in writing, or through various representations such as diagrams, pictures, or models. The fifth is the personal involvement in the construction of knowledge through the negotiation of meanings between the teacher's meaning of the concept and students' meaning of the same concept.

In addition, there are two components, directly influenced by the teacher, that facilitate the development of mathematical understandings. One is the mathematics task itself. The other is the tools used for instructional purposes.

Tasks with High Cognitive Demand

The task is central to the successful development of mathematical understanding; it should be rich enough so that students have the opportunity to use their intellect when solving problems. A task should require the use of high-level cognitive abilities. The students should be made to think and not just respond through repetitive exercises.

A task having high cognitive demand features students doing mathematics, such as creating a pictorial proof of the Pythagorean theorem, or following procedures with connections through problem solving, such as when a student sees a rationale for finding the slope of a linear equation in a *real-world situation*. In contrast, a task with low cognitive demand features students completing exercises that may require memorization and recall of facts and following procedures without connections such as simply identifying the components of a linear equation in the form of $y = mx + b$, where m is memorized to represent the slope with the traditional slope formula, and b is defined as the y-intercept.

Tools for Mathematical Understanding

Tools for teaching mathematics for understanding are essential. What tools can be used? The use of tools involves representing mathematical ideas in various ways. Tools can range from paper and pencil to computers and graphing calculators. *Manipulative* is a term used to describe a variety of objects. Many manipulatives may be used to teach mathematical concepts. Some may be commercially bought, while others can be made by the teacher or the students. Examples of commercial manipulatives include Cuisenaire Rods, geoboards, fraction tiles, pattern blocks, and algebra tiles, to name a few.

Homemade objects may include items like popcorn, which can be placed around the diameter of a circle to show the relationship between the circumference and the radius by tabulating the number of popped kernels placed on the circumference versus on the radius and finding the ratio of the circumference to the diameter regardless of whether or not the radius is pi. Students using construction paper can construct a cone with the same height and radius as a cylinder, fill the cone with rice, and then pour the rice from the cone to the cylinder to see that the cone's volume is one-third that of the cylinder. The source of homemade manipulatives is endless. The use of tools enables students to see concretely various mathematics concepts, such as the use of base ten blocks to represent place value concepts or Cuisenaire Rods to represent fraction concepts.

Building understanding with tools is a first step toward developing an abstract concept. For example, students first explore the Cuisenaire Rods by comparing sizes and seeing relationships among the different lengths. They might notice that the yellow rod has the same length as five white rods; hence, the concept of one-fifth is illustrated. Once students have become familiar with the tools, then the students are led to the next, transitional step, which is writing in symbols what can be represented by manipulatives.

For example, they could write a proportion to show the ratio of a purple rod (p) to a red rod (r) as p/r. They could use a similar proportion to represent the ratio of another rod (x) to a green rod (g) as x/g. If the two sets of rods have the same proportional relationship, then they could represent this knowledge by writing: $x/g = p/r$. The final step is to allow students to work with the symbols rather than manipulatives. For example, the ratios for the previous proportion could be $x/4 = 1/2$. Students could solve the problem to determine the length of the fourth rod (x).

Teaching mathematics for understanding is crucial for student success. When students have learned mathematical concepts using good mathematics tasks that encourage them to use knowledge to extend what they have previously learned, the result is students with persistence, understanding, and an ability to apply their knowledge in new situations. Students have learned to solve problems connected to various concepts and real-world situations. As a result, students become more motivated to learn mathematics and gain confidence as learners of mathematics.

Assessment

Assessment of student understanding is an important component of any mathematics classroom. It is through assessing students both formally and informally that teachers come to know what students have learned and how they have learned it. Assessment is defined as the process of collecting information from various sources to determine the degree to which students have obtained the necessary knowledge and skills. The design of an assessment program should go beyond assessing the accumulation of facts and procedures to ascertaining how the newly created relationships fit into previously existing knowledge structures, the use of knowledge in new situations, and the levels of reasoning applied when solving problems. There are three assumptions: (1) assessment is an ongoing process integrated with instruction, (2) multiple sources of information are needed to assess developing knowledge, and (3) as a process, assessment should also involve documenting classroom interaction from students' written work (Shafer and Romberg 1999). Teachers who approach assessment in this way are better able to make decisions regarding instructional sequences and activities.

Informal Assessment

One tier of an assessment design is the use of *informal assessment* gathered during instruction, besides the use of assignments, tests, or quizzes. Items embedded in instructional tasks or materials can be used. Often a good instructional task makes a good assessment item and vice versa. The instructional objectives of particular items may vary in focus from narrow views, examining whether students are able to apply a mathematical tool such as Cuisenaire Rods, to broader views of solving nonroutine problems, with or without tools. However, during assessment students should have available or have access to the tools they used to learn the concept.

A characteristic of an experienced mathematics teacher is being a good listener. Through careful listening, or informal interviews in which teachers ask thoughtful questions of students, teachers can assess students' level of understanding of a mathematical domain. A teacher may ask a student to explain her work or thinking; students often say, "Well I know it, but I cannot explain it." If a student can explain a concept, then that indicates a deeper level of understanding than just repeating a process or recalling a formula. If a student has difficulty explaining a concept, then in all likelihood, the student has a weak understanding of the concept.

In addition, good teachers are good observers. Making observations as students work on tasks provides teachers with insights into students' thought processes and solution strategies. This may be accomplished during independent work or while students are working in cooperative groups. The teacher can make notes on a checklist, ask probing questions, clear up misconceptions, and offer further guidance without revealing the process or solution.

It is difficult for teachers to let students struggle with a problem. Because of time pressures, some teachers feel it is necessary to do the work for students or give them an answer without letting the students use their own thinking. Teachers can ask students to check for errors in their work, encourage efficient solution pathways, and scaffold thinking by asking leading questions without directly providing the answer or solution process. Some of the questions can direct students to look for patterns or state and test conjectures as they move toward a generalization. The teacher, based on information gathered through informal procedures, can then alter instruction. For example, a teacher could make a simple problem more complex, alter a lesson's presentation strategy, or offer tasks that encourage multiple solution pathways. During the class, a teacher can analyze students' thinking through their written or oral explanations.

Typically, a benefit of informal assessment is improved instructional sequences both within the same class or for the next class period. When presenting the same concept to different classes, the teacher's first class may not go as planned, while the later classes go more smoothly because the teacher has had an opportunity, based on information obtained through informal assessments, to make changes in how the lesson is taught. These changes might include making the lesson less confusing, changing the types and quality of questions used for scaffolding, or making adjustments to required tasks.

Formal Assessment

When the phrase *formal assessment* is used, it more often than not refers to the standardized testing or high-stakes testing associated with schooling, where sanctions are placed on teachers, students, or schools if performance is not at the prescribed levels. In Texas, for example, the test used is the Texas Assessment of Knowledge and Skills (TAKS). The tests are administered at different grade levels and cover a variety of state standards, called the Texas Essential Knowledge and Skills (TEKS). Schools are rated based on the number of students who pass the exams.

Formal assessment used by mathematics teachers is related to end-of-unit activities (Shafer and Romberg 1999). Items should be designed to allow teachers to see what the students know and can do rather than what they cannot do. These assessments are linked to instructional objectives presented during the unit. The intent is to extend what was presented during the unit by introducing new contexts and permitting the use of tools. As a result, the teacher gains information about the ability of students to apply their knowledge and skills to new situations. Student work can be assessed through analyzing students' writing and their solution and thinking processes. These techniques may be used with *performance-based assessments*, during which students are required to demonstrate their knowledge and skills by solving an open-ended task that may have multiple solution pathways or more than one correct answer.

Performance-based assessment allows a teacher to see how students think about solving problems and at the same time communicates to the students what the teacher thinks is important about mathematics. For example, if students frequently experience tests or exercises that require very little time to solve, say a minute or so, then students begin to think that mathematics should be done in a hurry and if they cannot get an answer quickly, then they give up. This leads to a lack of persistence in students when solving mathematics problems. In real life, mathematicians take hours, days, or years to solve a problem. Performance-based assessments can communicate a different set of important attitudes, like persistence and the idea that it takes time to solve mathematics problems. Hence, performance-based assessments, either informal or formal, are critical for determining student thinking processes. These processes involve students in using different types of reasoning. Three levels of reasoning are described by Shafer and Romberg (1999). They are reproduction, connections, and analysis.

Reproduction • As student understandings grow within a particular domain, students begin to use the concepts and procedures associated with the domain in an increasingly more sophisticated manner. Reproduction is a basic level of mental activity that involves the recall of facts, procedures, and definitions. Examples include completing a calculation, constructing a graph, and using formulas. Items that elicit reproduction of knowledge and skills are often de-contextualized problems in a completion or short-answer format. Using reproduction items to assess basic facts, definitions, or procedures limits the type of information evaluated to low-level cognitive skills. The items are not well suited for assessing how students reason and communicate about their mathematical understandings.

Connections • A second level, connections, features assessing the extent to which students are able to connect mathematical concepts, make connections to other content areas, integrate different information, and make decisions regarding the use of tools to solve nonroutine problems. These items are usually contextualized by being set in real-world situations. There is usually one correct answer to a problem, but there are multiple solution pathways. Therefore, the students' responses may vary, illustrating different approaches to a problem and reflecting their understandings.

Analysis • The third level, analysis, assesses mathematical thinking at a more complex level than either reproduction or connections. In mathematics, this level is considered by Shafer and Romberg (1999) to include interpretation, analysis, and mathematical argumentation, mathematical modeling of situations, and generalization. These items are often set in real-world contexts, are open-ended, and require that students use discriminate thinking to choose appropriate strategies and tools for the solution. Students may develop innovative solutions that need to include their assumptions and reasoning that supports their conclusions. These items promote learning that encourages students to transfer their knowledge to new situations. This requires reflection, constructing relationships, extension and application of mathematical knowledge, and communication of their thinking.

Classroom assessment is an important part of a mathematics classroom. There is an adage that says, "You get what you test." This means that if you want to elicit particular mathematical thinking from students, then you need to assess those aspects. Classroom assessment is an important part of providing feedback to the students. It is with this feedback that students will come to know their strengths and weaknesses.

When asked whether he is good at mathematics, a student may respond, "Yes." A follow-up question may be "How do you know?" The student may respond, "Because I have an A average." This exchange illustrates that a student bases his mathematical worth on a grade rather than on his capabilities. Traditional classroom assessments usually focus on grades rather than on describing or communicating students' strengths and weaknesses. When teachers use assessment techniques mentioned in the preceding discussion, students will be able to come to know themselves as mathematics students and be able to describe what they are good at in mathematics and what they are not good at.

Standards-Based Math Unit

The following scenario represents a standards-based instructional unit. It has the features of high expectations and relating mathematics content to real life, problem solving, and critical thinking. The unit reflects sociocultural learning theory and capitalizes on students' interests, which assists in engaging students with the unit. Moreover, the unit allows all students to participate in mathematics regardless of language background, learning disability, or ethnicity.

Jim is a middle school mathematics teacher whose students are predominantly Mexican American. The unit centers on the issue of diet and health (Telese and Abete 2002). There has been a lot of publicity in the media about how important diet is for both young people and adults. Published reports have indicated that there are a great number of young people who are overweight. Jim planned a lesson that connected mathematics to daily-life activities like reading food labels and dieting. Jim included mathematical concepts related to standards that required students to demonstrate knowledge and skills in the areas of statistics, ratios, and proportions.

He began the unit by eliciting a discussion about the importance of a proper diet. This led to a discussion about the food pyramid. To raise further interest and connect the lesson to his students' lives, Jim asked the students to make collages of their favorite foods, using pictures from packages and placing them onto a poster board. The collages were helpful for students who had English as a second language (ESL) to present their favorite foods pictorially, as well as the other students, including those who had been identified for special education services. The ESL and special education students were creative with their collages. Many had themes that Jim and the other students could clearly identify. This activity gave Jim insight into the students' home life and the type of foods students ate. Students placed their collages around the room on the walls for display.

Jim presented a video on the importance of a healthy diet and what constitutes healthy eating habits. The video allowed a variety of students, including the ELLs and special education students, to learn visually the concepts related to diet. This discussion focused on aspects such as calories, proteins, carbohydrates, fat, and cholesterol. Also, Jim used graphic organizers throughout the lesson such as tables and charts to organize data and information. Students were provided data that related the percent of calories from fat in a diet to the amount of cholesterol in the blood in milligrams per thousand milliliters. Students were asked to interpret the graph. Their response was "The greater the percentage of fat in the diet, the more cholesterol there is in the blood."

This set the stage for Jim to introduce the concepts of ratios and proportions. Once Jim felt, through using informal assessments such as observations and interviews, that his students knew the major diet concepts, he began discussing ratios associated with those found on food labels. Here, he again used graphic organizers to illustrate the relationships. Graphic organizers help all students learn, especially ELLs and special education students. Students brought to class labels from packages found at home. Jim helped students determine that in one gram of fat there are nine calories. Then the students calculated the number of calories listed on their various food labels to determine the amount of calories from fat, carbohydrates, and proteins. Next, the students worked on finding the percent of the total calories associated with each of the three components. Students used informal reasoning like "Well, if there are ten grams of fat then that means there must be ninety calories."

Jim built on this idea by introducing the traditional way of finding the total calories. Students were asked to make a graph of this relationship, and a discussion ensued concerning the linear relationship between the amount of fat and total calories using the following equation: total calories = 9 calories/gram × (amount of fat in grams). Students used various representations of the ratio concept, representing it as a linear equation, a table, a graph, and in verbal or written descriptions. This allowed students to build connections in order to develop deeper understandings of the concepts. These different representations also allowed ELLs at different proficiency levels to show what they had learned.

The next aspect of the unit began with Jim using his favorite recipe for homemade tortillas. He presented the recipe to the students in a familiar situation, saying, "Here is my recipe for homemade tortillas given to me by my grandmother. Your father is going to have a surprise barbecue for your mother's birthday celebration. He needs tortillas made and wants you to figure out the amount of ingredients needed for various amounts of tortillas. Since the recipe makes 15 tortillas, find the amount of ingredients needed for 30, 45, and 135 tortillas. For example, the recipe for 15 tortillas calls for three cups of flour; how many cups do you need for 30 tortillas?" Jim gave students a few minutes to think about their answer. He encouraged students to write or draw something to represent what they were thinking. Giving special needs students and ELLs time to think before responding helps them to participate more fully in class discussions. Often, some students will answer quickly, but other students will also participate if given time to think first.

An ELL responded, "Six cups."

Jim asked, "How did you determine that number?"

She held up a drawing with three cups on it with fifteen tortillas and a second drawing with three cups and another group of fifteen tortillas and explained, "Well that is twice as many tortillas as the recipe makes, so I just thought that the flour needs to be twice as much too." She used her informal reasoning skills to explain the ratio of three cups of flour for fifteen tortillas. Jim then went on to capitalize on her explanation to illustrate the traditional mathematics of proportions,

$$\frac{3 \text{ cups}}{15 \text{ tortillas}} = \frac{n}{30 \text{ tortillas}}$$

The final phase of this unit involved a more direct connection to the students' lives by examining their school breakfast and lunch menus. Jim asked students how they would go about finding out what was planned for them for breakfast and lunch. The students took a few days and made inquires about how and where to find menus. Through their research, they learned that they needed to contact the district's food services department. The students obtained the menus for past and future weeks, which contained nutritional information similar to what was listed on the food labels they had brought to class.

Jim provided the students with a raw table for them to complete with column headings such as "Menu Item (Serving Size)," "Grams of Fat," and "Calories from Fat." Students tabulated items listed on the menus, filling in the cells of the table with calculated values using any means they thought appropriate, and they used tools like spreadsheets and graphing calculators as needed. These tools were made available throughout the unit. Students came to use particular tools as they deemed necessary. Jim only made the tools available; it was up to the students to decide whether they needed to use them or not. Once the tables were completed, Jim asked the students to analyze the data in the tables and make recommendations to the principal. With the supporting data, students wrote explanations about the data. They concluded that there was too much fat in their school menus and that they would like to see a healthier diet be provided to the students.

Through this unit, Jim showed his students how mathematics can be used to lead a healthy lifestyle, make good food choices, and most importantly improve their lives at school by becoming involved in an important social issue. Ultimately, the students used mathematics concepts as a basis for making a recommendation to the school principal. In Jim's class, students used mathematics in their efforts to make a change for the better.

Jim's unit reflects the principles of effective mathematics teaching. Jim followed the equity principle by holding high expectations for all his students. He also followed the teaching principle. He used informal assessments to determine what his students knew. He also found out what they needed to learn. He challenged them to learn it well in a supportive environment. He followed the learning principle as well by helping all his students, including his ELLs and special needs students, to develop a deep understanding of the mathematical concepts he taught them. His teaching reflected constructivist theories of learning, and his students came away from his class with a greater appreciation for mathematics.

Applications

1. In the beginning of the chapter, mathematics learning theories are presented. In your own words, describe each of the theories and how they could be applied in your classroom.

2. Choose a mathematics concept such as measurement, and trace how your local and state standards present how the topic should be taught from grades K through 12.

3. Describe the features that foster understanding in mathematics. Discuss the role of the task, the teacher, and the classroom environment.

4. Present an assessment plan to evaluate students in your mathematics classroom; include both informal and formal techniques.

5. Find a website that features virtual manipulatives, and design a lesson that incorporates a manipulative.

Key Terms and Acronyms

conjecture. An informal guess, resulting from making a series of observations, that has not been formally proven using mathematical logic.

constructivism. Briefly, a theory of learning based in cognitive psychology and social psychology. The major idea is that students construct knowledge from previous understandings, upon which new knowledge is built. The teacher's role is one of facilitator.

formal assessment. The process of collecting information concerning students' understandings and knowledge through standardized measures, such as a high-stakes accountability test. A student's performance is described in relation to a group, using scores like percentiles and stanines.

informal assessment. The process of collecting information concerning students' understandings and knowledge through the use of tests, quizzes, and questioning tied closely to instructional practices. They may be teacher-designed or published materials.

manipulatives. A generic term used to describe objects designed for teaching mathematics concepts. Examples include fraction tiles, Cuisenaire Rods, algebra tiles, base ten blocks, color tiles, and pattern blocks. Manipulatives may be purchased or may be handmade by the teacher. One website that offers patterns for handmade manipulatives is http://mason.gmu.edu/~mmankus/Handson/manipulatives.htm. There is also an online library of virtual manipulatives called the National Library of Virtual Manipulatives at http://nlvm.usu.edu/en/nav/vlibrary.html.

National Council of Teachers of Mathematics (NCTM). A professional organization dedicated to the improvement of mathematics teaching and learning from prekindergarten to high school. It was founded in 1920.

performance-based assessment. An assessment that requires students to do something. The student must respond with more than just an answer; she must illustrate the process or the application of knowledge, which may include solving open-ended tasks or developing a mathematical model of a real-world situation.

Principles and Standards for School Mathematics. Document published by NCTM in the year 2000, which offers both principles and standards for the teaching of school mathematics.

real-world situation. A term used to describe a mathematical problem-solving task reflecting a situation that one may encounter in daily life, such as determining the best cell phone deal between two companies.

reasoning. Characterized as having the ability to think analytically, noting patterns, structures, and regularities in real-word situations and symbolic objects, and make conjectures. It is often paired with the term *proof*, as in *reasoning and proof*. The result is being able to develop ideas, justify results, and use mathematical conjectures (NCTM 2000).

tool. Anything that can be used to assist in the teaching of mathematics concepts such as calculators, paper and pencils, compasses, protractors, and computers. A wide range of objects can be used as tools, limited only by the extent of the teacher's creativity.

10

Literacy in a Diverse Society

Paula Parson and Renée Rubin

What Is Literacy?

Reading and writing are important skills in today's society. But literacy is more than that. *The Literacy Dictionary* defines *literacy* as "minimal ability to read and write in a designated language, as well as mindset or way of thinking about the use of reading and writing in everyday life. [Literacy] therefore requires active, autonomous engagement with print and stresses the role of the individual in generating as well as receiving and assigning independent interpretations to messages"(Harris and Hodges 1995, 142). In the broader sense, literacy involves the ability to communicate effectively in order to participate and succeed in society. Readers must also be able to communicate through listening and speaking and interpret what they view as well as to represent their ideas in writing so others may understand.

Understanding for Communicating and Interpreting

Writing, representing through art, and speaking are often thought of as the creative and constructive parts of literacy because they are the expressive portions of literacy, but in reality all parts of literacy involve the creation of meaning (Rosenblatt 1994). Our culture and experiences shape how we understand what we hear and read. Reading involves much more than decoding or sounding out words. For example, we can all read the following five-word sentence: The child became an adult. However, the way that we interpret that sentence will vary greatly depending on our viewpoint.

For voting, joining the military, or obtaining credit cards, adulthood comes at eighteen years of age. For drinking, the rule is twenty-one in the United States. If you are a neurologist, you may think of brain development, which continues into the mid- or upper twenties (Zelazo 2005). Jewish boys and girls become adults when they have a bar or bat mitzvah at age thirteen. A Latina girl and her family may consider adulthood at fifteen years of age, when she has her *quinciñera*. The same five words can be interpreted in these and many other ways. Thus, reading goes well beyond saying the words in the sentence.

Many teachers tell us, "My students can read but they don't understand what they are reading." Our response is, "If someone could say the words on a medicine bottle but not know how much medicine to take, would that be considered reading? Would someone who could pronounce the words on a job application but not know how to fill it out be reading?" In life outside of school, we don't consider it reading unless people understand what they read. In other words, reading without comprehension is not really reading at all.

Yet many students can read well aloud but do not understand what they are reading. Often the students lack knowledge of the vocabulary or concepts in the text. This is especially true of English language learners (ELLs) and those who have come from other cultures. Even those raised in the United States may have difficulty with concepts that are not familiar to them. A child from Colorado who has not traveled much may have difficulty understanding the enormity of an ocean, and a child with limited experiences from Illinois may not be able to visualize a tall mountain.

"Our knowledge of words . . . determines how we understand texts, define ourselves for others, and define the way we see the world. A richer vocabulary does not just mean that we know more words, but that we have more complex and exact ways of talking about the world" (Stahl 1999, 1). The more words we understand, the more that we can read and write with meaning (Anderson and Freebody 1981).

When words represent a new concept, they are usually learned through *authentic*, or real, *contexts* (Schickendanz 1999). For example, if we want to teach students about condensation, it is better to have glasses with ice inside and allow students to watch as water condenses on the outside of the glasses than to try to explain the process of condensation to them or just have them read about the concept. When ELLs have already developed a concept in their native language, authentic context, pictures, or other experiences help the ELLs transfer the knowledge that they have in their native language to English and help them learn the new words in English for those concepts.

Instruction that emphasizes the pronunciation of words over the comprehension of the words may also contribute to reading problems. *Round-robin reading,* in which students take turns reading passages aloud, is particularly harmful for ELLs, who are so concerned about their pronunciation and accents that they do not pay attention to the meaning of the passage. The same thing is true of someone with a speech articulation problem. Think about someone who learns the steps of baking a cake but uses sawdust instead of flour. He understands and implements the steps of baking a cake perfectly, but he cannot eat it at the end. It is very similar for students who know all the steps in reading but do not understand what they read. They are left with nothing but a lump of sawdust when they finish reading.

Most reading that people do outside of school is silent reading, but teachers continue to use a large dose of oral reading in school to make sure students are really reading. There are several ways teachers can help all students read silently with comprehension.

Purcell-Gates (2001) explains that learning to read is much like learning to ride a bike or to swim because they are all processes that require the synthesis of many skills to be successful. Although a person can learn each skill separately, such as the letters and their sounds, the direction of print in English from top to bottom and left to right, and the meaning of words, it is only when the skills are put together that real reading occurs. Purcell-Gates says individual skills can be taught as "side of the pool" lessons, and then the students must return to the swimming pool to use the skills as they swim. Purcell-Gates, who worked with special needs students, writes, "Struggling readers make more progress, practicing and mastering the parts of the process in process, when they are reading for real purposes" (123).

Perhaps most important is to encourage students to read things that interest them and that are at a level where they can be successful. We all know that we are more motivated to do something when we like what we are doing and feel successful at it. Just because a student is in the fifth grade does not mean that she can read effectively at a fifth-grade level. We might compare reading to clearing the bar of a high jump. A student who is less than five feet tall might be able to jump a bar at two feet with little help and at two and a half feet with some guidance, but if someone suddenly lifted the bar to four feet, there is no way he could jump over the bar.

Within one classroom, a teacher may have students who are reading above and below grade level, students who are native English speakers and those who are just learning English, and students with a variety of experiences and interests. Therefore, teaching everyone the same skills with the same materials at the same time is no more appropriate than expecting someone who is five feet tall to jump as high as someone who is six feet tall with the same instruction and practice. One solution to the variety of abilities that naturally occur in any class is for a teacher to use books at different difficulty levels all related to the same theme. Organizing curriculum around thematic units and using text sets with books at different levels is one way to meet the needs of all students, including gifted and talented students, special needs students, and ELLs. All students in the class study the same theme but are able to read different texts about the theme and conduct different projects to indicate their knowledge.

The following sections explain how a teacher might help all her students develop higher levels of reading comprehension. Although reading is a recursive or circular process in which people may preview a text, read a little, preview again, and so forth, for practical purposes we have divided the reading process into three phases: before, during, and after.

Before

In order to improve reading comprehension, teachers should have two goals before reading. One is to introduce the topic or content of the reading and the other is to set a purpose for the reading or to help the readers set their own purposes for reading. Each of these goals can be achieved in many different ways.

If the concepts to be covered in the reading are new to most of the students in the class, then more extensive introduction of the content and vocabulary may be needed through experiential learning, DVDs, props, or pictures. If the concept is understood by most of the students, a simple discussion may be enough to remind the students of what they already know about the topic. Teachers can also use flexible groups to preview the content if there are great differences in background knowledge.

In addition, setting a purpose for reading is important. Often teachers simply tell their students to read certain pages in the text without giving them a reason for reading. For the students, this is like being asked to drive a car but not being told where to go. One way teachers can help students find a purpose for reading is to preview the text—that is, look at the cover, the title, pictures, graphics, and subheadings. If students are reading different texts, the teacher can model the process in a minilesson for everyone, and the students can apply these strategies individually or in small groups.

The teacher can also encourage students to make predictions of what the text will be about. As they are reading or being read to, the students can check their predictions. Students also can come up with questions of their own before they begin reading and look for the answers as they read. Each of these strategies helps to give the students a direction or road map to follow as they read.

During

Students should not be encouraged to stop frequently during reading because it disturbs concentration and comprehension. However, they can check to see if predictions are correct, look for answers to questions they wrote before reading, or exchange information about the reading with a partner.

Students also need to learn how to monitor their own comprehension during reading and take action if they do not understand what they are reading. Sometimes students don't have a purpose for reading other than getting through the required number of pages. Unfortunately, some students do this type of zombie reading most of the time. These students need strategies that will help them monitor their comprehension.

Think-alouds (Cunningham and Allington 2007) are one way that teachers can help students monitor and improve their comprehension. The teacher reads text that the students can see; it can be text from a big book, on chart paper, or projected from a computer or overhead projector. As the teacher comes to difficult words or sentences, she demonstrates what she would do to figure them out. This might involve using prefixes or suffixes, rereading the text, skipping the difficult part and coming back to it, or using cognates—words that are similar in the child's native language and English. The teacher demonstrates different strategies depending on the needs of the students.

After

After reading, there is a wide variety of activities students can do to increase their comprehension of the text. They can check predictions, relate what they read to their own experiences, or pose and answer questions. They can respond to the text through a variety of means including art, drama, music, and writing. This allows students with a variety of talents and needs to respond in their own way. A child who has difficulty writing or spelling may prefer to create a collage about the topic while another may write a song. Some outgoing students may want to create a skit and perform it for another class, while others may prefer a more individual approach, such as writing a poem. Still other students love to create bulletin board exhibits on the latest theme they are studying. All these are ways students can respond to a text.

Multicultural Literature

The landscape of America has changed and continues to change as people from the far reaches of the world make their homes in the United States. Faces that make up today's classrooms reflect this change. Students come speaking languages never before heard in our schools, bringing with them a broad range of cultural and linguistic backgrounds. Teachers can capitalize on these differences and, at the same time, help students develop reading proficiency by using literature that reflects the different cultures of their students. Although there are groups who are not represented in children's literature, more groups than ever before are depicted in modern children's books.

Use of high-quality *multicultural literature* allows children to see themselves represented positively and to see that others are just like them with the same feelings, thoughts, fears, dreams. As Maya Angelou expressed in her 1990 poem "From Human Family" (1994, 224–25),

> We are more alike, my friends,
> Than we are unalike.

Quality multicultural literature depicts the values, beliefs, and cultural backgrounds of cultural groups. As children see themselves in the stories they read, their self-esteem and pride in their own heritage increase. As children engage in experiences and adventures of characters in books, they learn about other cultures, breaking down barriers and reducing prejudices.

Selecting Quality Multicultural Literature

With such a wealth of literature to choose from, it is important for educators to select quality culturally relevant children's literature. Multicultural literature should encompass all of the characteristics of any high-quality literature. Books should "exhibit high literacy and artistic quality" (Lynch-Brown and Tomlinson 1999, 180). The culture should be represented accurately and authentically. The target culture should be evident as the story develops. Details should authenticate the cultural setting.

Language, traditions, clothing, food, and so on should not be stereotyped, nor should they just be superfluous to the story; rather, they should be integral to the story's action. Lynch-Brown and Tomlinson caution us to be alert "to any generalized portrayal of African Americans as course-featured, musical, and poor; of Asian Americans as sly, overly diligent and obsequious, of Hispanic Americans as lazy, holiday-minded, and impoverished; of Jewish Americans as greedy, aggressive, and penurious; and of Native Americans as savage, primitive, and war-like" (1999, 180).

Stereotypes are damaging and have no place in our classrooms. Racial, religious, and language minorities as well as traditional mainstream groups should be represented in the full range of characterization—the good, the bad, and the ugly. Not all Middle Easterners are terrorists. Not all Asians are smart and good in math. Not all blacks are natural athletes or great dancers. White men are not always the good guys, nor are those of color automatically the bad guys. Characters representing the minority group in the story should be well-rounded and dynamic rather than flat and static. Also important is ensuring that groups that may not be part of the classroom makeup are represented in the literature. Ignorance and unfamiliarity perpetuate prejudices. As we learn that we are more alike than we are different, we learn to accept and respect others.

Illustrations should also be accurate, authentic, and integral to the story. Educators need to exercise care to not be lured by illustrations of a target culture that portray the group with stereotypes and inaccuracies. Using quality literature in the classroom extends beyond expanding knowledge and creating enjoyment.

Teachers can integrate culturally relevant literature with content texts during thematic teaching. By choosing appropriate texts and using the before, during, and after approach to helping students build comprehension, teachers can meet the needs of the diverse students in their classes and help all their students become more proficient readers. In the following section, we describe a unit for beginning readers that incorporates effective literacy instruction.

Literacy in Kindergarten

Ms. Martínez is a kindergarten teacher in an English instruction class who has designed a unit for beginning readers that incorporates effective literacy instruction. For some students, this is their first time away from home, while other students have been in day cares and learning centers almost from birth. Some of the students have extensive knowledge about print and books, while others have received little exposure. Although most of her students are native English speakers, Ms. Martínez has five students who are native Spanish speakers but learned English in day care and prekindergarten. Their parents chose to place them in an English instruction class, but reinforcement in Spanish assists them. She also has two English language learners from the Philippines who speak Tagalog and some English. She has tried to arrange her classroom and her daily activities to provide support for all her students through thematic teaching, many hands-on activities, and centers designed for students of varying abilities.

Her room has many examples of original student work on the walls, books and writing materials almost everywhere, and a word wall to support students' reading and writing. There is a rug where the class meets at least twice a day for whole-group activities. There are tables for small-group activities and six learning centers.

Ms. Martínez has a writing center, math and science center, art center, block center, dramatic play center, and library center. She modifies the centers to correlate with her themes; the current theme is plants. Centers allow students to explore and discover on their own as well as reinforce what has been taught to the whole group. The centers are designed so that students with differing abilities can be successful and challenged.

Ms. Martínez assigns students to heterogeneous (mixed ability) groups to go to centers so that students can learn from each other. She tries to place English language learners with at least one other student with the same native language. Each group is assigned to two centers Monday through Wednesday. On Thursday and Friday, students can choose which centers they would like to attend as long as there are not more than four students at any one center at a time. During center time, Ms. Martínez sometimes meets with individuals or small groups on skills that they need or enrichment activities. She sometimes walks around the centers, listening to students and recording notes or anecdotal records about what they are doing. Ms. Martínez also asks questions and helps to extend students' oral language.

During the plant unit, the library center includes many favorite books that will stay in the library center all year. Ms. Martínez also added some books about plants in English and Spanish, such as *The Tiny Seed* (Carle 1991) and *Soy una hoja* (Marzollo and Moffatt 2002), for this theme. In addition to books, the library center has a listening center with books with tapes, a clipboard and writing materials, stuffed animals, and beanbag chairs. There is a flannel board with cutouts that students can arrange on the board. For this theme, Ms. Martínez has added flannel cutouts of plants at different stages of growth to go with books and to encourage students to make up their own stories.

The dramatic play center has been changed into a farmers market with plastic fruits and vegetables. It also has a cash register with play money and a small scale for weighing the fruits and vegetables. As with all centers, this one has writing materials and books. Ms. Martínez put two copies of *Fruits and Vegetables/ Frutas y vegetales* (Rosa-Mendoza 2002) in the dramatic play center so children can understand that reading is not just something to do at the library center.

The block center has a variety of blocks to encourage creativity. Ms. Martínez has added some plastic trees and flowers to the center so students can incorporate the theme into their creations if they would like. Students are encouraged to draw their creations and write about them so they will have a record of them before they have to tear them down. Sometimes Ms. Martínez even takes digital pictures of the creations, prints them out, and posts them on the wall with the students' names. She makes sure that everyone eventually has a picture on the wall.

Students are provided with various parts of plants, including bark, roots, leaves, and cut fruits and vegetables at the art center. They then use a sponge to apply tempera paint and make prints and patterns on colored construction paper. Students are provided with pens, pencils, and markers to write about their artwork.

The science center has lima beans that have been soaked and magnifying glasses so students can see the tiny plants inside. They draw and write about what they see. In addition, each child planted seeds before the unit began. They get their plants from the windowsill during their science center time, water them, and measure them with a simple ruler. Ms. Martínez has previously taught the class how to measure using a ruler. They also can draw a picture of their plant and write about it. Books about how plants grow are included at this center.

Finally, the writing center is a place where students are encouraged to write in their own way. Some may be scribbling, others spelling words with one or two letters, and some spelling many words correctly. Ms. Martínez has added some plant words, such as *seed, grow, leaves, flowers,* and *tree,* to the words already at the center to encourage students to write about plants. There are a variety of writing tools at the center, including letter stamps, ink pads, markers, colored paper, stationery, envelopes, and more.

Ms. Martínez integrates the theme throughout the day in many ways. She reads aloud to the students at least twice a day and often reads books related to the theme. When possible, Ms. Martínez reads the book in Spanish first to the native Spanish-speaking students in her class to provide a preview. For example, she reads and discusses *Sorpresas en el huerto* (Hall 2002) with the native Spanish speakers before reading the same book, *The Surprise Garden* (Hall 1998), in

Carle, Eric. 1991. *The Tiny Seed*. Parsippany, NJ: Simon and Schuster.
Hall, Zoe. 1998. *The Surprise Garden*. New York: Scholastic.
————. 2002. *Sorpresas en el huerto*. Trans. Nuria Molinero. New York: Scholastic.
Mora, Pat. 1994. *Pablo's Tree*. New York: Scholastic.
Marzollo, Jean, and Judith Moffatt. 2002. *Soy una hoja*. New York: Scholastic.
Rosa-Mendoza, Gladys. 2002. *Fruits and Vegetables/Frutas y vegetales*. Wheaton, IL: Me and Mi.

figure 10.1 Plant Unit Bibliography

English. This helps them relate their background knowledge in their native language to the English book.

The books often offer natural ideas for other activities as well. For example, in *Pablo's Tree* (Mora 1994), the grandfather decorates a tree that Pablo planted for his birthday. Each birthday the decorations are different. After reading the book, the teacher takes dictation from the class about how they would like to decorate their birthday tree. She writes down their exact words so they can see the relationship between speech and print. After she has written down several ideas, they read the text together. Then she asks students to point out certain letters that they have studied. Ms. Martínez also makes a tree with wrapping paper tubes and butcher paper. Students make their own decorations to place on the tree.

On other days, Ms. Martínez integrates the theme in math by having students sort different types of seeds by color, shape, size, and other characteristics. She brings in various types of fruits and helps students graph favorite fruits. Afterward, they make a fruit salad with the fruit.

Students role-play what it would be like to be a seed developing roots, poking out into the sunlight, growing leaves, getting bigger, getting rained on, and blowing in the wind. During each of these activities, Ms. Martínez is reinforcing much of the same vocabulary so that most of the students in the class understand what a seed, leaf, root, stem, and flower are and what they do by the end of the unit.

Ms. Martínez's classroom exemplifies the best practices discussed elsewhere in this chapter. The thematic unit provides multisensory opportunities for students with different learning styles to learn about the same topic. Vocabulary is developed through concrete experiences and repetition in a variety of contexts. The teacher reads aloud to the students frequently to reinforce the theme and their interest in reading. The emphasis during classroom instruction and during independent work at centers is on the construction of meaning rather than the pronunciation of words or perfect handwriting. The centers provide opportunities for students of varying abilities to participate and learn. Students also have opportunities to use both their native language and English as they read, write, and interact with others in the classroom.

Writing with Meaning

Reading informs our writing. Author and poet Alice Schertle says, "Every minute you spend reading is a minute you spend learning to write" (in Kasten et al. 2005, 317). The reading and writing processes are similar; thus skills used in one also transfer to the other. Good readers read like writers (Smith 1988). As they note what writers do well, they gain a deeper understanding of what they are reading but also learn to use those same techniques in their own writing.

Writing is hard for many. One of our graduate students told us her experience when she attended a writing workshop put on by the district. She remembered sitting around a table with other teachers writing to prompts that the workshop leader posed to the group. She watched others put their pencil to paper and write madly. They seemed to have a lot to write. She, on the other hand, struggled to think of something to write about. She remembered her own students writing to prompts that she posed to them. Did they experience the same struggle?

The workshop leader was guiding the group to write about the place where they lived, the people, traditions, the landscape, even the weather. This teacher had lived in the area for only a short time, and she had trouble writing about it. After struggling through several prompts, she decided to write about something she knew well, the place where she lived before moving here. Once she started writing about her experiences growing up in her hometown, words flowed from her pencil. This personal experience showed her that when teachers ask students to tap into their background experience and knowledge, they have lots to write.

Another problem that keeps students from writing is that often they feel like they don't have anything important to write about. They feel that they haven't had any dramatic, earth-shattering experiences. During a project in which we were collecting stories about the local area for Rural Voices Radio, a venture of the National Writing Project, we asked students to list names of people, events, or places that were important in some way. What did they remember about each? Once they made a short list, we asked them to pick one to write about, then gave them time to write about their chosen topic. Before starting to write, the students had several questions:

"Do we have to write in English?"

"Can we write about anything we want?"

"How long does it have to be?"

"How many paragraphs does it have to be?"

Once they understood that they could write in the language they were comfortable using, that they could include words and phrases in Spanish, that there were no limits or minimums in length or number of paragraphs required, they wrote. And wrote. And wrote. Their stories were amazing. As they read their stories to each other, we laughed, we cried, we held our breaths in anticipation, and we couldn't wait to hear the next. Each piece stimulated enthusiastic discussions as others eagerly shared similar stories. Clearly students were engaged in each other's stories. We asked if their writing always produced these wonderful stories. There was a resounding "No!"

"So," we asked, "what was different this time?"

"It's the first time we got to choose our own topic," volunteered one girl, to a chorus of agreement.

"It's the first time we had permission to use our own language," another said. "Yeah," another agreed. "We always have to write in English."

It was clear that these were not native English speakers, and writing in English was a challenge. When they were asked to write, writing was a struggle. By having to concentrate on getting words down in English, they lost focus as they struggled with words.

Research reveals that when ELLs are asked to write in a new language, they not only struggle to understand and master the grammatical task but must also take on a new identity. Freeman and Freeman (2001) conclude that effective school programs take into account factors from both the school and the societal contexts in planning curriculum for language-minority students. Clearly, for writing instruction to be effective, students' new identity in their school context must not be in conflict with their home culture. By permitting students to choose their own topics to write about and incorporate words and phrases in their home language to express their thoughts, instruction supports the students' home identity as they gain confidence and pride in expressing their ideas in writing. Not only is their language valued, but their stories are as well.

Additionally, students need opportunity to write extensively. Donald Graves commented that "if kids don't write more than three days a week, then they're dead, and it's very hard to become a writer" (in National Writing Project and Nagin 2003, 23). As students write more frequently, they begin to think about writing even when they're not doing it. Graves calls this "a state of constant composition" (23). The National Writing Project authors argue that not only should teachers require students to write more, but "they must also give students a rich and diverse array of writing experiences" (National Writing Project and Nagin 2003, 13).

Many teachers today use the writing workshop model. The work of Janet Emig (1971) and James Britton and colleagues (1975), who studied secondary students' writing process, and Donald Graves (1975), who found that seven-year-olds used the same strategies reported by Emig and Britton, defined the *writing process* much as we know it today. Writing workshop provides a structure that allows students to be in control of their own writing process. They select their own topics, draft, revise, conference with peers and the teacher, edit their work, and publish in a variety of ways. They learn that writing is recursive as they move through the writing process. Not every student is at the same point in the process on any given day. One might be prewriting, another revising a draft, others editing and preparing for publishing. Others might decide to start a new piece. Minilessons on procedure as well as skills are key components of the workshop model. Minilessons usually last ten to fifteen minutes (Atwell 1998).

An important element of the writing workshop is revision. Often, when teachers ask students to revise their written pieces, they simply copy everything neatly, correct some spelling errors, and turn in their "revised" work. One way to help students learn the revision process during writing workshop is to teach a minilesson on responding to other students' writing with good questions. Following the minilesson, the teacher can put students into small groups and have them read their pieces aloud to one another. Then, following the model from the minilesson, students can ask each other questions such as "What was her name?" "What color was the dress?" "What was he thinking?" or "I'd like to know more about . . ." and "What did he say?" These questions and comments help the authors to add interesting details.

In classes that use writing workshop, students are involved in a variety of activities. Students might revise by cutting their stories apart and then rearranging them, inserting new sections and taking out sections that no longer fit. With the help of minilessons, students learn to add dialogue, colorful details, imagery, and various other literary elements to their writing. They write or type their pages, illustrate them, and make covers to produce individual books that can go in the classroom library. Younger students might show their pride in their accomplishments during an authors' tea to which family, friends, administrators, and community members can be invited. Such events help students see themselves as writers.

Another common practice in classes with writing workshop is *author's chair*, a time when students can read their finished work to their classmates. The author's chair is powerful. Although it is often used as a way of generating peer response for the writer, it can also simply provide the opportunity for sharing written work. One teacher explained that author's chair changed her ELLs from nonwriters to enthusiastic writers. Once they experienced the author's chair, they came to class with pieces they'd written at home, eager to share. They were thinking about writing even when they weren't writing and then writing on their own. They began to see themselves as writers with something to share.

Another teacher had brought a rocking chair to her fourth-grade classroom for the author's chair. When she was leaving at midyear to take on another assignment, her students demanded to know if she was taking the author's chair. They negotiated. She agreed to leave the chair till the end of the year, at which time she would retrieve it.

Writing is thinking. Often writers don't fully know what they are writing about, but as they write, they discover their topic and are able to develop those ideas. Writing is fundamental in all subjects. The National Writing Project advocates journal writing as integral to content courses.

Students in a math class might write in journals daily to explain the math concepts and processes they are studying and to reflect on what they have learned. As they write, they clarify and solidify their understanding of those concepts and processes. The teacher can use the journals to pinpoint areas of fuzzy thinking and clarify misunderstandings and confusions and to plan future lessons. In a science class students can keep observation logs for their science experiments. They can use these logs when they write up their findings. Students in art classes can use journals to describe pieces of art they are studying. They can also try to reproduce different elements of art as they learn about line, color, texture, and perspective. Students in each content area can use writing to improve their thinking.

The key to effective writing instruction is to help students develop basic writing skills during writing workshop and to also use writing to improve thinking in all content area subjects. When students write each day in all their classes, their writing improves dramatically.

Encouraging students to write about what they know and have experienced, and allowing them to write in their first language, will also free them to write more confidently. All students at every age and step of development benefit from being immersed in reading and writing throughout the day and throughout the year. Much as a parent's embrace builds a child's general confidence, the embrace of good multicultural literature, engaging content texts, and an encouraging writing environment builds students' confidence in their literacy.

The Writing Process in Sixth Grade

Ms. Chen engages her sixth graders in the writing workshop three days each week. Half of her students have been in bilingual classes. Several entered the United States earlier this year and are at the beginner stage of English language development. A few were in bilingual classes the previous year only. They came to her class with varying levels of English proficiency.

Earlier in the year in a series of procedural minilessons, Ms. Chen's students learned the routine she expects them to follow. Each day her students pick up their writing journals, settle at their desks, and prepare for their writing. As soon as everyone is settled, Ms. Chen performs what Atwell (1998) terms the status of the class. As Ms. Chen quickly calls out their names, her students respond by stating their plan for the workshop period that day. As is typical, today several students indicate that they will work on revisions. Two girls report that they are ready for peer conferences, three students want to conference with the teacher, a few will edit, and three plan to begin working on new pieces.

Ms. Chen suggests that the two who are ready for peer response conferences meet together in the conferencing corner, where they will read their pieces to each other and provide responses that may help the writer during the revision process. Everyone gets right to work.

Ms. Chen has a word wall of words that students have used but have difficulty spelling. The word wall also includes colorful words that students have suggested for the wall.

Ms. Chen scans the room to ensure that all the students are engaged. She moves around the room, observing students at work. She crouches next to Jorge, who seems to be struggling, and asks, "How are things going?" Jorge frowns, then explains that he's writing a story about his brother who is in the army in Iraq. He misses him and really wants to express how special his brother is to him. He's written that his brother is special, that they've done lots of things together, and that he loves him so much.

Ms. Chen asks him some questions, then asks if there is one special time that he spent with his brother. His eyes light up. He turns to his writing and is on his way. Ms. Chen pats his shoulder and turns to another student. She makes contact with several students in similar brief exchanges and makes a point to touch base with the three students who had indicated that they wanted a teacher conference. James is experiencing a problem similar to Jorge's. Although he has written almost an entire page, most of it is in generalities. Ms. Chen asks him to circle the one word or phrase that he wants to describe in more detail. After reading over his piece, James circles a phrase. Ms. Chen suggests he focus on that and develop that idea. James seems relieved as he walks away.

Students are working at their own pace through the stages of the writing process. Most have four or five drafts as they work toward refining the content of their writing. Ms. Chen encourages her special needs students to use drawing for prewriting. They then are able to translate the drawing into sentences that describe their illustration. Ms. Chen knows that Javier will struggle to get his words on paper, so she has him dictate his story to another student, who records his dictation. During the revision process, these students are encouraged to make only one or two revisions.

Jennifer and Doug are both advanced writers and have decided to research on the Internet for background information that they might incorporate into their writing. Angelica, another advanced writer, is searching for places that she might submit her piece for publication.

During their peer response conferences, students provide valuable feedback. Ten minutes before the period ends, Ms. Chen asks for two or three students who are ready to read from the author's chair. Several eagerly volunteer. Students listen respectfully. At the end of each reading, students clap and say "thank you" along with words of praise and encouragement. As the bell signals the end of the period, students gather their writing portfolios, place them in the box designated for their period, and leave for their next class. As they leave, Ms. Chen overhears several telling each other about the pieces they worked on. Based on her brief conferences with students, she determines that a minilesson for the next workshop day should be on showing, not telling. She jots notes to herself and prepares to greet the next group of students.

Ms. Chen bases her lessons on the language arts standards. She demonstrates that she understands the foundation of the reading and writing processes. She plans her instruction to meet the academic as well as cultural and linguistic needs of her students. The writing workshop is an effective instructional approach for students to develop their writing skills. Ms. Chen includes minilessons to help students grow as writers, offering the support and structure they need. Students have control of their own writing as they make choices about what they will write about and how they shape their pieces with the support of their peers and their teacher. She helps all her students develop high levels of literacy that will serve them in all their classes.

Applications

1. Choose two short reading passages of equal difficulty that are appropriate for the person you will work with. Then write four comprehension questions for each passage. Hand the first passage to the reader and ask her to begin reading it aloud immediately. After she finishes reading it aloud, ask her the comprehension questions. Repeat the process, but this time have the person read the second passage silently before asking the questions. Was there a difference in comprehension? Why?

2. Select and read three picture books and two chapter books on a particular culture. Describe characteristics about that culture that you learn through the characters and their actions. How authentic are they? What biases or stereotypes do you detect? Discuss any of your beliefs about this culture that were confirmed or challenged through reading these books.

3. Writing for a real audience is important for young writers. Explore the Internet and locate three sites where students might be able to publish their writing. Describe each site, its accessibility, requirements, and limitations, and its acceptable use policy.

4. In this chapter we discuss how writing is hard, particularly when prompts are irrelevant to students' background and experiences. Write an essay describing a writing experience you had in school. The experience could have been negative or positive. Explain why it was so.

Key Terms and Acronyms

authentic contexts. Contexts that provide real experiences that help students to develop new concepts and related vocabulary.

author's chair. A place where students can sit to share their writing with others. The author's chair helps empower them to feel like real authors.

literacy. Understanding and interpreting the world, usually through reading and writing.

multicultural literature. Literature that depicts the lives of people from different cultures in an accurate and respectful manner. Students from different backgrounds can find themselves in this literature.

round-robin reading. When students take turns reading passages aloud from a text. The emphasis on pronunciation takes attention away from understanding and interpreting the text.

writing process. A recursive process that includes prewriting, drafting, revising, editing, and publishing. Writers work through the process at their own pace.

Resources for Further Study

International Reading Association: www.reading.org/

National Council of Teachers of English: www.ncte.org/

National Writing Project: www.writingproject.org/

Starfall website (ideas for teaching reading and writing): www.starfall.com/

11

Understanding the Human Experience Through Social Studies

Julio Noboa and Elsa Duarte-Noboa

Introduction: The Significance of Social Studies

Social studies teaching seeks to develop in students much more than the ability to memorize facts, name capitals, list presidents, or identify dates tied to historical events. Through social studies, the teacher provides students with opportunities to reflect on and understand the entire web of social, economic, and political relations that make up their daily lives.

Using historical approaches, social studies teachers encourage students to go beyond the specific conditions of their own lives and learn how others lived according to their particular time, place, and circumstance. Students also gain an ability to discover the commonalities as well as the differences among nations, cultures, and civilizations, and thus establish a foundation for understanding what it means to be human as well as what it means to be an American.

At the level of the *nation-state*, as in our own republic, having a literate, informed, and civic-minded citizenry is a well-established requirement for any democracy. Educators and most especially teachers of history, government, and civics play a vital role in shaping the political attitudes of citizens in a republic. Yet it is also vitally important that social studies educators provide to students the multicultural knowledge, skills, and understandings to compete in a *global economy*, one that is energized not only by the production and distribution of goods and services but also by the marketplace of ideas.

Social studies engages in this realm of ideas, especially those concerning democracy, equality, and freedom, yet it does so while firmly rooted in the landscapes of geography, the realities of economics, and the statutes of governance. Thus, the social studies teacher is challenged with the task of providing students not only with a considerable factual foundation of knowledge but also with the skills to analyze and interpret these realities to gain significant understanding of the human as well as the American experience. Perhaps one of the key challenges for teachers is to help students move beyond *ethnocentric* views, as many students prefer their own ethnic group's social traditions and cultural heritage and view these as superior to others.

That human experience in our nation is increasingly diverse in a variety of ways, as reflected in the growing demographic presence of Blacks, Latinos, Asians, and other ethnic minorities who have recently gained power and influence more commensurate with their numbers. Recent demographic data from the U.S. Census Bureau (2000) has confirmed that Latinos are now the largest ethnic minority in our nation, a reality that has begun to redefine the traditional Black-White paradigm of race relations in our nation and could potentially impact the teaching of social studies (Delgado and Stefancic 2001).

More than thirty-five million Hispanic Americans accounted for nearly 13 percent of the total U.S. population by the census year 2000, yet that figure does not include the millions of mostly Mexican undocumented workers nor the four million Puerto Ricans who are American citizens living on the island commonwealth. Not only are Latinos by far the largest minority, but they are among the youngest and fastest growing in our nation.

Some assimilationists are concerned that Latinos represent a threat to national unity by virtue of their Hispanic cultural and linguistic traditions (Huntington 2004). However, the fact that a majority of Latinos are bilingual speakers of two major international languages, and are bicultural citizens, capable of operating in two distinct cultural traditions, contributes to improved cross-cultural communication, a key source of unity within our nation and of understanding throughout the world.

Beyond ethnicity and race, diversity in the United States has several other key dimensions with strong historical roots, including gender, *social class*, religion, disability, citizenship, and sexual orientation. All of these impact the daily and future lives of our students. Social studies teachers are developing innovative approaches to impart among students a better appreciation of these differences as well as an understanding of how these interact at the individual and collective levels today and throughout history.

In response to the most recent research and practice, social studies educators have also developed ways to address the multiple intelligences of their students and provide appropriate pedagogy for students who are challenged by a variety of disabilities. Students with special needs have for more than a century included students who speak other languages at home, most particularly Spanish, a language with profound historical and cultural roots in many western and southwestern cities and states going back centuries (Rosales 1997; Kanellos 1998; Gonzalez 2000).

Considering bilingualism not as a disability but rather as an advantage, many multicultural educators encourage teachers to enrich their teaching or even to redefine it, by teaching in both languages and integrating bicultural elements from both the Anglo mainstream as well as the Latino experience into the classroom curriculum (Nieto 2004; Latham 1998; Valenzuela 1999).

As important as these and other current trends are, social studies teaching is still fundamentally guided by encompassing aims and specific objectives articulated more than a decade ago by the National Council for the Social Studies (NCSS 1994). These national curriculum standards have served as a model and resource for standards developed in almost every state. State social studies standards have then become the foundational guide not only for curricula but also for instructional methods and ultimately for the content of high-stakes assessments in the public schools of some states, tests that have taken on a greater significance since the establishment of No Child Left Behind (NCLB) as a federal mandate.

In this chapter, we identify the fundamental academic disciplines that constitute social studies and serve as sources of knowledge and as foundations for more specific secondary-level courses. We also provide background on the curriculum standards for social studies established by NCSS and define the organizing themes around which they are built. The discussion includes various state standards as well as some of the key political, religious, and ideological factors that have influenced their establishment.

Examples of research-based and culturally appropriate instructional methods are also provided with an emphasis on effective approaches for students with special needs, abilities, and disabilities. In addition we consider the influence of standardized testing on social studies teaching and identify some of the more authentic assessments being used today. The chapter then concludes with a scenario that demonstrates the use of effective and appropriate approaches to social studies teaching for diverse learners.

The Various Disciplines That Constitute Social Studies

There are a variety of social sciences and humanities disciplines that constitute the foundation for social studies. These disciplines serve as fountains of knowledge for social studies teaching and provide the specific facts and concepts as well as approaches to data-gathering methods used to obtain that knowledge.

Among these various disciplines are psychology, sociology, anthropology, political science, economics, and other social sciences as well as disciplines within the *humanities* such as art, literature, and history. For decades, the major disciplines reflected directly in the social studies curriculum that also served as organizing themes for integrating other branches of knowledge have been history, geography, economics, and government.

The concepts and elements from all of these disciplines are usually intertwined in the curricula at the level of the unit or even the lesson plan. More frequently, each of the four major disciplines is usually taught as several distinct courses such as U.S. history, world history, American government, and world geography, as well as introductory courses in such social sciences as economics, psychology, and anthropology.

One of the more interesting challenges for social studies teachers is to preserve on one hand the integrity of each discipline with its own concepts and methods of investigation and on the other to integrate these disciplines into a single meaningful lesson or unit. History and social studies teachers are aided in this task by the simple fact that many issues and problems do require solutions that utilize the knowledge derived from several disciplines. For this reason, good social studies teaching involves lessons using real-world situations, most particularly those involving civics or citizenship that are best understood using interdisciplinary approaches (NCSS 1994; *Executive Summary*).

National Social Studies Standards

The national curriculum standards for social studies are designed to answer for students, parents, educators, and policy makers several key questions, namely what students should be taught, how they will be taught, and how student achievement will be evaluated. The standards also specify the what, how, and when of social studies teaching for the early grades, middle school, and high school.

Social studies standards were developed concurrently with those of several other educational areas, most notably the closely related National Geography Standards (Geography Education Standards Project 1994) but also those in every major academic subject area. With the support of NCSS, educators were able to create a task force consisting of teachers from all levels, social studies supervisors, and teacher educators. The task force developed the standards from 1993 to 1994, and after considerable feedback and review, the standards were approved by the NCSS board in 1994. That fall, the standards were published in book form and disseminated throughout the nation, accompanied by discussions and training workshops at national, state, and local venues (NCSS 1994).

The Ten Themes

The basis of the social studies standards are ten thematic strands, each of which includes and integrates facts and concepts from the various social science and humanities disciplines. They are each briefly identified and described in Figure 11.1.

I. CULTURE: Social studies programs should include experiences that provide for the study of culture and cultural diversity.

II. TIME, CONTINUITY, AND CHANGE: Social studies programs should include experiences that provide for the study of the ways human beings view themselves in and over time.

III. PEOPLE, PLACES, AND ENVIRONMENTS: Social studies programs should include experiences that provide for the study of people, places, and environments.

IV. INDIVIDUAL DEVELOPMENT AND IDENTITY: Social studies programs should include experiences that provide for the study of individual development and identity.

V. INDIVIDUALS, GROUPS, AND INSTITUTIONS: Social studies programs should include experiences that provide for the study of interactions among individuals, groups, and institutions.

VI. POWER, AUTHORITY, AND GOVERNANCE: Social studies programs should include experiences that provide for the study of how people create and change structures of power, authority, and governance.

VII. PRODUCTION, DISTRIBUTION, AND CONSUMPTION: Social studies programs should include experiences that provide for the study of how people organize for the production, distribution, and consumption of goods and services.

VIII. SCIENCE, TECHNOLOGY, AND SOCIETY: Social studies programs should include experiences that provide for the study of relationships among science, technology, and society.

IX. *GLOBAL CONNECTIONS*: Social studies programs should include experiences that provide for the study of global connections and interdependence.

X. CIVIC IDEALS AND PRACTICES: Social studies programs should include experiences that provide for the study of the ideals, principles, and practices of citizenship in a democratic republic. (NCSS 1994, 2–12)

---

figure 11.1 The Ten Social Studies Themes

Political, Religious, and Ideological Influences

At every level, from the national to the state and local, the development, approval, and establishment of social studies standards into law involved contentious debates. Individual citizens, organizations, and academics who adhere to a variety of political, religious, and ideological views expressed widely differing opinions.

Although social studies teaching has long been a matter of much heated debate in our nation, especially in response to the questions of what to teach and whose version of history should be taught, the discussion rose to dramatic proportions with the controversy surrounding the National History Standards. Written by academic historians, experienced educators, and social science scholars under the auspices of the National Center for History in the Schools, these history standards also incorporated elements from the extraordinary blossoming of more recent historical research that finally included women and minorities into the historical narrative from which they had been systematically excluded for centuries.

Nevertheless, the National History Standards were widely criticized and condemned by conservative academics and in newspaper op-ed pieces, television talk shows, and on right wing radio throughout the country as being too politically correct, ignoring important historical figures, and giving too much attention to women and minority groups. Fueled by this intense propaganda campaign, even the Congress got involved and passed a sense-of-the-Senate resolution in January 1995, rejecting the standards in a ninety-nine-to-one vote (Nash, Crabtree, and Dunn 1997). It is interesting and perhaps ironic to note that when a tally of all the national figures mentioned in the National History Standards is taken, the majority of these are still white males, the same majority that is reflected in the U.S. Senate itself.

Responding to Diversity and Inequality

Much of the controversy surrounding social studies standards is generated by the need to respond to the growing diversity in our nation, affecting not only the content of the curriculum in terms of what is worth studying but also the instructional approaches used to reach students with diverse needs and characteristics.

The exclusion and marginalization of women and minorities from the content of history and social studies courses and textbooks, in particular, have been well documented for many decades (Garcia 1980, 1993). Although considerable progress has been made in recent years, certain groups, most significantly Latinos, are still relatively ignored and underrepresented in standards as well as in textbooks even in a state such as Texas, where Mexican Americans have had a cultural and historical presence for centuries (Noboa 2006).

Closely associated with the issues of racial, ethnic, and cultural diversity are the economic realities of poverty, underemployment, and substandard housing that, together with continued institutional discrimination, maintain structures of inequality for many minority groups. Among the educational implications of this inequality is that, because of the widespread use of property taxes as a basis for funding local school districts, most students of color today are in segregated schools with inadequate funding, meager resources, poorly qualified teachers, and inferior curricula (Kozol 2005).

In addition to these social and economic concerns that affect many students, social studies educators are also grappling with providing relevant and effective instruction to the diverse students in our classrooms, including English language learners (ELLs), immigrant and migrant students, students with a variety of disabilities, and students who are gifted and talented. History and social studies educators have found instructional strategies to respond to these challenges that have proven to be effective with a wide variety of students.

Instructional Strategies for Diverse Students

Social studies classes should naturally integrate all the social sciences and humanities including history, geography, literature, anthropology, and art. Successful teachers, especially at the elementary level, use social studies themes to integrate other subjects as well, such as math, science, and language arts, in their *interdisciplinary* units. Most children, including ELLs and special education students, are able to make learning connections among content taught in thematic units using interdisciplinary approaches (Jensen 1998; Wood 2005). Students labeled as gifted and talented also benefit from this approach.

Since the early 1990s, educators have been paying special attention to neuroscientific (brain) research, which points to the importance of creating a stimulating classroom environment. Other research has pointed to the value of ensuring that the classroom is also a caring environment where students feel appreciated and affirmed (Noddings 1984).

Jensen (1998) and Sylwester (1998) emphasize the role of emotion in the classroom. Education should be linked to emotion because the brain's emotional system drives learning and memory. Students can feel emotionally connected to their learning through such activities as debates, simulations, and storytelling. This approach is especially good for gifted and talented students, who can use their creativity to express new understandings. All of these strategies with the use of visuals have also been recognized as helping ELLs and special needs populations.

In addition, our diverse students exhibit multiple intelligences (Gardner 2006), and these different ways of learning may also be engaged or ignored in a teacher's particular instructional style. Teaching with the knowledge and recognition of multiple intelligences, be they linguistic, musical, naturalistic, kinesthetic, or any of the other five identified by Gardner thus far, allows teachers to see their students as complex individuals with many gifts as well as needs (Moran, Kornhaber, and Gardner 2006).

Also, understanding and recognizing the individual learning styles of students allows teachers to better assess their understandings, talents, and weaknesses (Dunn and Dunn 1978). Given the variety of instructional methods available to social studies teachers, they are in a perfect position to survey what their students' learning styles are and to create lessons that allow students to engage in their preferred styles.

Often a special education student labeled with a learning disability can draw the most significant picture in a cooperative learning project. When an English language learner comes out with the brilliant idea to represent freedom of speech in a TV ad, and the African American hip-hopper brainstorms a rap to illustrate the Bill of Rights, students are not only showing what they know but also demonstrating that they are being smart at what they do best. Teachers can be assured not only that their instruction is effective but that other students will also increase their understanding of concepts by learning from and with their peers (Mastropieri, Scruggs, and Berkeley 2007).

Relevancy and Culturally Relevant Pedagogy

Social studies and history in particular are subjects most American students dread because of the antiquated approaches some teachers still use (Shaughnessy and Haladyna 1985). Yet social studies can become the most relevant class because it deals with people as well as events that affect them, and students are naturally drawn to human stories of struggle. We encourage social studies teachers to relate historical events to current events as much as possible. Social studies educators should be informed about current events, especially in the specialized area(s) they teach. Civics and government teachers should empower their students not only to vote every two years but to analyze current issues that affect them, their community, their state, and the world.

Teachers should encourage students to take stands and approach the appropriate governmental agencies or officials to solve problems.

A four-year study titled *Quality 2000: Advancing Early Care and Education* contains eight recommendations with concomitant strategies based on national and international research. In presenting the highlights of this study, Kagan and Neuman (1997) describe the importance of implementing strategies that promote both cultural pluralism and sensitivity. These authors view the understanding and expression of one's own cultural values and beliefs as a springboard to learning about other cultures and ultimately to appreciating diversity.

Culturally relevant pedagogy, according to Ladson-Billings (1995), must provide a way for students to maintain their cultural integrity while succeeding academically. According to Violand-Sánchez and Hainer-Violand (2006), addressing the needs of Latino students means acknowledging and capitalizing on the cultural and linguistic strengths that students bring to the classroom. Schools should foster a positive ethnic identity by viewing bilingualism as an asset and immigration as a source of pride, empower Latino students through leadership roles within the school and community, and encourage student voice by having students speak and write from experience.

Learning to respect oneself and others is a major goal of social studies. Researchers have already proven how students' self-esteem affects their learning (Nieto 2004). Therefore, when teacher and students understand the importance of respect for all, collaboration, empathy, and learning will blossom.

Multiple and Multicultural Perspectives

History and social studies teachers should encourage students to see multiple perspectives in events, issues, and daily living. Teachers can bring in different readings, films, music, and other materials that illustrate what others might be feeling, thinking, and expressing. Teachers should go beyond mainstream media and access alternative media such as *Democracy Now!* on Free Speech cable TV; Alternet.org and TomPiane.com on the Internet; and *The Nation* or *Mother Jones* for print media. Primary documents and children's literature can bring in perspectives not covered in the mainstream textbooks. Students can also use critical thinking skills in comparing and contrasting political cartoons, journals or diaries, newspaper articles, and even their textbooks.

Understanding diverse perspectives is also one of the major objectives of multicultural education, an approach to curriculum and instruction that recognizes and integrates into classroom teaching the traditions, perspectives, and contributions of diverse cultures represented in our nation and throughout the world (Nieto 2004; Banks 1999). Although controversial and often vilified by *Eurocentric* and *Anglocentric* educators and academics who believe their European or Anglo-American cultures are in every way inherently superior to others, multicultural educators have continued to generate resources, research, and writings that despite influential opposition continue to impact public schooling in America (Schlesinger 1991; Loewen 1995; Levine 1996; Banks 2006). Effective social studies teachers who take multiple and multicultural perspectives incorporate a number of materials and techniques to make their teaching exciting and relevant to all their students, including the following:

Multicultural children's literature • Most children enjoy and learn from quality children's literature that is authentic and illustrates historical and cultural realities. Recently, there has been an explosion of children's literature that engages children's minds and hearts. A useful resource is the annual NCSS Notable Trade Books for Young People list as well as the ten guidelines by the Council on Interracial Books for Children (Rethinking Schools 1994).

In addressing the issue of school dropouts, Ramírez and Ramírez (1994) believe that it is only when Mexican American students learn through literature that celebrates their unique culture that education will seize their interest. They urge the publishers of children's books to offer stories that legitimize the Mexican American dual heritage as a way to help reduce the dropout rate. Teachers who value the Hispanic child's home and family preserve and build on the child's cultural values, thus raising that child's self-esteem. Like all other children, Hispanic children do well in warm, nurturing environments. Teachers who demonstrate tolerance for and interest in other cultures show how each person, adult or child, is valued.

Experiential exercises, simulations, and role-playing • There's an old Native American saying that claims in order to understand your neighbor, you must walk in his moccasins. We can understand things better when we feel conditions or events because we are drawn by our universal humanity to empathize with others. Teachers can use the powerful tool of experiential exercises or simulations, giving students opportunities to act out historical or cultural roles that produce deeper understanding of human reactions. Refer to the History Alive! website listed at the end of the chapter to access more sources for these exercises.

Critical thinking skills and writing • If social studies education is to prepare students to live harmoniously in a democratic society and with our global neighbors, then critical thinking skills become a priority. Analyzing the past, preparing for the future, making decisions, and engaging in civic projects require higher orders of thinking than the basics that were so popular in the 1970s.

Low-income schools that focus mostly on basic skills end up demotivating students to learn. Although teaching basic skills is important, it is also necessary to encourage our students to approach materials, events, literature, or media in a critical manner; otherwise, teachers are dumbing down the curriculum, something that students themselves will recognize and reject.

Students with disabilities, ELLs, and low-income students struggle with writing for many reasons. Immersing students in quality literature is a sure way of captivating students' interests. Encouraging students to respond and express themselves from the early grades on gives students confidence in their ability to communicate. Students should be encouraged to write daily in many different areas of the curriculum and for many different purposes. In the social studies, students can reflect on and write about a variety of sources, including their own experiences, historical events, interior monologues, historical retellings of events, journal entries, newspaper articles, and poetry.

Gentle feedback and revising should be encouraged and students should have opportunities to share their writings with others. Teachers must also model writing in the classroom and be aware of the connections between reading and writing (Bower, Lobdell, and Swenson 1994).

Cooperative learning and problem-solving group work • Researchers report that cooperative learning activities and problem-solving group work promote students' motivation, interaction, productivity, and understanding of content and concepts. Teachers are advised to design multiability groups in which all members are responsible for a task necessary to fulfill a designated goal. Once the groups are formed, teachers need to go over expected rules and procedures to guide students into collaborative and meaningful projects (Mastropieri, Scruggs, and Berkeley 2007). Cohen reminds us that "groupwork is an effective technique for achieving certain kinds of intellectual and social learning goals. It is a superior technique for conceptual learning, for creative problem solving, and for increasing oral language proficiency" (1986, 6).

Graphic organizers and representations • The students of the twenty-first century are extremely visual. Taking into consideration learning styles and multiple intelligences, teachers should keep in mind how important it is to illustrate graphically. Through the use of pictures, old paintings, political cartoons, films, maps, concept maps, and other visual aids, students are better able to make connections, understand concepts much more vividly, and analyze them more clearly.

Technology • Using technology, students can research issues, explore aspects that regular textbooks could never cover, and engage in voicing their opinions and concerns. Students become empowered by the newly discovered knowledge, and their activism affirms their civic responsibilities. Skillful use of appropriate and relevant technology can generate global connections and learning for students and also promote multicultural literacy (Cummins and Sayers 1995).

Unfortunately, because of the expense of hardware and software, those in low-income schools and homes are not able to provide the technology students deserve to use and master. There are many available grants to help underfunded schools or classroom teachers acquire technology. At school, teachers should capitalize on any and all opportunities to use technology with students. Yet teachers also must be very careful about assigning homework that requires technology not accessible to all students. Schools serving low-income students should allow students to use computers and other resources before and after school in order to help balance the economic inequities over which students have little control.

Standardized Testing and Appropriate Assessment

For decades, there has been much discussion and controversy regarding the influence that high-stakes standardized tests have on the teaching of social studies and other subject areas, and the disagreements on this matter show no signs of abating. The critics of standardized testing, most particularly Madaus (1988), almost two decades ago warned that teachers would teach to the test and adjust their instruction to its format and, ultimately, that the control over the curriculum would be transferred over to the test developers.

Since the establishment of the No Child Left Behind mandates in 2001, educators in many states have been grappling with the fact that, especially at the elementary level, social studies teaching has been considerably diminished or ignored altogether because more time and effort are focused on the tested subjects such as math, science, and language arts (Brewer 2006; Bustamante Jones 2006).

Beyond these concerns, many diverse students who derive particular benefit from multicultural approaches to instruction are especially affected by the negative influences standardized testing has on multicultural teaching. Since there's no way of knowing precisely which facts will be covered on the test, teaching history or social studies becomes a sort of memory Olympics, thus leaving no time for more in-depth understanding that is the foundation of teaching multiculturally (Bigelow 2006).

Typically, social studies teachers have used multiple-choice and true-or-false questions in exams that test low-level skills. More effective teachers, however, use a variety of approaches to assess their students. There are alternative types of assessments that go beyond memorization and the regurgitation of factoids as measured by worksheets, quizzes, short answers, and multiple-choice tests. These multiple-ability assessments are designed to permit students with different abilities to demonstrate their skills and knowledge in a variety of ways. Among these are engaging activities that involve using technology, such as preparing a travel brochure for a historic site, creating a cartoon or visual metaphor, or videotaping a reenactment of a historical event (Bower, Lobdell, and Swenson 1994).

Students could be asked to respond spontaneously to a simulated historical event or situation, or they could work in cooperative learning groups to explore a provocative question. At a more individual level, students could be challenged with a culminating project in addition to the usual final test, such as an oral history project or museum project. These types of assessment approaches engage students in a process of research, writing, evaluation, and presentation that expands their knowledge, deepens their understanding, and develops their social studies skills.

While there is no assurance that the particular knowledge students gain from these more authentic assessments will be on the state standardized tests, the teacher can use the established curriculum standards upon which the test is based to identify much of the information most likely to be tested. Using this strategy, history and social studies teachers can enrich their approaches to instruction, better prepare all their students for the high-stakes standardized tests, and provide lessons and assessments more relevant and appropriate for diverse students.

Secondary Social Studies Scenario

As can be surmised from the previous discussion, social studies teachers have a wide repertoire of approaches, strategies, and methods available to them, as well as abundant sources to draw from in print, on video and DVD, and on the Internet. The following scenario, from the secondary level, illustrates how methods and resources as well as valuable learning objectives can be combined to create an effective lesson for diverse learners.

Multiple Perspectives on the Mexican American War

Students are very aware of the struggles of the African Americans who suffered great injustices as slaves in the United States. Upon learning about this era, students are moved and sometimes passionate about the human suffering that took place before and during the Civil War. However, another historically pivotal conflict, namely the Mexican American War, is usually covered by too many teachers who use the official textbook in a very superficial way while ignoring the human suffering on both sides of that war. Thus, American students miss a key opportunity to understand the historical roots and early struggles of the Mexican American people, one of the largest, oldest, and fastest growing ethnic minorities in our nation. In this scenario, a history teacher, Elsa, provides a student-centered lesson integrating some of the strategies mentioned earlier to impart to her students a deeper understanding of social and historical perspectives.

She begins by asking, "What do you know about the Mexican American War?" Elsa uses this question not only to spark the students' interest but also to assess what students already know, or think they know, about the topic. She then asks her students to read the version in their history textbook. After a brief discussion and summary of the textbook version, she introduces her students to a variety of texts retelling the story of the Mexican American War.

Elsa guides her students toward considering the different perspectives presented in the various texts. Then she introduces students to several primary sources, including letters and diaries written by Mexican and American soldiers, newspaper articles expressing the positions of President Polk, General Taylor, and congressmen from both the Democrat and the Whig parties. Statements from organizations such as the American Anti-slavery Society, influential writers such as Henry David Thoreau and Ralph Waldo Emerson, as well as Protestant and Catholic churches are also included. She integrates brief excerpts from Mexican textbooks, websites, newspapers, and historical accounts into this initial discussion as well.

Next, Elsa forms heterogeneous groups, carefully choosing students with complementary talents and skills as well as diverse genders and backgrounds to work together. She gives each group a perspective to research and analyze. After the groups conduct their research, they present their findings to the entire class. Elsa encourages the students to use different ways to demonstrate what they have learned. She suggests they produce as an essay, song, poem, political cartoon, recruiting poster, diary entry, letter, newspaper article, or short skit. Besides capturing their perspective and illustrating it in a presentation, the students are also responsible for creating a page or two of talking points to be distributed among their classmates, presenting a clear statement of their assigned perspective along with sources and references.

At the end of the project, after the groups conduct and present their research, Elsa asks each student to reflect on a collection of sources expressing various perspectives on the Mexican American War. For this phase of the unit, she guides students in the strategic use of their own school library and the Internet to secure both primary and secondary resources. Elsa encourages students with Spanish literacy skills to seek Mexican historical sources, including Internet sites, discussing the "United States Invasion." She assists special education students so they can participate as much as possible. Altogether, the student groups will be responsible for presenting at least six to eight different perspectives, with at least two expressing a Mexican view. Instead of making group assignments, Elsa lists the multiple perspectives from which student groups can choose, making sure that all key perspectives are included.

This project takes about two weeks. During this student-centered project, Elsa acts as guide, coach, and facilitator for her students. She is responsible for helping her students access appropriate and credible resources and for designing an equitable and project-specific evaluation rubric with significant student input. This unit reflects practices that align with the social studies standards and with best practices for all students. Figure 11.2 lists sources for this project.

Background Information for Teachers on the Mexican American War

Bigelow, Bill. 2006. "The U.S.–Mexico War Tea Party." Teaching activity. In *The Line Between Us: Teaching About the Border and Mexican Immigration*, 43–51. Milwaukee, WI: Rethinking Schools.

Public Broadcasting System. 1995. *U.S. Mexican War.* Video series. www.pbs.org/kera/usmexicanwar/index_flash.html.

Zinn, Howard. 2006. "We Take Nothing by Conquest, Thank God." In *The Line Between Us: Teaching About the Border and Mexican Immigration*, by Bill Bigelow, 53–59. Milwaukee, WI: Rethinking Schools.

Other Suggested Perspectives to Investigate

General Santa Ana	General Winfield Scott
Mariano Paredes y Arrillaga	John Quincy Adams
Melchor Ocampo	John L. O'Sullivan
Los Ninos Heroes de Chapultepec	St. Patrick's Battalion
poor Mexican farmers	poor Americans lured to enlist
Benito Juarez	Abraham Lincoln

figure 11.2 Background Information for Teachers on the Mexican American War

Applications

1. Tracing a Concept: Select a concept such as democracy, equality, or revolution that has a long history in a wide variety of cultures, and trace either its origins, dissemination, variations, or social and economic implications. Search out information from many print, audiovisual, and Internet sources, and create a written report or electronic slideshow presentation with references that summarizes your most significant findings. Throughout the entire process, utilize primary and secondary sources, incorporate social studies disciplines such as history and geography, and apply methods from these disciplines to gather, organize, and present your knowledge and understanding about this topic.

2. Evaluating U.S. History Textbooks: Obtain a history textbook for U.S. history and do a content analysis and, to the extent possible given your time and resources, focus on one or more of the following:

   a. Compare the number of individuals and events as well as pages dedicated to men versus women.

   b. Determine and compare the space, text, and illustrations focusing on Latinos, African Americans, and Native Americans.

   c. Determine the extent to which the experiences of women and/or minorities are valued, or given importance.

   d. Determine the extent to which the women and/or ethno-racial minorities are represented as actors in history who exert some positive influence on society.

   e. Determine the extent to which the views, opinions, and perspectives of women and/or minorities are presented in a fair and objective way either as a group or through their leaders.

3. Evaluating World History Textbooks: Obtain a world history textbook and conduct similar analyses to those mentioned in the previous activity, focusing on the representation of women throughout history or on the representation of peoples, cultures, and civilizations of Africa, Asia, the Middle East, or Latin America.

4. Evaluating Standards: Obtain the social studies standards for your own or another state, and focus on a specific elementary grade level or on a secondary-

level U.S. or world history course. Conduct an analysis of the individuals, groups, concepts, and events related to women and/or to people of color in the context of that grade level or within the scope of that course.

Key Terms and Acronyms

Anglocentric. A form of bias that assumes the inherent superiority of English and Anglo-American society, culture, and language.

ethnocentric. Having a strong preference for your own ethnic group's social traditions and cultural heritage and viewing these as superior to others.

Eurocentric. A form of bias that assumes the inherent superiority of European and European American societies, cultures, and languages.

global connections. The cultural and communicative links among individuals, societies, and nations across geographic boundaries and distances, enhanced by the Internet and modern technology.

global economy. The economic interaction and interchanges of raw materials, capital, energy, manufactured goods, and a variety of services on a worldwide scale.

humanities. Generally refers to all the fields of human thought and creativity, including the arts, music, dance, drama, literature, history, and philosophy.

interdisciplinary. Involving the combined use of knowledge, concepts, and methods from different disciplines such as ecology, history, and mathematics in classroom instruction.

nation-state. A political entity defined by geographic boundaries, a common central government, and a particular historical and cultural tradition.

NCLB. The federal No Child Left Behind Act, authorized in 2001, whose mandates include standardized testing as the primary tool for educational assessment.

NCSS. National Council for the Social Studies. The primary national organization for social studies education.

social class. Term used to describe the variations of power and wealth among individuals and families based on income, occupation, and level of education.

Resources for Further Study

Internet sources for social studies are increasingly abundant. For a comprehensive and detailed guide, see *Surfing Social Studies* (Braun and Risinger 1999).

California History–Social Science Standards: www.cde.ca.gov/be/st/ss/hstmain.asp

Education Minnesota: www.educationminnesota.org/index.cfm?PAGE_ID=9441

Educators for Social Responsibility: www.esrnational.org/

History Alive! online resources: www.teachtci.com/resources/onlHistory.aspx

Illinois Learning Standards for Social Science: www.isbe.state.il.us/ils/
social_science/standards.htm

National Association for Multicultural Education: www.nameorg.org/

National Center for History in the Schools: http://nchs.ucla.edu/

National Council for the Social Studies: www.ncss.org/

National Geographic EdNet: www.ngsednet.org/

National Standards for History: http://nchs.ucla.edu/standards/

National Standards for World History: http://w3.iac.net/~pfilio/part1.html

New York Social Studies Standards: www.emsc.nysed.gov/ciai/socst/socstands/
socstand.html

Population Connection education resources: www.populationeducation.org/

Rethinking Schools resources: www.rethinkingschools.org/

Texas social studies standards: www.tea.state.tx.us/rules/tac/chapter113/index.html

References

Aldridge, David, and Wolfgang Schmid. 2004. "Active Music Therapy in the Treatment of Multiple Sclerosis Patients: A Matched Control Study." *The Journal of Music Therapy* 41 (3): 225–40.

Ambert, Alba N., and Sarah E. Melendez. 1985. *Bilingual Education: A Sourcebook.* New York: Teachers College Press.

Anderson, Paul. 2007. "What Is Web 2.0? Ideas, Technologies, and Implications for Education." *JISC Technology and Standards Watch.* Retrieved December 20, 2007, from www.jisc.ac.uk/media/documents/techwatch/tsw0701b.pdf.

Anderson, Richard, and Peter Freebody. 1981. "Vocabulary Knowledge." In *Comprehension and Teaching: Research Reviews,* ed. J. T. Guthrie, 77–117. Newark, DE: International Reading Association.

Angelou, Maya. 1994. *The Complete Collected Poems of Maya Angelou.* New York: Random House.

Anzaldúa, Gloria. 1987. *Borderlands/La Frontera: The New Mestiza.* San Francisco: Aunt Lute.

Archambault, Francis S., Karen L. Westberg, Scott W. Brown, Bryan W. Hallmark, Christine Emacons, and Wanli Zang. 1993. *Regular Classroom Practices with Gifted Students: Results of a National Survey of Classroom Teachers.* Research Monograph 93102. The National Research Center on Gifted and Talented. Storrs: University of Connecticut.

Atwell, Nancie. 1998. *In the Middle.* 2d ed. Portsmouth, NH: Heinemann.

Banks, James A. 1993. "Multicultural Education for Young Children: Racial and Ethnic Attitudes and Their Modification." In *Handbook of Research on the Education of Young Children*, ed. Bernard Spodek, 236–50. New York: Macmillan.

———. 1999. *An Introduction to Multicultural Education*. 2d ed. Boston: Allyn and Bacon.

———. 2006. *Cultural Diversity and Education: Foundations, Curriculum, and Teaching*. Boston: Allyn and Bacon.

Banks, James, Marilyn Cochran-Smith, Luis Moll, Anna Richert, Kenneth Zeichner, Pamela LePage, Linda Darling-Hammond, Helen Duffy, and Morva McDonald. 2005. "Teaching Diverse Learners." In *Preparing Teachers for a Changing World: What Teachers Should Learn and Be Able to Do*, ed. Linda Darling-Hammond and John Bransford, 232–74. San Francisco: Jossey-Bass.

Berliner, David. 2005. "If the Underlying Premise for No Child Left Behind Is False, How Can That Act Solve Our Problems?" In *Saving Our Schools: The Case for Public Education*, ed. Kenneth Goodman and Yetta Goodman, 167–84. Berkeley, CA: RDR.

Bernal, Ernesto. 2003. "To No Longer Educate the Gifted: Programming for Gifted Students Beyond the Era of Inclusion." *Gifted Child Quarterly* 47 (3): 181–91.

Bigelow, Bill. 2006. *The Line Between Us: Teaching About the Border and Mexican Immigration*. Milwaukee: Rethinking Schools.

Bird, Marsha, Vicky Libby, Latosha Rowley, and Joseph Turner. 2002. "Plan for Making Meaning." *Primary Voices* 10 (3): 25–30.

Booth Olson, Carol. 2007. *The Reading/Writing Connection: Strategies for Teaching and Learning in the Secondary Classroom*. 2d ed. Boston: Allyn and Bacon.

Bower, Bert, Jim Lobdell, and Lee Swenson. 1994. *History Alive: Engaging All Learners in the Diverse Classroom*. Teachers Curriculum Institute. Menlo Park, CA: Addison-Wesley.

Braun, Joseph A., Jr., and C. Frederick Risinger. 1999. *Surfing Social Studies: The Internet Book*. Washington, DC: National Council for the Social Studies.

Bredekamp, Sue, and Carol Copple, eds. 1997. *Developmentally Appropriate Practice in Early Childhood Programs*. Rev. ed. Washington, DC: National Association for the Education of Young Children.

Brewer, Ernest A. 2006. "Keep Social Studies in the Elementary School." *Childhood Education* 82 (5): 296–98.

Bridgeland, John, John Dilulio, et al. 2006. *The Silent Epidemic: Perspectives of High School Dropouts*. Washington, DC: Civic Enterprises.

Britton, James, Tony Burgess, Nancy Martin, Alex McLeod, and Harold Rosen. 1992. *The Development of Writing Abilities* (11–18). Urbana, IL: National Council of Teachers of English.

Bruner, Jerome. 1960. *The Process of Education*. Cambridge: Harvard University Press.

————. 1996. *The Culture of Education*. Cambridge: Harvard University Press.

Burton, Sara, and Linda C. Edwards. "Creative Play: Building Connections with Children Who Are Learning English." *Dimensions of Early Childhood* (Spring/Summer): 3–9.

Bussert-Webb, Kathy. 2001. "I Won't Tell You About Myself, but I Will Draw My Story." *Language Arts* 78 (6): 511–19.

————. 2005. "An After-School Cultural Arts Program." *Academic Exchange Quarterly* 9 (3): 24–29.

————. 2006. "Community Words." *State of Reading Online Journal* (Fall). Retrieved March 18, 2007, from www.tsra.us/state_of_reading.htm.

Bustamante Jones, E. 2006. "What Happened to Social Studies and Civics Education? Looking at the Effects of Accountability on Immigrant Children, Second-Language Learners, and the Urban Poor." In *Language and Literacy in Schools*, ed. Robert T. Jimenez and Valerie Ooka Pang. Westport, CT: Praeger.

Canclini, Nestor García. 1995. *Consumidores y ciudadanos: Conflictos multiculturales de la globalización*. Mexico: Grijalbo.

Carbone, Eric. 2001. "Arranging the Classroom with an Eye (and Ear) to Students with ADHD." *Teaching Exceptional Children* 34 (2): 72–81.

Carlson, Judith K., Dorothy Gray, and Janalea Hoffman. 2004. "A Musical Interlude: Using Music and Relaxation to Improve Reading Performance." *Intervention in School and Clinic* 39 (4): 246–50.

Carolan, Jennifer, and Abigail Guinn. 2007. "Differentiation: Lessons from Master Teachers." *Educational Leadership* 64 (5): 44–47.

Carpenter, Thomas, and Richard Lehrer. 1999. "Teaching and Learning Mathematics with Understanding." In *Mathematics Classrooms That Promote Understanding*, ed. Elizabeth Fennema and Thomas Romberg, 19–54. Mahwah, NJ: Lawrence Erlbaum.

Casares, Oscar. 2003. *Brownsville: Stories*. Boston: Back Bay.

Castañeda, Juan. 1999. "La cultura: Una señora grande y gorda de la que todos hablan y nadie ha podido conocer." In *La cultura como principio de organización*, ed. R. S. Gómez Zúniga and M. Marmolejo Marmelejo, 18–23. Cali, Colombia: Universidad del Valle.

Chamberlain, Steven P. 2003. "An Interview with Evelyn Green and Perry Green." *Intervention in School and Clinic* 38 (5): 297–306.

————. 2005. "Recognizing and Responding to Cultural Differences in the Education of Culturally and Linguistically Diverse Learners." *Intervention in School and Clinic* 40 (4): 195–211.

Chang, Ji-Mei. 2001. "Monitoring Effective Teaching and Creating a Responsive Learning Environment for Students in Need of Support: A Checklist." *NABE News* 24 (3): 17–18.

Chapman, Alan. 2007. *Howard Gardner's Multiple Intelligences.* Retrieved April 20, 2007, from www.businessballs.com/howardgardnermultipleintelligences.htm.

Chau, Michelle, and Ayana Douglas-Hall. 2007. *Low Income Children in the United States: National and State Trend Data, 1996–2006.* New York: Task Force for National Center for Children in Poverty.

Chen, Jie-qi. 2004. "Theory of Multiple Intelligences: Is It a Scientific Theory?" *Teacher's College Record* 106 (4): 17–23.

Cisneros, Sandra. 1984. *The House on Mango Street.* Philadelphia: Chelsea House.

Clasen, Donna R., James A. Middleton, and Timothy J. Connell. 1994. "Assessing Autistic and Problem-Solving Performance in Minority and Nonminority Students Using a Nontraditional Multidimensional Model." *Gifted Child Quarterly* 38 (1): 27–32.

Cogangelo, Nicholas, Susan G. Assouline, and Miraca U. M. Gross. *A Nation Deceived: How Schools Hold Back America's Brightest Students.* Iowa City: University of Iowa Press.

Cogangelo, Nicholas, and Gary Davis, eds. 1990. *Handbook of Gifted Education.* Boston: Allyn and Bacon.

Cohen, Elizabeth. 1986. *Designing Groupwork: Strategies for the Heterogeneous Classroom.* New York: Columbia University, Teachers College Press.

Collier, Virginia. 1989. "How Long? A Synthesis of Research on Academic Achievement in a Second Language." *TESOL Quarterly* 23 (3): 509–32.

———. 1992. "A Synthesis of Studies Examining Long-Term Language Minority Student Data on Academic Achievement." *Bilingual Research Journal* 16 (1 and 2): 187–212.

Collier, Virginia, and Wayne Thomas. 2004. "The Astounding Effectiveness of Dual Language Education for All." *NABE Journal of Research and Practice* 2 (1): 1–19.

Columbus Group. 1991. Unpublished Transcript of the Meeting of the Columbus Group. Columbus, Ohio.

Conquergood, Dwight. 2002. "Performance Studies Interventions and Radical Research." *The Drama Review* 46 (2): 145–56.

Crawford, James. 1991. *Bilingual Education: History, Politics, Theory, and Practice.* Los Angeles: Bilingual Education Services.

———. 2004. *No Child Left Behind: A Misguided Approach to School Accountability for English Language Learners.* Washington, DC: National Association for Bilingual Education.

Creative Commons. Retrieved December 23, 2007 from www.creativecommons.org.

Csikszentmihalyi, Mihaly. 1990. *Flow: The Psychology of Optimal Experience*. New York: Harper & Row.

Cummins, Jim. 1981. "Empirical and Theoretical Underpinnings of Bilingual Education." *Journal of Education* 163 (1): 16–29.

———. 2000. "Biliteracy, Empowerment, and Transformative Pedagogy." In *The Power of Two Languages 2000: Effective Dual-Language Use Across the Curriculum*, ed. Josefina V. Tinajero and Robert A. DeVillar, 9–19. New York: McGraw-Hill School Division.

Cummins, Jim, and Dennis Sayers. 1995. *Brave New Schools: Challenging Cultural Illiteracy Through Global Learning Networks*. New York: St. Martin's.

Cunningham, Patricia M., and Richard L. Allington. 2007. *Classrooms That Work: They Can All Read and Write*. 4th ed. Boston: Pearson.

Curtis, Deb, and Margie Carter. 2006. *Designs for Living and Learning: Transforming Early Childhood Environments*. New York: Redleaf.

Darling-Hammond, Linda. 1996. "What Matters Most: A Competent Teacher for Every Child." *Phi Delta Kappan* 78 (3): 193–200.

Dauber, Susan L., and Camilla P. Benbow. 1990. "Aspects of Personality and Peer Relations of Extremely Talented Adolescents." *Gifted Child Quarterly* 34: 10–15.

Davis, Gary, and Sylvia Rimm. 2004. *Education of the Gifted and Talented*. 5th ed. Boston: Pearson Education.

Davis, Robert, Carolyn Maher, and Nel Noddings. 1990. "Introduction: Constructivist Views on the Teaching and Learning of Mathematics." In *Constructivist Views on the Teaching and Learning of Mathematics. JRME Monograph*, ed. Robert Davis, Carolyn Maher, and Nel Noddings, 7–18. Reston, VA: National Council of Teachers of Mathematics.

Delgado, Richard, and Jean Stefancic. 2001. *Critical Race Theory: An Introduction*. New York: New York University Press.

Delpit, Lisa D., and Joanne Kilgour Dowdy, eds. 2002. *The Skin We Speak: Thoughts on Language and Culture in the Classroom*. New York: New Press.

Deshler, Donald D., and Jean B. Schumaker. 2006. *Teaching Adolescents with Disabilities: Accessing the General Education Curriculum*. Thousand Oaks, CA: Corwin.

Dettmer, Peggy. 2006. "New Blooms in Established Fields: Four Domains of Learning and Doing." *Roeper Review* 28 (2): 70–82.

Dewey, John. 1897. "My Pedagogic Creed." *The School Journal* 54 (3): 77–80.

———. 1916. *Democracy and Education*. New York: McMillan.

Diamond, Jared. 1999/2003. *Guns, Germs, and Steel: The Fates of Human Societies.* New York: W. W. Norton.

Diaz-Rico, Lynne T., and Kathy Z. Weed. 2006. *The Cross-Cultural Language and Academic Development Handbook: A Complete K–12 Reference Guide.* 3d ed. New York: Pearson.

Drews, E. 1972. *Learning Together: How to Foster Creativity, Self-Fulfillment, and Social Awareness in Today's Students and Teachers.* Englewood Cliffs, NJ: Prentice Hall.

Dulay, Heidi, and Marianna Burt. 1974. "Natural Sequences in Child Second Language Acquisition." *Language Learning* 24: 37–53.

Dunn, Rita Stafford. 1993. *Teaching Secondary Students Through Individual Learning Styles: Practical Approaches for Grades 7–12.* Boston: Allyn and Bacon.

Dunn, Rita Stafford, and Kenneth Dunn. 1978. *Teaching Students Through Their Individual Learning Styles: A Practical Approach.* Englewood Cliffs, NJ: Prentice Hall.

D'Youville College. No date. *Health Services Administration: Learning Preferences.* Buffalo, NY: Author. Retrieved March 12, 2007, from http://ddl.dyc.edu/~hsa/learningstylesmar7.htm.

Early Learning Standards: Creating the Conditions for Success; A Joint Position Statement of the National Association for the Education of Young Children (NAEYC) and the National Association of Early Childhood Specialists in State Departments of Education (NAECS/SDE). 2002. Washington, DC: NAECS.

Educause. 2005. Seven Things You Should Know About Wikis. Retrieved December 23, 2007, from www.educause.edu/ir/library/pdf/ELI7004.pdf.

Ellis, Edwin S., and Patricia Friend. 1991. "Adolescents with Learning Disabilities." In *Learning About Learning Disabilities*, ed. Bernice Y. L. Wong, 505–61. San Diego, CA: Academic Press.

Emig, Janet. 1971. *The Composing Processes of Twelfth Graders.* Champaign, IL: National Council of Teachers of English.

Englebright-Fox, Jill. 2006. "Back to Basics." *Early Childhood News* (March/April): 12–15.

Epstein, Seymour. 1998. *Constructive Thinking: The Key to Emotional Intelligence.* Westport, CT: Praeger.

Fasko, Daniel, Jr. 2001. "An Analysis of Multiple Intelligences Theory and Its Use with the Gifted and Talented." *Roeper Review* 23 (3): 126–31.

Fiedler, Ellen D., Richard E. Lang, and Susan Winebrenner. 1993. "In Search of Reality: Unraveling the Myths About Tracking, Ability Grouping, and the Gifted." *Roeper Review* (16): 4–7.

Fielding, Cheryl. 2004. "Low Performance on High-Stakes Test Drives Special Education Referrals: A Texas Survey." *The Educational Forum* 68 (Winter): 126–32.

Fountas, Irene C., and Gay Su Pinnell. 2001. *Guiding Readers and Writers (Grades 3–6): Teaching Comprehension, Genre, and Content Literacy.* Portsmouth, NH: Heinemann.

Fraiser, Mary M. 1989. "Poor and Minority Students Can Be Gifted Too!" *Educational Leadership* 46 (6): 16–18.

———. 1991. "Disadvantaged and Culturally Diverse Gifted Students." *Journal for the Education of the Gifted* 14: 234–45.

———. 1995. *Educators' Perceptions of Barriers to Identification of Gifted Children from Economically Disadvantaged and Limited-English Proficient Backgrounds.* Report No. RM-95216. Storrs, CT: National Research Center on the Gifted and Talented. ERIC Document Reproduction Service No. ED402-707.

Fraiser, Mary M., Jaime H. Garcia, and A. Harry Passow. 1995. *A Review of Assessment Issues in Gifted Education and Their Implications for Identifying Gifted Minority Students.* Storrs: National Research Center on the Gifted and Talented, University of Connecticut.

Frank, Gwen. 2007. The Effect of Elementary Teachers' Professional Development Activities Intended to Increase the Number of Migrant Student Nominations for Gifted and Talented Programs. Final diss., University of Houston, May.

Freedman, Joshua, and Anabel Jensen. 2006. "Joy and Loss: The Emotional Lives of Gifted Children." Retrieved from www.kidsource.com/kidsource/content4/joy.loss.eq.gifted.html.

Freeman, David E., and Yvonne S. Freeman. 2001. *Between Worlds: Access to Second Language Acquisition.* Portsmouth, NH: Heinemann.

———. 2006a. Developing Academic Language for School Success. Paper presented at the International Reading Association Conference, May, Chicago.

———. 2006b. "Teaching Language Through Content Themes: Viewing Our World as a Global Village." In *Supporting the Literacy Development of English Learners: Increasing Success in All Classrooms,* ed. Terrel Young and Nancy Hardaway, 61–78. Newark, DE: International Reading Association.

———. 2007. *English Language Learners: The Essential Guide.* New York: Scholastic.

Freeman, Yvonne S., Ann Freeman, et al. 2003. "Home Run Books: Connecting Students to Culturally Relevant Texts." *NABE News* 26 (3): 5–8, 11–12.

Freeman, Yvonne S., and David E. Freeman. 1998. *ESL/EFL Teaching: Principles for Success.* Portsmouth, NH: Heinemann.

———. 2000. "Preview, View, Review: An Important Strategy in Multilingual Classrooms." *NABE News* 24 (2): 20–21.

———. 2002. *Closing the Achievement Gap: How to Reach Limited Formal Schooling and Long-Term English Learners.* Portsmouth, NH: Heinemann.

———. 2004. "Connecting Students to Culturally Relevant Texts." *Talking Points* 15 (2): 7–11.

Freeman, Yvonne S., David E. Freeman, and Sandra P. Mercuri. 2005. *Dual Language Essentials.* Portsmouth, NH: Heinemann.

Freire, Paulo. 1998. *Teachers as Cultural Workers: Letters to Those Who Dare Teach.* Oxford: Westview.

Frost, Joseph, Sue Wortham, and Stuart Raeifel. 2007. *Play and Child Development,* 2d ed. New York: Merrill Prentice Hall.

Fuchs, Douglas, Devery Mock, Paul L. Morgan, and Caresa L. Young. 2003. "Responsiveness-to-Intervention: Definitions, Evidence, and Implications for the Learning Disabilities Construct." *Learning Disabilities Research and Practice* 18 (3): 157–71.

Gagne, Francoys. 1995. "From Giftedness to Talent: A Developmental Model and Its Impact on the Field." *Roeper Review* 18: 103–17.

Gallagher, John, and Susan Gallagher. 1994. *Teaching the Gifted Child.* Boston: Allyn and Bacon.

García, Gilbert. 2000. *Lessons from Research: What Is the Length of Time It Takes Limited English Proficient Students to Acquire English and Succeed in an All-English Classroom?* Washington, DC: National Clearinghouse for Bilingual Education.

García, Jaime H. 1994. "Nonstandardized Instruments for the Assessment of Mexican American Children for Gifted and Talented Programs." In *Addressing Cultural and Linguistic Diversity in Special Education: Issues and Trends.* Reston, VA: Division of Culturally and Linguistically Diverse Exceptional Learners, Council for Exceptional Children (ED 379–814).

Garcia, Jesus. 1980. "Hispanic Perspective: Textbooks and Other Curricular Materials." *The History Teacher* 14 (1): 105–20.

———. 1993. "The Changing Image of Ethnic Groups in Textbooks." *Phi Delta Kappan* 75 (1): 29–35.

García, Shernaz B., and Alba A. Ortiz. 2006. "Preventing Disproportionate Representation: Culturally and Linguistically Responsive Prereferral Interventions." *Teaching Exceptional Children* 38 (4): 64–68.

Gardner, Howard. 1983. *Frames of Mind: The Theory of Multiple Intelligences.* New York: Basic.

———. 1986. "The Theory of Multiple Intelligences." *Annals of Dyslexia: An Interdisciplinary Journal of the Orton Dyslexia Society* XXXVII (November): 19–35.

———. 1993. *Multiple Intelligences: The Theory in Practice.* New York: Basic.

———. 1999. *Intelligence Reframed: Multiple Intelligences for the 21st Century.* New York: Basic.

———. 2006. *Multiple Intelligences: New Horizons*. New York. Basic.

Gardner, Howard, and T. Hatch. 1994. "Multiple Intelligences Go to School: Educational Implications of the Theory of Multiple Intelligences." *Educational Research* 18 (8): 4–9.

Gay, Geneva. 2000. *Culturally Responsive Teaching: Theory, Research, and Practice*. New York: Teachers College Press.

Gee, James P. 2004. *What Video Games Have to Teach Us About Learning and Literacy*. New York: Palgrove.

Geography Education Standards Project. 1994. *Geography for Life: National Geography Standards*. Washington, DC: National Geographic Research and Exploration.

Gestwicki, Carol. 2006. *Home, School, and Community Relations*. 6th ed. New York: Thompson-Delmar Learning.

Goleman, Daniel. 1995. *Emotional Intelligence: Why It Can Matter More Than IQ*. New York: Bantam.

Gómez, Leo, Yvonne S. Freeman, and David E. Freeman. 2005. "Dual Language Education: A Promising 50/50 Model." *Bilingual Research Journal* 29 (1): 145–64.

Gómez, Richard. 2006. "Promising Practices: Dual Language Enrichment for ELL Students, K–12." *Texas Association for Bilingual Education (TABE)* 9 (1): 46–65.

Gonzalez, Juan. 2000. *Harvest of Empire: A History of Latinos in America*. New York: Viking.

González, Norma, L. C. Moll, and C. Amanti, eds. 2005. *Funds of Knowledge: Theorizing Practices in Households, Communities, and Classrooms*. Mahwah, NJ: Lawrence Erlbaum.

Gonzalez-Jensen, Margarita, and Diane Gara-Weiner. 2000. "Using Art to Teach Language." *School Arts* 99 (8): 56–60.

Goodman, Ken, Patrick Shannon, Yetta Goodman, and Roger Rapoport, eds. 2005. *Saving Our Schools: The Case for Public Education; Saying No to "No Child Left Behind."* Berkeley, CA: RDR.

Google Earth™. n.d. Explore, Search and Discover. Retrieved December 24, 2007, at http://earth.google.com/.

Gordon, Raymond G., Jr., ed. 2005. *Ethnologue: Languages of the World*. 15th ed. Dallas: SIL International.

Gottleib, Margo. 2006. *Assessing English Language Learners: Bridges from Language Proficiency to Academic Achievement*. Thousand Oaks, CA: Corwin.

Grant, Steven. 1990. *The Count of Monte Cristo*. Illus. Dan Spiegle. Originally written by Alexandre Dumas. Chicago: Berkley.

Graves, Donald H. 1975. "An Examination of the Writing Processes of Seven-Year-Old Children." *Research in the Teaching of English* 9: 227–41.

Greene, Jay. 1998. *A Meta-Analysis of the Effectiveness of Bilingual Education.* Claremont, CA: Tomas Rivera Policy Institute.

Greenhawk, Jan. 1997. "Multiple Intelligences Meet Standards." *Educational Leadership* 55 (1): 62–64.

Gronlund, Gaye. 2006. *Make Early Learning Standards Come Alive.* St. Paul, MN: Redleaf Press.

Hadaway, Patricia. 1995/2000. "Cultural Diversity in Texas Schools." In *Education in Texas: Policies, Practices, and Perspectives,* 9th ed., ed. C. W. Funkhauser, 161–69. New York: Prentice-Merrill.

Haley, Marjorie Hall. 2004. "Learner-Centered Instruction and the Theory of Multiple Intelligences with Second Language Learners." *Teachers College Record* 106 (1): 163–80.

Hall, Christopher J. 2005. *An Introduction to Language and Linguistics: Breaking the Language Spell.* London: Continuum.

Harris, Theodore L., and Richard E. Hodges, eds. 1995. *The Literacy Dictionary.* Newark, DE: International Reading Association.

Harste, Jerome C., Kathy Gnagey Short, and Carolyn Burke. 1995. *Creating Classrooms for Authors and Inquirers.* 2d ed. Portsmouth, NH: Heinemann.

Helm, J. H., and L. Katz. 2001. *Young Investigators: The Project Approach in the Early Years.* New York: Teachers College Press; Washington, DC: NAEYC.

Hirsch, E. D., Joseph F. Kett, and James Trefil. 2002. *The New Dictionary of Cultural Literacy.* 3d ed. Boston: Houghton Mifflin.

Huntington, Samuel P. 2004. "The Hispanic Challenge." *Foreign Policy* (March/April): 30–45.

Hyson, Marilou. 2001. "Better Futures for Young Children, Better Preparation for Their Teachers: Challenges Emerging from Recent National Reports." *Young Children* 56 (January): 60–62.

———. 2003. *Preparing Early Childhood Professionals: NAEYC's Standards for Programs.* Washington, DC: NAEYC.

———. 2004. *The Emotional Development of Young Children: Building an Emotion-Centered Curriculum.* 2d ed. New York: Teachers College Press.

Jensen, Eric. 1998. *Teaching with the Brain in Mind.* Alexandria, VA: Association for Supervision and Curriculum Development.

———. 2000. *Brain-Based Learning.* San Diego: Brain Store.

Jobling, Anne, and Karen B. Moni. 2004. "'I Never Imagined I'd Have to Teach These Children': Providing Authentic Learning Experiences for Secondary Preservice Teachers in Teaching Students with Special Needs." *Asia-Pacific Journal of Teacher Education* 32 (1): 5–22.

Johnson, James, James Christie, and Francis Wardle. 2005. *Play, Development, and Early Education*. Boston: Pearson Education.

Joyce, Bruce, Marsha Weil, and Emily Calhoun. 2000. *Models of Teaching*. 6th ed. Needham Heights, MA: Allyn and Bacon.

Kagan, Spencer L., and M. J. Neuman. 1997. "Highlights of the Quality 2000 Initiative: Not by Chance." *Young Children* 52 (6): 54–62.

Kampwirth, Thomas J. 2003. *Collaborative Consultation in the Schools: Effective Practices for Students with Learning and Behavior Problems*. 2d ed. Upper Saddle River, NJ: Merrill Prentice Hall.

Kanellos, Nicolas. 1998. *Thirty Million Strong: Reclaiming the Hispanic Image in American Culture*. Golden, CO: Fulcrum.

Kasten, Wendy C., Janice V. Kristo, Amy A. McClure, and Abigail Gathwaite. 2005. *Living Literature*. Upper Saddle River, NJ: Prentice Hall.

Katz, Jennifer, Pat Mirenda, and Stan Auerbach. 2002. "Instructional Strategies and Educational Outcomes for Students with Developmental Disabilities in Inclusive 'Multiple Intelligences' and Typical Inclusive Classrooms." *Research and Practice for Persons with Severe Disabilities* 27 (4): 227–38.

Katz, Lilian, and Sylvia Chard. 2005. *Engaging Children's Minds: The Project Approach*. 2d ed. Greenwich, CT: Ablex.

Kids Count National Statistics. 2006. Baltimore: Annie E. Casey Foundation.

Klingner, Jeanette K., and Sharon Vaughn. 1996. "Reciprocal Teaching of Reading Comprehension Strategies for Students with Learning Disabilities Who Use English as a Second Language." *The Elementary School Journal* 96 (3): 275–93.

Kozol, Jonathan. 2005. *The Shame of the Nation: The Restoration of Apartheid Schooling in America*. New York: Crown.

Krashen, Stephen D. 1982. *Principles and Practice in Second Language Acquisition*. New York: Pergamon.

———. 1991. "Bilingual Education: A Focus on Current Research." *NCBE FOCUS: Occasional Papers in Bilingual Education*. Retrieved June 13, 2002, from www.ncbe.gwu.edu/ncbepubs/focus/focus3.htm.

———. 2000. "The Two Goals of Bilingual Education: Development of Academic English and Heritage Language Development." In *The Power of Two Languages 2000: Effective Dual-Language Use Across the Curriculum*, ed. Josefina V. Tinajero and Robert A. DeVillar, 20–29. New York: McGraw-Hill School Division.

————. 2003. *Explorations in Language Acquisition and Use.* Portsmouth, NH: Heinemann.

Kronowitz, Ellen L. 2007. *The Teacher's Guide to Success.* Boston: Pearson Education.

Ladson-Billings, Gloria. 1995."Multicultural Teacher Education: Research, Practice, and Policy." In *Handbook of Research on Multicultural Education*, ed. James Banks, 747–63. New York: Simon and Schuster.

Lankshear, Colin, and Michele Knobel. 2003. *New Literacies: Changing Knowledge and Classroom Learning.* Philadelphia: Open University Press.

Lara-Alecio, R., and B. Irby. 1997."Identification of Hispanic, Bilingual, Gifted Students." *Tempo* 17 (2): 20–25.

Larkin, Martha J., and Edwin S. Ellis. 1998."Adolescents with Learning Disabilities." In *Learning About Learning Disabilities*, ed. Bernice Y. L. Wong, 505–61. San Diego: Academic.

Latham, Andrew S. 1998."The Advantages of Bilingualism." *Educational Leadership* 56 (3): 79–80.

Leland, Christine H., Jerome C. Harste, and Karen Smith. 2005. "Out of the Box: Critical Literacy in a First-Grade Classroom." *Language Arts* 82 (4): 257–68.

Leont'ev, Alexi. 1975. *Dejatel'nost', licnost', soznaanie* [Activity, Personality, Consciousness]. Moscow: Izd-vo Političeskoj Literatury.

Lessow-Hurley, Judith. 2005. *The Foundations of Dual Language Instruction.* Boston: Allyn and Bacon.

Levine, L. 1996. *The Opening of the American Mind: Canons, Culture, and History.* Boston: Beacon.

Lindholm, Kathryn J., and Rosa Molina. 2000."Two-Way Bilingual Education: The Power of Two Languages in Promoting Educational Success." In *The Power of Two Languages 2000: Effective Dual-Language Use Across the Curriculum*, ed. Josefina V. Tinajero and Robert A. DeVillar, 163–74. New York: McGraw-Hill School Division.

Loewen, James W. 1995. *Lies My Teacher Told Me: Everything Your American History Textbook Got Wrong.* New York: New Press.

Low, G. R., and D. B. Nelson. 2005."Emotional Intelligence: The Role of Transformative Learning in Academic Excellence." *Texas Study of Secondary Education* 14 (2): 41–44.

Lucile Packard Children's Hospital at Stanford. 2006. *Anatomy and Function of the Liver.* Palo Alto, CA: Lucile Packard Children's Hospital at Stanford. Retrieved November 18, 2006, from www.lpch.org/DiseaseHealthInfo/HealthLibrary /transplant/liverant.html.

Lynch-Brown, Carol, and Carl M. Tomlinson. 1999. *Essentials of Children's Literature.* 3d ed. Boston: Allyn and Bacon.

Machado, Antonio. 1982. *Selected Poems*. Translated and with an introduction by Alan S. Trueblood. Cambridge, MA: Harvard University Press.

Madaus, George. 1988. "The Influence of Testing on the Curriculum." In *Critical Issues in Curriculum: 87th Yearbook of the NSSE, Part 1*, ed. L. Tanner. Chicago: University of Chicago Press.

Maffi, Luisa, ed. 2001. *On Biocultural Diversity: Linking Language, Knowledge, and the Environment*. Washington, DC: Smithsonian Institution Press.

Magliaro, Susan G., Barbara B. Lockee, and John K. Burton. 2005. "Direct Instruction Revisited: A Key Model for Instructional Technology." *Educational Technology Research and Development* 53 (4): 41–55.

Malakoff, Marguerite, and Kenji Hakuta. 1990. "History of Language Minority Education in the United States." In *Bilingual Education: Issues and Strategies*, ed. Amado M. Padilla, Halford H. Fairchild, and Concepción M. Valadez, 27–44. Newbury Park, CA: Sage.

Mann, Charles C. 2006. *1491: New Revelations of the Americas Before Columbus*. New York: Vintage.

Markham, Thom, John Larmer, and Jason Ravitz. 2003. *Project-Based Learning Handbook*. Oakland, CA: Wilshed and Taylor Publishing Services.

Martín-Barbero, Jesús. 2001. Introduccíon. In *Cuadernos de nacion: Pensar en medio de la tormenta*, 7–10. Bogotá, Colombia: Ministerio de Cultura.

Mastropieri, M. A., T. E. Scruggs, and S. L. Berkeley. 2007. "Peers Helping Peers." *Educational Leadership* 64 (5): 54–58.

McCarty, Teresa L., Eunice Romero-Little, and Ofelia Zepeda. 2006. "Native American Youth Discourses on Language Shift and Retention: Ideological Cross-Currents and Their Implications for Language Planning." *International Journal of Bilingual Education and Bilingualism* 9 (5): 659–77.

McCourt, Frank. 2005. *Teacher Man*. New York: Scribner.

McGinnis, Ellen, and Arnold P. Goldstein. 1997. *Skillstreaming the Elementary School Child: New Strategies and Perspectives for Teaching Prosocial Skills*. Rev. ed. Champaign, IL: Research.

McIntyre, Ellen, Ann Rosebery, and Norma González. 2001. *Classroom Diversity: Connecting Curriculum to Students' Lives*. Portsmouth, NH: Heinemann.

Meier, Deborah, and George Wood, eds. 2004. *Many Children Left Behind: How the No Child Left Behind Act Is Damaging Our Children and Our Schools*. Boston: Beacon.

Mercer, Cecil D., and Ann R. Mercer. 2005. *Teaching Students with Learning Problems*. 7th ed. Columbus, OH: Merrill.

Moll, Luis C. 1991. "Funds of Knowledge for Teaching: Using a Qualitative Approach to Connect Homes and Classrooms." *Theory into Practice* 31 (1): 132–41.

Moran, S., M. Kornhaber, and H. Gardner. 2006. "Orchestrating Multiple Intelligences." *Educational Leadership* 64 (1): 22–27.

Morse, A. 2003. *Language Access: Helping Non-English Speakers Navigate Health and Human Services*. Washington, DC: National Conference of State Legislatures Children's Policy Initiative.

Moses, Robert. 1995. "Algebra, the New Civil Right." In *The Algebra Initiative Colloquium*. vol. 2, ed. C. B. Lacampagne, W. Blair, and J. Kaput, 53–69. Washington, DC: U.S. Department of Education, Office of Educational Research and Improvement.

Muñoz Cruz, Héctor, ed. 2002. *Rumbo a la interculturalidad en educación* [Toward Interculturality in Education]. Mexico: Universidad Autonoma Metropolitana.

Murillo, Luz Alba. 2004. "Educación de gestión local: La experiencia educativa en una comunidad indígena Arhuaca [Education for Local Action: The Educational Experience of an Arhuaco Community]." *Estudios de lingüística aplicada* número 39, Universidad Nacional Autónoma de México, 94–106.

Nash, G. B., C. Crabtree, and R. E. Dunn. 1997. *History on Trial: Culture Wars and the Teaching of the Past*. New York: Alfred A. Knopf.

National Association for the Education of Young Children (NAEYC). 1996. "Responding to Linguistic and Cultural Diversity: Recommendations for Effective Early Childhood Education." *Young Children* 51 (2): 4–12.

National Center for Early Development and Learning (NCEDL). 2000. *Early Childhood Teacher Preparation Programs in the United States*. Chapel Hill: National Pre-kindergarten Center, FGP Development Institute, University of North Carolina at Chapel Hill.

National Clearinghouse for English Language Acquisition. 2006. "The Growing Numbers of Limited English Proficient Students 1993/94–2003/04." Retrieved February 6, 2007, from www.ncela.gwu.edu/.

National Council for the Social Studies. 1994. *Expectations of Excellence: Curriculum Standards for Social Studies*. Washington, DC: NCSS. Retrieved March 21, 2007, from www.socialstudies.org/standards.

National Council of Teachers of Mathematics (NCTM). 2000. *Principles and Standards for School Mathematics*. Reston, VA: NCTM.

National Research Council. 2001. *Eager to Learn: Educating Our Preschoolers*. Committee on Early Childhood Pedagogy. Ed. B. T. Bowman, M. S. Donovan, and M. S. Burns. Commission on Behavioral and Social Sciences and Education. Washington, DC: National Academies Press.

———. 2006. *Multiple Origins, Uncertain Destinies: Hispanics and the American Future*. Washington, DC: National Academies Press.

National Science Foundation. 2006. *Discovery Research K–12 (DR-K12)*. Retrieved March 1, 2007, from www.nsf.gov/pubs/2006/nsf06593/nsf06593.pdf.

National Writing Project and Carl Nagin. 2003. *Because Writing Matters: Improving Student Writing in Our Schools.* San Francisco: Jossey-Bass.

Needleman, Rafe. March 15, 2007. Newbie's Guide to Twitter. Retrieved December 19, 2007, from www.webware.com/8301-1_109-9697867-2.html.

Nelson, Darwin B., and Gary R. Low. 2003. *Emotional Intelligence: Achieving Academic and Career Excellence.* Upper Saddle River, NJ: Prentice Hall.

Nettle, Daniel, and Suzanne Romaine. 2000. *Vanishing Voices: The Extinction of the World's Languages.* New York: Oxford University Press.

Newby, Timothy J., Donald A. Stepich, James D. Lehman, and James D. Russell. 2000. *Instructional Technology for Teaching and Learning. Designing Instruction, Integrating Computers, and Using Media.* 2d ed. Upper Saddle River, NJ: Prentice-Hall.

Nieto, Sonia. 2004. *Affirming Diversity: The Sociopolitical Context of Multicultural Education.* 4th ed. Boston: Allyn and Bacon.

Noboa, Julio. 2006. *Leaving Latinos Out of History: Teaching U.S. History in Texas.* New York: Routledge.

Noddings, Nel. 1984. *Caring: A Feminine Approach to Ethics and Moral Education.* Berkeley: University of California Press.

Norton, Donna E. 2001. *Multicultural Children's Literature: Through the Eyes of Many Children.* Upper Saddle River, NJ: Prentice Hall.

Norton, Priscilla, and Karin Wiburg. 2003. *Teaching with Technology: Designing Opportunities to Learn.* 2d ed. Belmont, CA: Wadsworth/Thomson Learning.

Novick, Rebecca. 1996. Developmentally Appropriate and Culturally Responsive Education: Theory in Practice. Paper prepared for Child and Family Program, Northwest Regional Educational Laboratory, Portland, OR.

Office of Civil Rights. 1970. *DHEW Memo Regarding Language Minority Children.* Washington, DC. Retrieved March 13, 2007, from www.ed.gov/print/about/offices/list/ocr/docs/lau1970.html.

———. 1985. *Policy Regarding the Treatment of National Origin Minority Students Who Are Limited English Proficient.* Washington, DC. Retrieved March 13, 2007, from www.ed.gov/print/about/offices/list/ocr/docs/lau1990_and_1985.html.

———. 1991. *Policy Update on Schools' Obligations Toward National Origin Minority Students with Limited-English Proficiency.* Washington, DC. Retrieved February 22, 2007, from www.ed.gov/print/about/offices/list/ocr/docs/lau1991.html.

———. 2000. *The Provision of an Equal Education Opportunity to Limited-English Proficient Students.* Washington, DC. Retrieved February 22, 2007, from www.ed.gov/print/about/offices/list/ocr/eeolep/index.html.

Office of Educational Research and Improvement (OERI). 1993. *National Excellence: A Case for Developing America's Talent.* Washington, DC: U.S. Government Printing Office.

Olsen, Laurie, and Ann Jaramillo. 1999. *Turning the Tides of Exclusion: A Guide for Educators and Advocates for Immigrant Students*. Oakland, CA: California Tomorrow.

Ovando, Carlos J., Mary C. Combs, and Virginia P. Collier. 2006. *Bilingual and ESL Classrooms: Teaching in Multicultural Contexts*. 4th ed. Boston: McGraw-Hill.

Parker, W. D. 1997. "An Empirical Typology of Perfectionism in Academically Talented Children." *American Educational Research Journal* 34: 545–62.

Partnership for 21st Century Skills. 2002. Learning for the 21st Century: A Report and Mile Guide for 21st Century Skills. Retrieved December 18, 2007, from www.21stcenturyskills.org/images/stories/otherdocs/p21up_Report.pdf.

Piaget, Jean. 1952. *The Child's Conception of Number*. New York: Norton.

———. 1977. *The Development of Thought: Equilibration of Cognitive Structures*. New York: Viking.

Pinker, Steven. 2002. *The Blank Slate: The Modern Denial of Human Nature*. New York: Viking.

Porter, Bernajean. 2006. About Digital Storytelling. Retrieved September 24, 2006, from www.digitales.us/about/index.php.

Prensky, Marc. 2001. "Digital Natives, Digital Immigrants." *On the Horizon* 9 (5). Retrieved December 20, 2007, from www.marcprensky.com/ (click on "writings").

Purcell-Gates, Victoria. 2001. "What We Know About Readers Who Struggle." In *Reading Researchers in Search of Common Ground*, ed. Rona F. Flippo, 118–28. Newark, DE: International Reading Association.

Ramírez, Gonzalo Jr., and Jan Lee Ramírez. 1994. *Multiethnic Children's Literature*. Albany, NY: Delmar.

Ramírez, J. David. 1991. *Final Report: Longitudinal Study of Structured English Immersion Strategy, Early-Exit and Late-Exit Bilingual Education Programs*. Washington, DC: U.S. Department of Education.

Ramírez, J. David, Sandra D. Yuen, and Dena R. Ramey. 1991. *Executive Summary of Final Report: Longitudinal Study of Structured Immersion Strategy, Early-Exit and Late-Exit Transitional Bilingual Education Programs for Language-Minority Children*. San Mateo, CA: Aguirre International.

Ramírez, Robert. 2004. *We the People: Hispanics in the United States*. Washington, DC: U.S. Census Bureau.

Raver, C. C., and J. Knitzer. 2002. *Ready to Enter: What Research Tells Policymakers About Strategies to Promote Social and Emotional School Readiness Among Three and Four Year-Old Children*. New York: National Council on Children in Poverty.

Rehabilitation Act of 1973. 29th United States Congress. 794.

Reid, Carol, and Brenda Romanoff. 1997. "Using Multiple Intelligence Theory to Identify Gifted Children." *Educational Leadership* 55 (1): 71–74.

Renzulli, J. S. 1978. "What Makes Giftedness: Re-examining a Definition." *Phi Delta Kappan* (60): 180–81.

———, ed. 1986. *Systems and Models for Developing Programs for the Gifted and Talented*. Mansfield Center, CT: Creative Learning.

Renzulli, J. S., and S. Reis. 1985. *The School-Wide Enrichment Model: A Comprehensive Plan for Educational Excellence*. Mansfield Center, CT: Creative Learning.

Rethinking Schools. 1994. *Rethinking Our Classrooms: Teaching for Equity and Justice*. Vol. 1, 7th print. Milwaukee: Rethinking Schools.

Richardson, Will. 2005. RSS: A Quick Start Guide for Educators. Retrieved December 21, 2007, from www.weblogg-ed.com/wp-content/uploads/2006/05/RSSFAQ4.pdf.

Rodríguez, Luis. 1997. *América Is Her Name*. Willimantic, CT: Curbstone.

Rolstad, Kellie, Kate Mahoney, and Gene V. Glass. 2005. "The Big Picture: A Meta-Analysis of Program Effectiveness Research on English Language Learners." *Educational Policy* 19 (4): 572–94.

Rosaldo, Renato. 1993. *Culture and Truth: The Remaking of Social Analysis*. Boston: Beacon.

Rosales, Arturo F. 1997. *Chicano! The History of the Mexican American Civil Rights Movement.* Houston: Arte Publico.

Rosenblatt, L. M. 1994. "The Transactional Theory of Reading and Writing." In *Theoretical Models and Processes of Reading*, 4th ed., ed. R. B. Ruddell, M. R. Ruddell, and H. Singer, 1057–92. Newark, DE: International Reading Association.

Rueda, Robert, Margaret A. Gallego, and Luis C. Moll. 2000. "The Least Restrictive Environment: A Place or a Context?" *Remedial and Special Education* 21 (2): 70–78.

Saavedra, Elizabeth R. 1999. "Transformative Learning Through a Study Group." In *Making Justice Our Project: Teachers Working Toward Critical Whole Language Practice*, ed. C. Edelsky, 303–15. Urbana, IL: National Council of Teachers of English.

Sadowski, Michael. 2006. *Core Knowledge for PK–3 Teaching: Ten Components of Effective Instruction*. New York: Foundation for Child Development.

San Miguel, Guadalupe, Jr. 1997. "Roused from Our Slumbers." In *Latinos and Education: A Critical Reader*, ed. Antonia Darder, Rodolfo D. Torres, and Henry Gutiérrez, 135–57. New York: Routledge.

Schickendanz, Judith A. 1999. *Much More than the ABCs: The Early Stages of Reading and Writing*. Washington, DC: National Association for the Education of Young Children.

Schlesinger, Arthur M., Jr. 1991. *The Disuniting of America: Reflections on a Multi-cultural Society.* Knoxville, TN: Whittle Direct.

SchwabLearning.org Editorial Staff. 2006. "Accommodations, Modifications, and Alternate Assessments: How They Affect Instruction and Assessment." Retrieved March 9, 2006, from www.schwablearning.org/articles.aspx?r=306.

Shafer, Mary, and Thomas Romberg. 1999. "Assessments in Classrooms That Promote Understanding." In *Mathematics Classrooms That Promote Understanding,* ed. Elizabeth Fennema and Thomas Romberg, 159–84. Mahwah, NJ: Lawrence Erlbaum.

Shaughnessy, J. M., and T. M. Haladyna. 1985. "Research on Student Attitude Toward Social Studies." *Social Education* 49: 692–95.

Shearer, Branton. 2004. "Using a Multiple Intelligences Assessment to Promote Development and Student Achievement." *Teachers College Record* 106 (1): 147–62.

———. 2006. *Multiple Intelligences Developmental Assessment Scales* (MIDAS). Kent, OH: M. I. Research and Consulting. Retrieved March 17, 2007, from www.miresearch.org.

Shonkoff, J. P., and D. A. Phillips, eds. 2000. *From Neurons to Neighborhoods: The Science of Early Childhood Development.* Report of the National Research Council. Washington, DC: National Academies Press.

Short, Deborah, and Shannon Fitzsimmons. 2007. "Double the Work: Challenges and Solutions to Acquire Language and Academic Literacy for Adolescent English Language Learners." Interactive presentation. New York: Carnegie Corporation.

Short, Kathy Gnagey, and Carolyn Burke. 1991. *Creating Curriculum: Teachers and Students as a Community of Learners.* Portsmouth, NH: Heinemann.

Skemp, Richard. 1976. "Relational Understanding and Instrumental Understanding." *Mathematics Teaching* 77: 20–26.

Sleeter, Christine E. 1996. *Multicultural Education as Social Activism.* Albany: State University of New York Press.

Slocumb, P., and R. Payne. 2000. *Removing the Mask: Giftedness in Poverty.* Highlands, TX: Aha! Process.

Smith, Frank. 1988. *Joining the Literacy Club: Further Essays into Education.* Portsmouth, NH: Heinemann.

Smith, Patrick H., and Robert T. Jiménez. 2006. "Literacy Lessons for Both Sides of the Border: Views of Reading and Writing in a Mexican Community." In *Race, Ethnicity, and Education: Language, Literacy, and Education,* vol. 2, ed. R. T. Jiménez and V. O. Pang, 75–94. Westport, CT: Praeger.

Stahl, Steven A. 1999. *Vocabulary Development.* Vol. 2, Reading Research to Practice. Cambridge, MA: Brookline.

Stainback, Susan, and William Stainback. 1996. *Inclusion: A Guide for Educators.* New York: Brookes.

Stanford, Pokey. 2003. "Multiple Intelligences for Every Classroom." *Intervention in School and Clinic* 39 (2): 80–85.

Steinberg, Jacques. 2000. "Arizona Teachers Look to End of Bilingual Era." *New York Times* (December 18): A12.

Sternberg, Robert J. 1991. "Giftedness According to the Triarchic Theory of Human Intelligence." In *Handbook of Gifted Education,* ed. N. Colangelo and G. A. Davis, 45–54. Boston: Allyn and Bacon.

Sternberg, Robert J., and Elena L. Grigorenko. 2004. "Successful Intelligence in the Classroom." *Theory into Practice* 43 (4): 274–80.

Sternberg, Robert J., and L. Zhang. 1995. "What Do We Mean by Giftedness? A Pentagonal Implicit Theory." *Gifted Child Quarterly* (39): 88–94.

Sullivan, Danny. n.d. Searches per Day. Retrieved December 23, 2007, from http://searchenginewatch.com/showPage.html?page=2156461.

Swick, Kevin J. 2004. "The Dynamics of Families Who Are Homeless: Implications for Early Childhood Educators." *Childhood Education* 80 (3): 116–20.

Sylwester, Robert. 1998. "Art for the Brain's Sake." *Educational Leadership* 56 (3): 31–35.

Taylor, Steven J. 2004. "Caught in the Continuum: A Critical Analysis of the Principle of the Least Restrictive Environment." *Research and Practice for Persons with Severe Disabilities* 29 (4): 218–30.

Telese, James, and Jesus Abete. 2002. "Diet, Ratios, and Proportions." *Teaching Mathematics in the Middle School* 8 (1): 8–16.

Texas Education Agency. 2006. Texas Examinations of Educator Standards. Preparation Manual for Field 130: Pedagogy and Professional Responsibilities, 8–12, Competency 002. Retrieved September 24, 2007, from www.texes.ets.org/assets/pdf/testprep_manuals/130_pedprofresp8_12_55013_web.pdf.

Texas Education Code. 1995. "Home Language Survey 19, TAC Chapter 89, Subchapter BB 89. 1215: Bilingual Education and Special Language Programs." Austin: Texas Education Agency. Retrieved February 4, 2007, from www.tea.state.tx.us/curriculum/biling/tec.

Texas Essential Knowledge and Skills—Fifth Grade. n.d. Retrieved December 31, 2007, from www.tea.state.tx.us/teks/grade/Fifth_Grade.pdf.

Thomas, John W. 2000. A Review of Research on Project-Based Learning. Retrieved December 10, 2007, from https://www.bie.org/files/researchreviewPBL.pdf.

Thomas, Wayne P., and Virginia P. Collier. 2002. *Executive Summary of Final Report: A National Study of School Effectiveness for Language Minority Students'*

Long-Term Academic Achievement. Berkeley, CA: Center for Research on Education, Diversity and Excellence. Retrieved June 13, 2002, from www.crede.ucsc.edu/.

Tomlinson, Carol Ann. 2005. *How to Differentiate Instruction in Mixed-Ability Classrooms*. 2d ed. Upper Saddle River, NJ: Pearson Education.

Tompkins, Gail E. 2005. *Language Arts: Patterns of Practice*. 6th ed. Upper Saddle River, NJ: Prentice Hall.

U.S. Census Bureau. 2000. "Census 2000 Redistricting Summary File, Tables PL1 and PL2." Washington, DC: U.S. Census Bureau.

U.S. Congress. 1973. Section 504 of the *Rehabilitation Act of 1973*. Public Law 93-112. *U.S. Code* 29 § 794.

———. 1975. *Education for All Handicapped Children Act of 1975*. Public Law 94-142. *U.S. Code* 20 § 1400 et seq.

———. 1998. *Assistive Technology Act of 1998*. Public Law 105-394. S 2432.

———. 2002. *No Child Left Behind Act of 2001*. Public Law 107-110. *U.S. Code* 20 § 6301 *et seq.*

———. 2004. *Individuals with Disabilities Education Improvement Act of 2004*. Public Law 108-446. *U.S. Statutes at Large* 118: 2647.

U.S. Court of Appeals for the Fifth Circuit. 2006. *United States v. Texas*. No. 05-41205. Retrieved August 22, 2006, from www.tea.state.tx.us/pmi/eeo/resources /072406_Reversal_of_Judgement_CA5281.pdf.

U.S. Department of Education, National Center for Educational Statistics. 2000. *Statistics in Brief: March 2000; Home Literacy Activities and Signs of Children's Emerging Literacy; 1993–1999*. Washington, DC: U.S. Government Printing Office.

Valdés, Gina. 1982. *Puentes y fronteras: Coplas chicanas*. Los Angeles: Castle Lithographs.

Valenzuela, Angela. 1999. *Subtractive Schooling: U.S.-Mexican Youth and the Politics of Caring*. Albany: State University of New York Press.

van Oers, Bert. 1996. "Learning Mathematics as a Meaningful Activity." In *Theories of Mathematical Learning*, ed. Leslie Steffe, Pearla Nesher, Paul Cobb, Gerald Goldin, and Brian Greer, 91–113. Mahwah, NJ: Lawrence Erlbaum.

Van Tassel-Baska, J. 1993. "Theory and Research on Curriculum Development for the Gifted." In *International Handbook of Research and Development of Gifted and Talented*, ed. K. A. Heller, F. J. Marks, and A. H. Passow, 365–81. New York: Pergamon.

———, ed. 1990. *A Practical Guide to Counseling the Gifted in a School Setting*. 2d ed. Reston, VA: Council for Exceptional Children.

Varenne, Hervé, and Ray McDermott. 1999. *Successful Failure: The Schools America Builds*. Boulder, CO: Westview.

Violand-Sánchez, Emma, and Julia Hainer-Violand. 2006. "The Power of Positive Identity." *Educational Leadership* 64 (1): 36–40.

Wagmeister, Jane, and Ben Shifrin. 2000. "Thinking Differently, *Learning* Differently." *Educational Leadership* 58 (3): 45–48.

Walsh, Catherine. 2003. "Entrevista con Walter Mignolo. Las geopolíticas del conocimiento y la colonialidad del saber [Interview with Walter Mignolo: The Geopolitics of Knowledge and the Coloniality of Knowledge]." *Revista on-line de la Universidad Bolivariana de Chile*, 1 (4): 1–26. Retrieved August 22, 2006, from www.revistapolis.cl/4/wal.pdf#search=%22Walter%20Mignolo%20Walsh%22.

Warlick, David. n.d. Setting Up a del.icio.us Social Bookmarks Account. Retrieved December 10, 2007 from http://landmark-project.com/workshops/handouts/delicious_setup.pdf.

Wiley, T. G. 1994. "Estimating Literacy in the Multilingual United States: Issues and Concerns." Washington, DC: Adjunct ERIC Clearinghouse for ESL Literacy Education.

Winner, E. 1996. *Gifted Children: Myths and Realities.* New York: Basic.

Wolfson, Nessa. 1989. *Perspectives: Sociolinguistics and TESOL.* Boston: Heinle.

Wood, Karlyn E. 2005. *Interdisciplinary Instruction: A Practical Guide for Elementary and Middle School Teachers.* Columbus, OH: Pearson, Merrill Prentice Hall.

Wortham, Sue. 2006. *Early Childhood Curriculum: Developmental Bases for Learning and Teaching.* Columbus, OH: Pearson Merrill Prentice Hall.

Zelazo, Philip D. 2005. "Brain Growth and the Development of Executive Function." Retrieved March 20, 2007, from www.aboutkidshealth.ca/.

Zhang, W. 1993. *Regular Classroom Practices with Gifted Students: Results of a National Survey of Teachers.* Research monograph 93102. Storrs, CT: National Research Center of the Gifted and Talented.

Zinn, Howard. 1997/2006. "We Take Nothing by Conquest, Thank God." In *The Line Between Us: Teaching About the Border and Mexican Immigration,* ed. Bill Bigelow, 53–59. Milwaukee, WI: Rethinking Schools.

Contributors

Kathy Bussert-Webb is an associate professor of reading in the Department of Curriculum and Instruction at the University of Texas at Brownsville. Her research interests include using multiple intelligences approaches with culturally and linguistically diverse students.

Janice Wilson Butler is an assistant professor of educational technology in the Department of Curriculum and Instruction at the University of Texas at Brownsville. In education for nineteen years, seventeen of which were in K–12, she continues to be interested in the impact of technology integration into current curriculum. Believing that systemic change will begin with higher education and teacher education programs, she has made the impact of educational technology a research priority.

Steve Chamberlain is an associate professor of special education at the University of Texas at Brownsville. His research interests include different ways culture influences teacher-student and teacher-parent interactions in schools and culturally responsive assessment and instruction for students with disabilities.

Georgianna Duarte is a professor of early childhood education in the Department of Curriculum and Instruction at the University of Texas at Brownsville. Her research interests include early literacy, migrant education, outdoor learning environments, and emergent curriculum.

Elsa Duarte-Noboa, MEd, is a lecturer-supervisor in the Department of Curriculum and Instruction at the University of Texas at Brownsville. She taught for twenty-three years at the elementary, middle school, and high school levels, sixteen years as a bilingual and ESL education teacher, and seven as a secondary social studies teacher.

David E. Freeman is a professor of reading and ESL in the Department of Curriculum and Instruction in the School of Education at the University of Texas at Brownsville. His research and writing center on literacy for English language learners, linguistics, academic language development, second language acquisition, bilingual education, and dual language. He has published numerous articles and book chapters as well as twelve books on the topics of second language teaching, biliteracy, bilingual education, linguistics, and second language acquisition.

Yvonne S. Freeman is a professor of bilingual education in the Department of Curriculum and Instruction in the School of Education at the University of Texas at Brownsville. Her research and writing center on second language acquisition, academic language development, biliteracy, bilingual education, dual language, and approaches for teaching English language learners. She has published articles and book chapters as well as twelve books on the topics of second language teaching, biliteracy, bilingual education, linguistics, and second language acquisition.

Richard Gómez Jr. is an associate professor of bilingual education in the Department of Curriculum and Instruction at the University of Texas at Brownsville. His research specialization is the implementation and development of dual language enrichment education programs.

Luz A. Murillo is an educational anthropologist who trains future teachers about cultural and linguistic diversity at the University of Texas Pan American. Her research interests include indigenous schooling, ethnographic descriptions of dual language programs and other culturally diverse schools, and transnational literacies.

Darwin Nelson is a professor of educational leadership and counseling and a doctoral faculty member in the College of Education at Texas A&M University–Kingsville. His research interests include the assessment of emotional intelligence, the development of personal excellence, and transformative learning. He has authored positive assessment and emotional learning materials used worldwide for the positive development of human potential.

Julio Noboa is an assistant professor of curriculum studies in the Department of Curriculum and Instruction at the University of Texas at Brownsville. Among his research interests are the teaching of history, social studies, multicultural education, biculturalism, and Latino identity.

Paula Parson is a professor of literacy and ESL in the Department of Curriculum and Instruction at the University of Texas at Brownsville. She also serves as codirector of the Sabal Palms Writing Project. Her research interests include examining the efficacy of cooperative learning strategies in her graduate and undergraduate classes and working with children's writing.

Reynaldo Ramírez, chair of the Department of Curriculum and Instruction, is an associate professor of secondary and science education in the Department of Curriculum and Instruction at the University of Texas at Brownsville. His research interests include teaching science through recreation, science education leadership, and environmental education.

Alma Dolores Rodríguez is an assistant professor of ESL and bilingual education in the Department of Curriculum and Instruction at the University of Texas at Brownsville. Her research interests include the preservation and development of the Spanish language in South Texas and the integration of authentic literature in the teaching of English as a second language.

Renée Rubin is an associate professor of literacy and English as a second language and principal investigator of the Early Childhood Educator Professional Development Program at the University of Texas at Brownsville and Texas Southmost College. Her research interests include the writing development of bilingual students, preparing preservice and inservice teachers to work with Latino families, and instructing day care providers in the preparation of young bilingual students for school.

Patrick H. Smith is a professor of biliteracy in the Department of Curriculum and Instruction at the University of Texas at Brownsville. His research interests include transnational and Mesoamerican literacies, funds of linguistic knowledge, and the use of Spanish and English in bilingual and dual language education programs.

James A. Telese is an associate professor of secondary and mathematics education in the Department of Curriculum and Instruction at the University of Texas at Brownsville. His research interests include student attitudes and beliefs, algebra teaching, and assessment in mathematics.

of these groups? Next, have students make a list of all the things that they are good at or know how to do. In addition to academic skills, be sure they include home activities and responsibilities like cooking, taking care of children, helping out in the family business, language and translating skills, family chores, music or arts abilities, sports, hobbies, and other interests. Compare the list of assumed deficits or problems with the list of strengths compiled by your students. What are the differences between them?

2. Learners often take for granted what they already know how to do, especially in regard to their out-of-school activities. At first, it might be difficult for your students to imagine that what they know is important. To help them think about this, you can ask them to write about how they help their families by responding to the following prompt. We've filled it in here with an example of the kind of response a student might write:

> When people in my *family* need to *write a song*, they ask me because I am *really good at making up the words for songs*. One time . . .

You can use this prompt as the beginning of a story or composition in which students write about a time they showed someone how to do or make something.

Applications for Challenge 4

1. Ask parents about their own education backgrounds. Be ready to explain how things are different in the school where you work with their children. For example, parents who expect homework to be assigned daily in each subject may be surprised if their child isn't assigned daily homework. Similarly, parents may be accustomed to particular forms of written schoolwork that stress products (copying, dictation, writing sentences or words in a list). For example, literacy programs that stress process and development (such as invented spelling, creative writing, and writing multiple drafts of the same assignment) may need to be explained to noneducators, particularly to parents who attended schools where such practices were not common.

2. Make sure that your students understand what the class is doing and why, and have them explain and show their work to their parents. Borrowing a technique from Mexican public schools, you can write individual notes to parents in children's notebooks. Framing your notes in question form will invite parents to respond back in writing or to call or visit the school if they have questions.

on a time line you provide. You can begin by asking students to guess where you are from, where you went to university, what languages you speak, and so on, as well as why they have reached these (perhaps faulty) conclusions.

2. Ask students to write or talk about themselves. Depending on students' age and literacy proficiency, they can prepare oral or written autobiographies like the one you model in class. Be aware that some students are shy and that those students who are already feeling different might be reluctant to share their stories with classmates at first. The important thing is not that all students' stories become immediate classroom knowledge—it might take longer for some students to feel comfortable about sharing their stories in public—but that all feel valued and important in your class.

Applications for Challenge 2

1. What groups do you belong to? List all the characteristics that you believe compose your identity (for example, woman, heterosexual, Asian American, college student, etc.). Add any groups that you feel are truly important for understanding who you are as a person. As you compile your list, you may wish to show it to a classmate to get new ideas or to keep it private, only for yourself. When you are finished, add the names of other people you feel belong (like you) to each of these categories.

2. Are new cultural groups forming? Go back to the section where we discuss "What is cultural diversity?" In 1989 Renato Rosaldo listed several cultural groups (environmentalists, feminists, gays and lesbians, Native Americans, African Americans, Chicanos, and Puerto Ricans). Rosaldo claimed that ideas about cultural diversity have been shaped by social movements that have organized to protect the rights and interests of key groups. Looking at his list, what other groups would you add today? Are there some you would subtract based on their assimilation into a larger U.S. culture or other factors? What are some of their defining characteristics, in your opinion? What is your evidence for adding or removing these groups from a contemporary version of the list?

Applications for Challenge 3

1. Make a list of all the labels that might be used to describe the children in your classes. What problems or deficits are typically associated with members